A *Chorus* OF CRANES

A *Chorus*

OF CRANES

THE CRANES OF NORTH AMERICA
AND THE WORLD

Paul A. Johnsgard

With photographs by Thomas D. Mangelsen

Drawings and maps by P. A. Johnsgard

UNIVERSITY PRESS OF COLORADO
Boulder

Published by University Press of Colorado
5589 Arapahoe Avenue, Suite 206C
Boulder, Colorado 80303

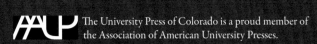 The University Press of Colorado is a proud member of
the Association of American University Presses.

The University Press of Colorado is a cooperative publishing enterprise supported, in part, by Adams State University, Colorado State University, Fort Lewis College, Metropolitan State University of Denver, Regis University, University of Colorado, University of Northern Colorado, Utah State University, and Western State Colorado University.

∞ This paper meets the requirements of the ANSI/NISO Z39.48-1992 (Permanence of Paper).

ISBN: 978-1-60732-436-2 (pbk)
ISBN: 978-1-60732-437-9 (ebook)

The University Press of Colorado gratefully acknowledges the generous support of the Iain Nicolson Audubon Center at Rowe Sanctuary, Audubon Nebraska, Ron and Judy Parks, Wagon Tongue Creek Farm, and the Trull Foundation toward the publication of this book.

Library of Congress Cataloging-in-Publication Data

Johnsgard, Paul A.
  A chorus of cranes : the cranes of North America and the world / Paul A. Johnsgard ; with photographs by Thomas D. Mangelsen ; drawings and maps by P.A. Johnsgard.
    pages cm
  Includes bibliographical references and index.
  ISBN 978-1-60732-436-2 (pbk.) — ISBN 978-1-60732-437-9 (ebook)
1. Cranes (Birds) 2. Cranes (Birds)—North America. 3. Cranes (Birds)—Pictorial works. 4. Sandhill crane. 5. Sandhill crane—North America. 6. Sandhill crane—Pictorial works. 7. Whooping crane. 8. Whooping crane—North America. 9. Whooping crane—Pictorial works. I. Mangelsen, Thomas D. II. Title. III. Title: Cranes of North America and the world.
  QL696.G84J57 2015
  598.3'2—dc23

                        2015011316

        24 23 22 21 20 19 18 17 16 15   10 9 8 7 6 5 4 3 2 1

Cover and text design by Daniel Pratt

To George W. Archibald,

cofounder of the International Crane
Foundation and an inspiration to
crane-lovers worldwide.

Contents

Illustrations

Maps

Drawings (by Paul A. Johnsgard)

Photographs (by Thomas Mangelsen)

Preface

IT HAS NOW BEEN ALMOST FOUR DECADES since I wrote my *Cranes of the World* monograph. During that time many changes have occurred in the world's crane populations and in our knowledge of crane biology. At the time I wrote my book in the late 1970s and early 1980s, for example, only about 100 whooping cranes existed in the wild, and a joint Canadian-American effort to establish a separate population using foster-reared birds in Idaho were just getting under way. At that same time the first important crane sanctuaries had recently been established on the Platte River, and a variety of privately and federally supported studies on the ecology of the river and its spring sandhill crane populations were being initiated. Although the whooping and sandhill cranes' populations have improved since then, nearly all of the other cranes of the world are literally losing ground.

Shortly after finishing that book, I was asked to write a general essay on crane biology and some accompanying short accounts of the cranes of the world, to be published in conjunction with a series of life-sized oil paintings of cranes done by the late English artist Philip Rickman and owned by my friend Christopher Marler. That project never materialized, and my manuscript was filed away and forgotten for a few years. Then in 1988 an editor from the Smithsonian Institution Press asked me if I would consider doing a trade book for them. I suggested that an account of cranes, especially the North American cranes, might make a worthwhile topic. I was already working on a script for a television documentary on sandhill cranes to be filmed by Thomas Mangelsen, and it seemed to me that an expanded version of that text, along with a comparable one on the whooping crane, and earlier unpublished crane manuscript materials might all easily be put together and converted into a short, nontechnical book. This was the origin of *Crane Music*.

Although several popular books on the whooping crane and its precarious history have been published, the sandhill crane has been relatively neglected. This situation is surprising, in view of the sandhill crane's much greater abundance and more widespread occurrence throughout North America, although it lacks the rarity appeal and mystique of the whooping crane. Additionally, the sandhill crane touches special heartstrings for me because, more than any other bird species, I associate it with Nebraska and the Platte River, both of which are very dear to me. Nebraska is my adopted home, and its most important river, the Platte, is my favorite of all the hundreds of rivers of the world that I have seen, from the Amazon to the Yukon. Just as the whooping crane is an endangered species, the Platte is a threatened if not endangered river. One of my major reasons for writing this book was to point out once again the inextricable ecological links connecting the sandhill and whooping cranes, the Platte (and countless other wetlands), and humanity.

My passion for sandhill cranes began in the spring of 1962, shortly after I had arrived to begin a teaching position at the University of Nebraska, after completing postdoctoral studies in England. On a magical Saturday in March, I drove with one of my students out to the central Platte Valley west of Grand Island, as much to witness the famous spring waterfowl migration, and perhaps also see sandhill cranes. At that time the cranes had not received any publicity as a birding attraction, but I had been told by my Nebraska-born student that they were said to be common along the central Platte River. It was perhaps just as well that I wasn't emotionally prepared for the sight of countless cranes. They punctuated the sky from horizon to horizon, and gracefully wheeled about overhead as if they were caught in some ultra-slow-motion whirlwind, their vibrato calls drifting downward like the music of an angelic avian chorus. Not since the days of my boyhood, when I first saw vast migrating spring flocks of snow geese and Canada geese dropping into eastern North Dakota's prairie marshes, was I so completely enthralled. It was certainly on that particular day of epiphany that I realized that cranes would become as important to my mental well-being as were my beloved waterfowl.

Now, five decades after first seeing sandhill cranes on the Platte, witnessing their return in spring is still as much a part of my annual semireligious rituals as are Christmas and Thanksgiving, and perhaps even more rewarding. Like Christmas giving, I savor the sandhill cranes of the Platte Valley most completely when I can present them to others as a special gift and observe in them the same sense of discovery and enormous pleasure that I know so well and feel so deeply. It is for reasons such as this that *Crane Music* was written in 1991. Since then I have written several other books that relate in varying degrees to cranes, their habitats, and their biology.

After recovering the copyright for *Crane Music* from Smithsonian Institution Press, which had allowed the University of Nebraska Press to print a softback reprint, I decided in 2013 that an updated and substantially expanded version was badly needed. Many ecological changes affecting the world's fifteen species of cranes have occurred since the 1990s, and there have been many associated changes on crane populations and distributions. I decided that a new book was needed, summarizing the new information now available on the biology and status of the two North American cranes, plus more abbreviated summaries on the status and biology of the other thirteen crane species of the world. Happily, I was able to convince the University Press of Colorado to publish the book and conned Tom Mangelsen into helping me illustrate it.

FIGURE 0.1. *Sandhill cranes in flight*

Acknowledgments

IN THE COURSE OF WRITING THIS BOOK, MANY
people helped me. Most importantly, my friend and onetime
student Tom Mangelsen provided a host of wonderful photographs that add immeasurably to this book's value and appeal.
All of the drawings and maps in the text are by me and are copyrighted
by me; unless otherwise indicated, the photographs are by Thomas
Mangelsen and are copyrighted by him.

I must also sincerely thank Dr. George Archibald, cofounder and
director of the International Crane Foundation (ICF), for his good
advice and helpful comments on the manuscript. He and our common
friend, the late Ron Sauey, also treated me to the ICF facilities at various times, and they and their works have provided a rallying point
for all crane biologists and conservationists to gather around. Under
George's leadership the ICF has become the world's cynosure for crane

lovers and crane biologists. I especially also thank Claire Mirande and Jim Harris of the ICF for sending me still-unpublished data on the Old World cranes, and to the ICF librarian Betsy Dedrickson for countless favors over the years and for reviewing my text.

Since publishing *Crane Music* in 1991 I have benefited from hundred of hours watching cranes and from the knowledge and friendships of many people who love them as much as I do. Among these are such old friends as Tom Mangelsen and George Archibald, as well as many newer ones, including biologists and crane enthusiasts such as Jeb Barzen, Linda Brown, Jackie Canterbury, Rod Drewien, Vladimir Flint, Mike Forsberg, Joan Garden, Karine Gil-Weir, Brina Kessel, Tommy Moore, Amy Richart, Elizabeth Smith, Bill Taddiken, Warwick Tarboton, Paul Tebble, Larry Walkinshaw, and many others. Betsy Dedrickson and Linda Brown both provided valuable editorial comments on this book's manuscript. George and Christy Yunker Happ supplemented my material on the sandhill crane with their personal observations and very kindly reviewed my relevant text.

Tom Mangelsen and I wish especially to thank Darrin Pratt and his editors and staff of the University Press of Colorado for mastering the challenge of producing a large and extensively illustrated book in the mold of our earlier *Yellowstone Wildlife: Ecology and Natural History of the Greater Yellowstone Ecosystem.*

All of these people, and others whom I might equally well have mentioned, have the kind of passionate love for cranes that I can understand and I share. I hope that in the course of reading this book a few additional people might develop those same feelings for cranes and their special habitats, which are becoming ever more threatened every year. Since long before medieval times cranes have been considered messengers of the gods, calling annually from on high to remind humans below of the passing years and of their own mortality. Now it is up to humans to take responsibility for controlling our own fate and also to cry out to protect, not only cranes, but all the other wonderful creatures that share our increasingly fragile and threatened planetary ecosystem with us.

A *Chorus*

OF

CRANES

ONE

Crane Magic

CRANES—WHOSE VOICES PENETRATE the atmosphere of the world's wilderness areas, from arctic tundra to the South African veld, and whose footprints have been left on the wetlands of the world for the past 60 million years or more—are the stuff of magic. They have served as models for human tribal dances in places as remote as the Aegean, Australia, and Siberia. Whistles made from their wing bones have given courage to Crow and Cheyenne warriors of the North American Great Plains, who ritually blew on them as they rode into battle. These birds' wariness, gregariousness, and regularity of migratory movements have stirred the hearts of people as far back as medieval times and probably long before, and their sagacity and complex social behavior have provided the basis for folklore and myths on several continents. Their large size and humanlike appearance have perhaps been a major reason

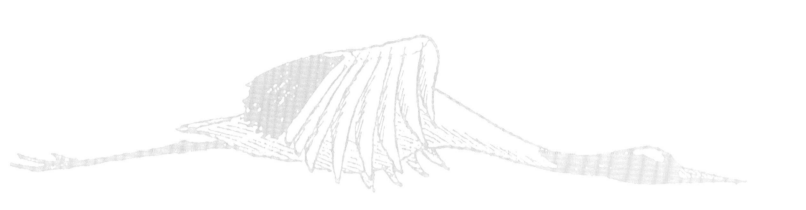

"*And beauty, touched by love, is
somehow transformed into magic.*"
P. JOHNSGARD

why we have so often been in awe of cranes and why we have tended to
bestow so many human attributes upon them.

Cranes have provided the basis for a surprising number of English
words that we no longer associate with them. The Greek word for cranes,
geranos (or *gereunos*), apparently was based on the myth that cranes
constantly wage warfare on a tribe of Pygmies, the ruler of whom was
named Gerania and had been transformed into a crane by Juno and
Diana for neglecting the gods. (A similar myth in India refers to warfare between dwarfs and the fabulous garuda bird.) The geranium plant
is so named because of the similarity of the long and pointed seed cap-
sule to a crane's bill. The Romans referred to the cranes as *grues*, apparently from the sound of their calls. The related Latin word *congruere*.
meaning to agree, is the basis for the modern English word "congru-
ence," and both derive from the highly coordinated and cooperative

behavior typical of cranes. Likewise, the English word "pedigree" is derived from the French *pied de grue*, meaning "foot of a crane," and is based on the characteristic branching pattern of a genealogy. Finally, "hoodwinking" is derived from the practice of sewing shut the eyes of captured cranes in order that they can be more readily tamed and fattened for the pot.

Cranes have been mythically credited with the derivation for several of the letters of the Greek alphabet. Thus, the hero Palamedes supposedly was able to devise several Greek letters simply by watching the convolutions of crane flocks. A similar myth gives the god Mercury credit for inventing the entire Greek alphabet by watching the flights of cranes.

The migratory flights of cranes have probably been observed with interest by humans for millennia, perhaps because cranes generally migrate by day, and also because they typically are organized into coordinated formations during such flights. Edward Topsell (1572–1625), who collected all of the then-available information on the natural history of birds, mammals, and other animals known to the ancient world, wrote at length about crane formations. He believed that the foremost bird in such a formation acted as captain and that all the subordinate birds of the group organized themselves in such a way as to avoid obscuring its view. Various older birds would reputedly take turns at being the flock leader. Topsell erroneously believed that, should a flock member become tired, it would be supported in flight on the backs, wings, or outstretched legs of other flock members. It has also been widely believed in many cultures that cranes will help transport smaller birds on their migrations by carrying them on their backs.

Various early writers proposed the idea that cranes probably swallowed heavy stones or sand before they began a long flight, with the view that such stones would serve as ballast and prevent the birds from being tossed about by gusts of wind. It was believed that at the end of these flights the birds would cast up the stones or sand. Other writers believed that the stones were carried by the feet, from which they could be easily dropped when they were no longer needed.

An equally widely held and appealing view was that a flock of cranes would sleep at night only after posting one or more "watch birds," which would stand on one leg and hold a heavy stone in the claws of the other foot. Should such a bird fall asleep, it would drop the stone, thus helping to awaken both itself and the other birds of the flock. This idea gave rise to a Christian morality tale, to the effect that Christians must have faith, imitate cranes in their watchfulness, and avoid falling into sin as a crane avoids falling asleep by holding fast to a heavy stone. With such a belief anchor, the faithful could find their way through life safely, and upon arrival in heaven their weighty ballast would be turned to gold. Indeed, in heraldry and in the stone carvings of some medieval cathedrals the images of stone-carrying cranes can often be found.

Even more commonly than in the Christian church, cranes have permeated the religions and mythologies of ancient Eurasian cultures. In central Anatolia, at a Neolithic culture site (Çatalhöyük) dating from 7300 to 6200 BC, modified middle wing bones of a Eurasian crane have been found. Cut marks and holes on the radius bone suggest that they could have been used to attach the wing to the shoulder of a dancer (Russell and McGowan 2003). A "dance of the white cranes" was performed in China at least as early as 500 BC, and in that country it was generally believed that cranes and dragons transported to heaven those souls who were destined for immortality. It was also believed that old pine trees sometimes were transformed into cranes, or vice versa, both being extremely long-lived. Indeed, in both Chinese and Japanese art there is a recurrent theme of associated pine trees and cranes, and these icons have generally come to symbolize long life, happiness, steadfastness, and love. Because of the belief that cranes help support a soul to paradise, a crane-shaped hairpin may be placed in the hair of a deceased woman, and a representation of a crane may be hung in the window of a house where there has been a death.

Because of their venerated status, cranes were rarely if ever killed and eaten in the Orient, although in India they were sometimes sacrificed. In Egypt the birds were captured for food, together with other waterfowl. Furthermore, in the Temple of Deirel-Barari there is a wall painting of captive cranes walking between slaves, with each crane's bill tied down toward its neck, thus upsetting its balance and making it unable to fly. Other illustrations of demoiselle cranes in captivity occur in Egyptian tombs dating from the fifth to the eighteenth dynasty.

Cranes were also captured and domesticated in ancient Greece, for on a Grecian vase in the Hermitage Museum at Leningrad a scene is depicted of a woman offering a tidbit to a domesticated or captive crane. At least as early as the late Ice Age in Great Britain cranes were killed and eaten by humans; British cave deposits of this era have yielded crane bones, and the bones of a now-extinct crane the size of a sarus crane have been found in human-associated deposits of the late Pleistocene in Britain and France, of the Neolithic period in Germany, and of the Bronze and Iron ages in Britain. Because these bones include crane remains of varied sizes, it has been suggested that perhaps the inhabitants of these sites may have raised crane chicks for their consumption. At least as early as the Chou period, some 2,200 years ago, Chinese royalty raised cranes in captivity.

The tales of ancient Greece include many stories of cranes. For example, it was noted that in Thessaly cranes and storks would sometimes feed on snakes and thus help to protect the people there. As a result, the people of that region were forbidden to kill these birds, a practice that was referred to as *antipalargia* (from the Greek *palargos,* or stork). Similarly, a mountain on the Magaris Peninsula was named Gerania (now Yerania) because the people there followed the calls of cranes to higher ground following a flood.

The story of the death of Ibycus is even better known; this poet of Rhegium was attacked by robbers and mortally wounded. As he lay dying, he saw a flock of migrating cranes over-head, and with his last breath told the robbers that the cranes had seen his murder and would avenge his death. Later, in the Corinth market one of the robbers happened to see a flock of cranes overhead and called out in fear to his friends, "Behold the cranes of Ibycus!" On being overheard, the men were questioned and arrested, and later confessed to the murder of Ibycus.

In a somewhat similar fashion, the sighting of cranes has been associated with death in various other cultures. For example, slaves of the American South believed that if a crane should circle over a house three times, somebody in that house would soon die. An ancient counterpart of this belief may be Pliny's story that the oldest of a flock of cranes would fly around in a circle three times before the flock was due to leave on migration, and then fall down and die of exhaustion. Perhaps these and similar stories derive from the fact that prior to migration cranes do indeed spend much time circling in thermals on sunny days and ride thermals to great heights immediately prior to setting out on long migratory journeys.

The actual migratory journeys of cranes are no less interesting than they were imagined to be by the peoples of medieval times. In recent years it has been possible to follow these movements very closely by using radar or radio telemetry or by following migrating flocks in small airplanes. It is now known, for example, that Eurasian cranes, and probably most other cranes as well, maximally utilize their soaring abilities during migration by exploiting the lifting potential of thermal winds and then gliding in close formation for great distances while seeking out another thermal. Eurasian cranes may thus soar to heights of more than 6,500 feet while in thermals, and their thermal-assisted climbing abilities are especially valuable between about 1,500 and 5,000 feet. Using radio telemetry, it has been found that greater sandhill cranes can fly nonstop as far as 360 miles during a 9.5-hour period, averaging nearly 40 miles per hour. This generally agrees with estimated air speeds for Eurasian cranes of from 37 to 52 miles per hour. Observations on migrating whooping cranes indicate that similar daily migration patterns occur, with single-day trips of up to 510 miles reported, but with most daily movements of less than 200 miles and lasting about 6.5 hours.

In the case of the sandhill crane, the birds prefer to fly only on clear or partly cloudy days. They normally land before dark and usually begin to arrive at roosting sites by about sundown. Nearly all migratory flight in this species occurs at elevations below 6,000 feet, generally between about 1,000 and 3,000 feet, but some greater sandhill cranes must fly over a Colorado mountain pass (North Pass or Cochetopa Pass) at an altitude of 10,000 feet or higher. Sandhills in central Alaska regularly fly past the face of Mount McKinley, but their east-west route does not take them over its crest.

No doubt the demoiselle cranes migrating over the Himalayas from Asia to India encounter much higher elevations than these that must be traversed, as do black-necked cranes migrating to wintering grounds in Bhutan. Black-necked cranes breed at altitudes as high as 4,900 meters (nearly 16,000 feet), so they are no doubt well adapted to survive and migrate at such high altitudes. The Eurasian alpine or yellow-billed chough breeds at still higher altitudes, to about 6,500 meters (over 20,000 feet). This remarkable capacity for alpine survival reflects the inherent capacity of birds to survive at low temperatures and very low oxygen levels as a result of their extremely efficient respiratory system, the high oxygen-carrying capacity of their blood, and their highly effective feathered insulation.

Altitudes used by migrating cranes are high enough that landmarks are visible from great distances and place the birds well above ground turbulence or obstacles. Cranes also choose those days for migratory flights when they can exploit following winds rather than face crosswinds or headwinds. On rare occasions when sandhill cranes have been observed migrating during inclement weather, barometric pressures have been rising in those areas toward which the birds were flying. Equally remarkably, sandhill cranes have been observed to terminate a migration leg early in the day, apparently sensing the approach of bad weather well before it has actually has arrived.

Flock sizes of migrating cranes vary greatly, probably influenced by such factors as total population size, levels of social tolerance or gregariousness in the species, degrees of disturbance on roosting and foraging areas, and time of year. In whooping cranes the average flock size is usually of less than five birds and rarely more than ten, probably consisting of a single pair and one or more cohorts of their offspring. Migrating flocks of sandhill cranes often number in the thousands, but field-foraging flocks often have no more than fifty birds, within which the most common social units are of two or three birds, probably representing pairs or family units. However, the roosting flocks of sandhill cranes are usually much larger. At times these assemblages may contain 70,000 or more individuals, especially in areas of extensive sandbars ands very low human activity. These massive roosts are restricted to the relatively few areas of the Platte River that still comprise ideal roosting habitats; as a result, birds are crowded into confined stretches of river. Sandhill cranes tend to return to the same roosting sites day after day and also tend to exhibit year-to-year site fidelity.

The main factor affecting the daily timing of roosting flights is the light intensity, with the majority of the birds arriving at the roost by sunset, nearly all of them within fifteen minutes after sunset. Delayed returns to the roost most often occur under conditions of a moonlit clear sky, moderate to high temperatures, and no wind. Similarly, morning departures from roosts are associated with sunrise; more than half of the birds usually leave the roost by a half hour after sunrise, and nearly all will have left during the first hour. However, heavy clouds, fog, rain, and strong winds will delay morning departures, and the birds may even remain on the roost all day long. Judging from observations of other crane species, much the same pattern of diurnal activity seems to be typical of cranes in general.

Cranes take flight from a running start into the wind, finally springing into the air and slowly gaining altitude. In flight they present an appearance distinctly different from that of geese, in that the wingbeat is shallower and the upstroke is noticeably more rapid than the downstroke. This rapid upstroke is especially conspicuous among frightened birds trying to gain altitude quickly. Furthermore, perhaps because of their less labored flight than that of generally heavier birds such as geese or swans, they rarely maintain a fixed formation for any length of time, except when migrating at high altitudes. Instead, the flock pattern is constantly undulating and changing, without any definite lead bird. At fairly close range the long and trailing legs of cranes also visually set them apart from geese. However, during cold weather it is not uncommon for some of the flock members, especially young birds, to tuck their legs forward into their flank feathers and thus assume a rather gooselike flight profile, albeit with a slower wingbeat and flight speed.

Landing is done into the wind, with the legs dangled pendulum-like, providing for a lowered center of gravity and increased stability, as the tail is spread and the wings cupped. In this way the birds descend parachute-like almost vertically to their roost, finally breaking their descent during the last few seconds by wing flapping. Cranes are unable to match the abilities of ducks and geese to lose altitude by acrobatically flipping their bodies from side to side ("wiffling"), so that their wings' lifting abilities are lost and a falling-leaf maneuver is created, although occasionally cranes will ineffectively attempt this remarkable behavior.

While flying, and especially during landings and takeoffs, cranes utter a constant clamoring, enabling pair and family members to maintain vocal contact amid the confusion of flock movements. Although it remains to be proven, there seems little doubt that cranes must be able to recognize their mates or other family members by their vocal traits alone, for pairs often maintain "conversational" contact with one another when they are out of each other's sight. When lone birds have somehow been separated from their social groups, it is common to see them flying back and forth over roosting flocks, calling almost constantly.

FIGURE 1.1. *Crane flight behavior (red-crowned crane), including takeoff (T), flight (F), and landing (L) (after Masatomi and Kitagawa 1975)*

Of all the cranes' visual and vocal signals, it is the mutual "unison-call" display sequence of paired cranes that is most important and provides a basic key to the understanding of their social bonding. No observer of cranes can begin to understand their interactions without some appreciation of the importance of this complex behavior. Although there are several other calls that cranes utter between pair members, the most important of these is the "unison call." This call, which develops during the second or third year of life, is a complex and extended series of notes uttered by paired birds, with associated species-specific and sex-specific posturing. It is uttered in a time-coordinated sequence, with the birds typically also standing in a specific spatial relationship to one another. This posture is always an erect and alert one, with the wings folded and the primaries often drooped while the inner variably elongated and ornamental innermost secondary ("tertial") feathers are raised, forming a visual "bustle." The birds are usually oriented side by side or facing one another, and the male initiates the call sequence (Figure 1.2).

The unison-call sequence may last from only a few seconds to a minute or more, depending in part on the species and in part on the intensity of the display. The associated vocalizations are typically the loudest and most penetrating of any of the species' calls. In the more anatomically generalized cranes, such as the African crowned cranes, the trachea barely penetrates the anterior end of the sternum's keel, and these species of cranes typically have fairly high-pitched voices without much volume.

By contrast, in adults of probably all of the species of the genus *Grus* the trachea is highly elongated, penetrating the keel of the sternum nearly to the end of the keel (Figure 1.3), increasing its length and enhancing both its vocal resonating capabilities and its volume (Johnsgard 1981). In the whooping crane, with a tracheal length of about 150 cm (62 in.), the unison call has three to four well-developed harmonics (Lewis 1993). In adult sandhill cranes, having a tracheal length of 55–60 cm (23–25 in.), the call has little harmonic development evident (Johnsgard 1981; Tacha, Nesbitt, and Vohs 1992). Sandhill crane calls often contain a distinctive pulsed or rattle-like component, produced at the rate of about twenty-five pulses per second.

Still unpublished acoustic research on several species of cranes by Bernhard Wessling (n.d.) has shown a high degree of individual variations in the acoustic characteristics of crane voices. Study of sonographic "voiceprints" of the unison calls of Eurasian, whooping, sandhill, black-necked, and white-naped cranes has allowed him to identify individual pairs by voice alone. The Siberian crane's voice required including some additional time-dependent traits of its calls for him to determine individual identification. There can be no doubt that cranes can readily recognize the voices of their mates and offspring, and perhaps even less closely related members of their assemblages.

Although there are considerable differences among crane species, it is typical for a male to initiate the call; very shortly the female joins in, often calling in counterpoint to its mate. Most often the female utters shorter calls, and in the genus *Grus* the female usually utters two calls for every call of the male, beginning almost simultaneously with the male so that their calls overlap. However, in the more anatomically "primitive" genera of cranes, the call notes tend to be fairly short in duration, and both sexes utter notes of about the same length. In most of these non-*Grus* cranes, such as the crowned, Siberian, and wattled cranes,

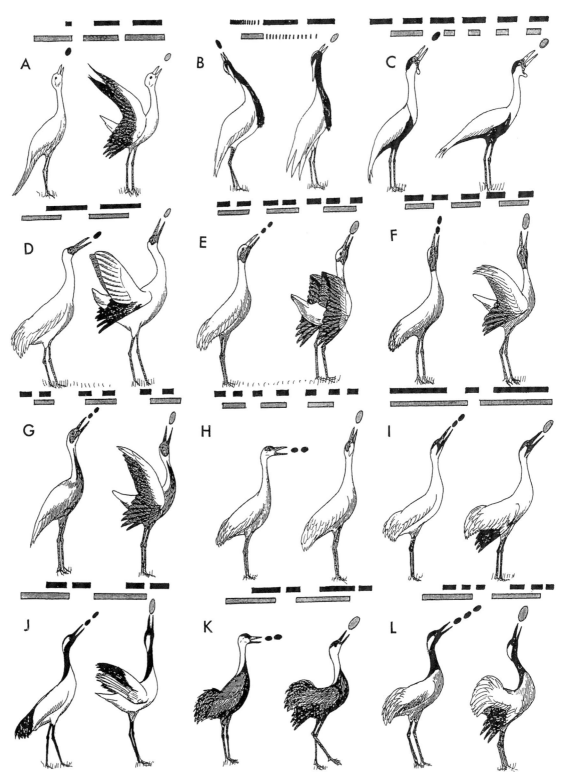

FIGURE 1.2. *Unison-call postures of the cranes of the world: blue (A), demoiselle (B), wattled (C), Siberian (D), Australian (E), sarus (F), white-naped (G), sandhill (H), whooping (K), red-crowned (J), and Eurasian (K); durations of male (shaded) and female (inked) vocalizations are indicated by overhead bars; "balloons" indicate number of female calls per male call (after Archibald 1975).*

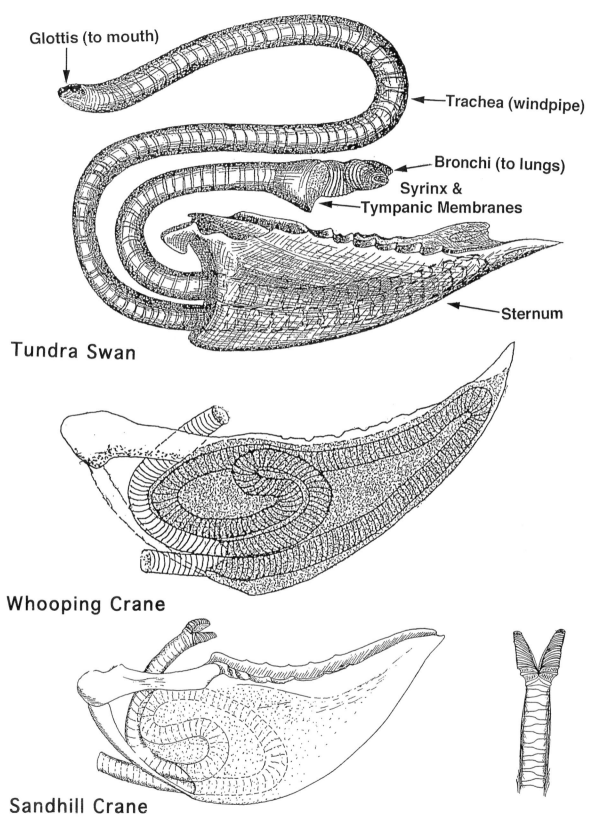

Glottis (to mouth)

Trachea (windpipe)

Bronchi (to lungs)

Syrinx &
Tympanic Membranes

Sternum

Tundra Swan

Whooping Crane

Sandhill Crane

FIGURE 1.3. *Tracheal and sternal anatomy of the tundra swan, whooping crane, and sandhill crane. A dorsal view of a sandhill crane's syringeal structure is also shown (in part after Johnsgard 1981).*

the vocalizations typically lack resonance and have little associated harmonic development. Increased tracheal length in cranes is correlated with increased volume and resonance of their primary vocalizations. The crane species with the loudest and most penetrating unison calls (the whooping, red-crowned, and sarus cranes) are those that combine relatively large size, conspicuous plumage patterning, high levels of territoriality, and low social tolerance during nesting, in addition to having greatly elongated tracheal structures. Similar kinds of correlations apply to those swans that have variably elongated tracheal structures, such as the trumpeter and tundra swans.

These observations and correlations suggest that the unison call has a variety of social functions. Perhaps most importantly, it seems to be a basic mechanism for individual pair bonding and pair maintenance, and at least in some species it may also serve as an important sex-recognition device. Partly because of their tracheal complexity, crane voices also vary enough in pitch and harmonic characteristics that individual recognition within families and possibly among other flock members can be achieved by their vocal attributes alone. At least in captive whooping cranes, the unison call is uttered throughout the year. It is most prevalent from October to April and is least common during molting, suggesting its importance in pair-bond maintenance.

At least in sandhill cranes, the unison call also serves as a territorial advertisement call and as a general threat call, as it is often stimulated by the intrusion of a potential enemy into the breeding area of an established pair. It might also serve as a synchronizing mechanism for the pair members, helping to bring them into reproductive condition simultaneously. Males are evidently brought into reproductive condition by increasing day length; ovarian development in females evidently requires further stimulation through unison calling behavior with their mates.

A variety of other call types occur in most cranes; studies by Dr. George Archibald (1975) suggest that in the genus *Grus* there are three calls that are uttered only by chicks, as compared with eight that are characteristic of adults. In species that have especially loud and penetrating adult voices, the young birds go through a "voice break" period near the end of their first year, when the high-pitched peeping voices of the young are replaced by much lower and louder calls. By this age most or all of the tracheal coiling in the sternum has usually already occurred, so the physiological/anatomical mechanism for this permanent vocal change remains obscure. George Archibald has concluded that up to sixteen different calls exist, varying in length, intonation, repetition, and other variables, providing an almost infinite amount of potential information diversity.

Besides their generally similar call characteristics, cranes share a number of "egocentric" or individualistic behavior patterns that are fairly uniform throughout the entire group (Figures 1.2–1.6). All cranes older than chicks usually sleep while standing, often with one leg raised. However, both young and adult birds may sometimes rest or sleep in a sitting posture, with the legs folded underneath and the abdomen resting on the substrate. This posture is also assumed during incubation, with the head resting comfortably on the breast or lowered almost to the ground when the incubating bird is trying to avoid detection. While sleeping, the birds often tuck their bills into their scapulars, but during incubation they rarely if ever sleep, and the incubating bird seems constantly alert to danger. Occasionally, a

FIGURE 1.4. *General crane behavior (sandhill crane): preening (O), wing-stretching (W), bow-stretching (B), flight-intention (F), drinking (D), and attack (A) (after Voss 1976)*

standing crane may rest on its "heels," although this posture is not nearly so common as it is among some heavier long-legged birds such as storks.

Like nearly all birds, cranes drink by dipping their bills, then quickly tilting them upward to swallow (Figure 1.4). Seeds and insects are obtained from the substrate by pecking or by digging and probing with the tip of the bill. Prior to taking off, cranes often assume an "intention" posture in which the head and extended neck are gradually lowered to a diagonal angle or even almost horizontal position. This distinctive posture may help to coordinate departure in a group, or at least warn others nearby that one of their flock members is about to take off. Cranes also perform several stretching behaviors that are common to most if not all birds. These include the simultaneous stretching of one wing and the leg on the same side of the body, a double wing stretch above the back, with the head and neck simultaneously lowered and stretched forward, and a similar double wing stretch but without out head lowering.

All cranes preen in a consistent manner. This involves extensive nibbling, drawing of the feathers through the slightly opened bill, and associated oiling behavior. In a few species of cranes (especially sandhill cranes and, to a lesser degree, Eurasian cranes) there is an interesting related behavior that is performed by breeding adults immediately prior to nesting. In sandhill cranes the birds "paint" almost their entire body plumage with mud or rotting vegetation that they probe for with their bills, gradually staining their basically grayish plumage into a brownish to reddish brown color. In this way the entire bird eventually assumes an appearance that closely matches the color of their dead-grass nesting substrate. During fall and winter these stained feathers are gradually molted, so the process must be repeated annually. The Eurasian crane paints itself less extensively than does the sandhill, and probably hooded and black-necked cranes paint to some degree. Only one essentially white-plumaged crane, the Siberian, is known to exhibit similar behavior, and in this species the staining is mostly limited to the lower neck region.

Preening, feather ruffling, and similar body care activities also occur in a social or "display" context in most and probably all cranes. These movements often scarcely differ from their normal nondisplay counterparts performed in nonsocial situations and are usually overlooked by the casual observer. However, they are among the most important of the visual signals of cranes, and careful watching will often allow the observer to gain a keen insight into the social interactions of a crane flock as well as judge crane responses to humans or other animals.

Common social displays of cranes in aggressive situations consist of an expansion of the bare crown skin, followed by strutting toward the opponent with rhythmic steps, the neck stretched and the elongated innermost wing feathers (tertials) variably lifted. All cranes perform "ritualized" preening movements, which are usually are directed toward the back feathers as one wing is lowered, exposing some of the primary feathers. These preening movements are performed silently, but the preening bird rarely if ever takes its eyes off the individual toward whom the display is directed. The preening is often interspersed with generalized feather ruffling and shaking of all the body feathers.

A very common aggressive-defensive display is to spread or variably lower both wings while facing the opponent, especially by those birds defending their nest site or young.

FIGURE 1.5. *Crane social behavior (sandhill crane), including tertial-raising (T), appeasement (A), crouch-threat (C), and charge (Ch). After Voss (1976).*

This display sometimes grades into "broken-wing" behavior, in which the displaying bird attempts to decoy the intruder away from the immediate vicinity while assuming the appearance of being partly disabled (Figure 1.5).

An aggressive "ruffle-bow" display begins with an exaggerated body-shake and ends with the bird bending its head down toward its breast. The bare head skin is maximally exposed and directed toward the opponent and intensely red during this display. During a stiff-legged, march-like aggressive approach, the crane likewise tilts its head downward so that its bare crown is directed toward the other individual. In some cranes the bird may even sink to the ground in a "crouch-threat," with the wings somewhat spread and the bare crown skin greatly expanded.

During an actual face-to-face attack, the two birds will individually or simultaneously jump upward and strike out at each other, attempting to rake it with their feet, a behavior that otherwise closely resembles "dancing." This is the "jump-rake" display as described by Christy and George Happ, who have provided photos, names, and descriptions of more than forty social signals of sandhill cranes (Happ and Happ 2011).

Of all the social displays of cranes, none is more interesting or complex than "dancing" (Figure 1.6). Dancing behavior has been observed in all crane species, but it has been carefully studied in only a few, and its functions are still both controversial and perhaps manifold. Although dancing varies greatly in speed and intensity among cranes (smaller species such as the demoiselle dance with greater speed and vigor than larger ones), it seems to have a few common components in all.

The two major ones consist of a lowering of the head nearly to the ground while simultaneously lifting and spreading the wings, followed by a sudden return of the head upward and down-stroking of the wings. Actual jumping often accompanies this return phase, in which the bird may also pick up and throw upward a stick or piece of vegetation. Sometimes two birds perform these activities in synchrony or near synchrony while facing one another or standing side by side. At other times a single bird may dance, or a large group may participate in the activity to varying degrees. The behavior tends to be contagious, and a period of intense dancing may quickly spread through a social group.

While dancing alone, a crane may make a series of three rapid jumping movements, turning with each jump, so that a complete rotation occurs in a series of three jumps (the jump-turn, or "*tour-jeté*" in the Happs' terminology. Or a mated pair may rotate while jumping together (the "minuet" display).

Dancing sometimes leads to flying, especially when it is stimulated by a threatening outside source, such as the appearance of a potential predator. Dancing also sometimes leads to fighting among the participants. It can occur at any time of year and among birds of all age groups. It is prevalent among birds that are forming or have recently formed pair bonds, so its possible role in this general process cannot be dismissed. However, dancing often seems to reflect a general sense of excitement or limited aggression among cranes, and as such it has broader and less circumscribed functions than simple courtship.

Whatever the possible roles of dancing, it is not a direct prelude to fertilization. Copulation is apparently rather infrequent in cranes and is limited to the period immediately associated with egg laying. Judging from several published descriptions, copulatory

FIGURE 1.6. *Crane social behavior (sandhill crane), including bowing (B), tossing vegetation (T), and distraction (D) behavior. In part after Voss (1976).*

FIGURE 1.7. *Crane copulatory behavior (Eurasian crane): male's preliminary "march" posture (1), female's receptive posture (2), and treading sequence (3–5) (after Glutz 1973)*

behavior can be initiated by either sex, but most often by the male (Figure 1.7). He walks toward his mate in a distinctive "parade-march" posture with his tertial feathers raised, his crown expanded, and his bill pointed upward, all of which presents an appearance of dominant hostility.

The female, if receptive, responds by spreading her wings somewhat and holding her neck and body in a somewhat diagonal posture and her wings horizontally spread. This provides a rather flattened surface on which the male is able to stand, after first leaping onto her back. He bends his toes around the leading edge of the female's wings and flaps his wings to maintain his balance while trying to achieve cloacal contact. Following copulation, both sexes usually participate in a postcopulatory display that may last up to about twenty seconds. This consists of various forms of ritualized threat display, such as feather ruffling, preening, and crown expansion. In the red-crowned crane, an elaborate mutual bowing and neck arching are invariable postcopulatory displays, and a similar mutual wing-lowering and neck-arching posture is performed by the Siberian crane. Postcopulatory bowing may also occur in sandhill cranes.

Cranes are unusually long-lived birds and tend to place their nests each year in the same or nearly the same location as they did the year before. Based on studies of color-banded whooping cranes, it appears that experienced pairs return to the same "composite nesting area" (the collective territories used in past years) to reestablish their nesting sites and that other birds are unable to force resident pairs from these areas. Nests are constructed of herbaceous vegetation and are usually fairly close to water or at times even surrounded by shallow water. Nests that are built in water tend to be bulkier than those constructed on land, and both of the species that nest on dry land (blue and demoiselle cranes) construct little or no actual nests, placing their eggs in a shallow depression that may at most contain a few straws or pebbles. In all cranes incubation begins with the laying of the first egg, and both sexes participate fairly equally in it. The eggs are attended from the beginning of incubation until hatching occurs, which varies from 27 to 40 days in different species, averaging 31–33 in most.

Since crane eggs are incubated from the time they are laid and since they are usually laid about two days apart, the young typically hatch on different days. Usually the first-hatched chick will remain on the nest for much of its first day of posthatching life, although it may leave the nest for a short time and be tended by the nonincubating parent (typically the male at this period) while the other continues to incubate. Except in the crowned cranes, two eggs constitute the maximum clutch; crowned cranes may have as many as four, and wattled cranes frequently have single-egg clutches. The nest is typically abandoned soon after the hatching of the second egg, or even after the first egg has hatched, in the case of wattled cranes. Shortly after the last youngster has hatched, the chicks are led away from the nest site by both parents, often into heavier cover. Because it is rare for both offspring to survive until fledging, fledgling cranes are sometimes accused of performing siblicide (the killing of one younger or weaker sibling by another). Although a limited amount of antagonistic behavior between the young has been noted in wild sandhill cranes, there have apparently been no cases of actual sibling-killing observed in sandhill cranes.

During the long fledging (preflying) period of about 55–150 days, the young birds gradually acquire their buffy-tinted juvenile plumage and flight feathers, while at the same time their parents typically undergo their annual molt. Adults of most species of cranes lose their major flight feathers rather abruptly during this postbreeding molting period and thus become flightless for a time. Flightlessness appears to be quite variable, even within species.

In a few crane species (at least the demoiselle and the crowned cranes), however, there is no actual flightless period, since the period of wing molt is much more prolonged. In yet other cranes there seem to be age-related and possibly also race-related or individual variations in the pattern of wing molting, and thus the degree or extent of flightlessness. George and Christy Happ (personal communication) observed that the Alaskan pair they have watched for nearly ten years became flightless only once, after a failed nesting effort.

In addition, it has been suggested that some cranes may molt their flight feathers only on alternate years. In the case of the sandhill crane it is now evident that second-year sub-adult birds usually do not replace any of their flight feathers except for a few inner secondaries, and thus do not become flightless at all during that year. They also retain some of their juvenile wing coverts, which are buffy-tipped and provide easy in-hand recognition of young birds. During their third year all of the secondaries and a few inner primaries are replaced, but the outer juvenile primaries are still retained. Buffy-tipped primary coverts are only rarely present in this age class. Finally, after their third year, there is an irregular molting pattern of wing feathers, and these older birds thus exhibit intermixed worn and unworn primaries representing differing molt periods and feather generations. In nonmigratory Florida sandhill cranes the molt of flight feathers begins in April after the start of nesting, and the growth of new body feathers ends in October. A similar seasonal time frame exists for Florida whooping cranes. In the sandhills, the period of regrowth of primary and secondary feathers last about 45–70 days, or longer than the corresponding period in whooping cranes (38–46 days) (Nesbitt, and Schwikert 2008).

Because of the very long incubation and fledging periods of cranes, not surprisingly, only one breeding cycle is completed per year. However, there may well be a still-unknown incidence of renesting by pairs that fail to hatch their first clutch, at least in those species or races living in fairly temperate climates. For example, the Florida race of the sandhill crane exhibits a seven-month spread of egg records, whereas the Alaskan population exhibits only a four-month spread. The mostly tropical wattled crane of Africa has a twelve-month spread, with a poorly defined peak of egg records between May and August.

Not only do cranes have a single reproductive effort each year, but they also exhibit a pattern of deferred reproductive maturity. There is little information on the average age of initial breeding among most wild cranes, but among cranes raised in captivity it is unusual for breeding to occur less than four years after hatching. The average for eleven males and fourteen females of various crane species raised in captivity was slightly over seven years, with male breeding averaging slightly sooner than females. However, the artificial conditions of captivity are not a close reflection of the situation in nature, and thus it is probable that individuals of at least some cranes regularly breed in their third year of life. With improved rearing and management techniques, captive Siberian cranes now breed at four to six years of age, when previously they were typically at least seven years old at initial breeding.

Studies on wild whooping cranes indicate that two three-year-old males attempted to breed unsuccessfully but fathered chicks the following year. One female produced chicks

FIGURE 1.8. *Adult whooping crane in threatening posture*

when five years old, and another at five or six years. Laying by females as young as two years old have been reported in captive wattled, red-crowned, sarus, and sandhill cranes. The youngest pairs rearing young among twenty-eight pairs of greater sandhill cranes were three years old, including four of seventeen pairs of this age class. On the other hand, among Florida sandhill crane pairs the youngest pairs rearing young were five years old. Thus, there may be racial or geographic differences in the attainment of reproductive maturity in this species.

Surprisingly little is known of relative age structures in most wild crane populations, in spite of the fact that several of these are rare or endangered and that it is usually fairly easy to determine visually the incidence of young birds in wild flocks, an accurate measurement of the past season's breeding success and the long-term outlook for the species.

Given the small clutch size and the apparently low hatching and fledging success rates of cranes, it is not surprising that they have some of the lowest recruitment rates of all birds that are legally considered game birds in North America. This statistic represents the proportion of young birds entering the population each fall and is an important measure of reproductive success. It is unusual for more than about 10 percent of most wild crane populations to consist of first-year birds, which means that the adult mortality rate cannot rise above 10 percent per year for prolonged periods without significant adverse effects on populations.

In the case of greater sandhill cranes, the incidence of young in fall populations has recently ranged from only about 5 percent (in a declining Central Valley population of California) to about 14 percent (in the expanding eastern population). Over the three-decade period 1972–2011, the stable Rocky Mountain population of greater sandhill cranes had an average recruitment rate of 8.1 percent. Lesser sandhill fall recruitment rates have generally averaged 7–12 percent.

Whooping cranes seem to have generally higher recruitment rates than sandhills, perhaps as a result of their protected status. These rates have remained fairly uniform over the decades in the Wood Buffalo–Aransas flock. For the nearly seven-decade period 1938–2006 their collective average annual fall recruitment rate was 12 percent. The fifty-five-year fall–winter recruitment rate in this population from the 1940s until the mid-1990s was 13.9 percent, with about 8 percent of the pairs successfully bringing two young to Aransas (Lewis 1993).

Annual survival rates among whooping cranes that have been surveyed annually at Aransas (thus excluding all juveniles that didn't live long enough to reach Texas) averaged about 87 percent during the period 1945–65, compared with 92 percent for the period 1965–85 and 83 percent for the period 1985–2005. It would seem that postjuvenile and adult whooping cranes have annual survival rates of about 87 percent, or nearly the same as non-hunted sandhill cranes

Survival rates among juveniles prior to arrival in Texas are substantially lower. For example, estimated survival rates of chicks from hatching to fledging at Wood Buffalo National Park have ranged from 25 to 86 percent in various years. In 2012 and 2013, 47 and 38 percent respectively of the nesting pairs at Wood Buffalo managed to raise offspring to fledging or near-fledging.

Approximately three-fourths of the newly fledged juveniles typically survive their first fall migration to Aransas National Wildlife Refuge, making this initial migration one of the most

FIGURE 1.9. (PREVIOUS PAGE)
Paired whooping cranes performing unison-call display, Patuxent Wildlife Research Center, Maryland

FIGURE 1.10. (OVERLEAF)
Sandhill cranes mating on a Platte River roost, Nebraska

hazardous phases of their life. Overall survival from the time of banding of nearly-fledged whooper young through the following twelve months of life is probably about 60–65 percent. Thus, of all the whooping crane eggs that are produced at Wood Buffalo National Park, probably no more than about 35–45 percent of them hatch and survive to fledging, and perhaps only 20–25 percent of the hatched chicks survive through their first year of life. Based on later subadult mortality rates, it is further likely that fewer than 10 percent of all newly hatched chicks live long enough to begin breeding at about four or five years of age.

Although 85–90 percent of whooping crane deaths are from unknown causes, evidence suggests that the most common known cause of postfledging mortality in whooping cranes is collision with elevated objects, especially overhead wires such as electrical transmission lines. Deaths from hunting mistakes or purposeful vandalism are also probably a secondary but often purposefully hidden cause of mortality, for the typical federal fine for killing an endangered species such as a whooping crane is $20,000, plus supplemental penalties.

Most persons find ways of avoiding such severe penalties, but a South Dakota man who knowingly shot a migrating adult whooping crane in April 2012 was charged $85,000 in restitution, plus two years of probation, forfeiture of his rifle, and a two-year ban from hunting, fishing, or trapping. In Kansas three whooping cranes were mistakenly shot by sandhill crane hunters in 2004. As a result, more restrictive hunting hours were put in place in 2005 to reduce the likelihood of such mistakes, only to have Kansas's state wildlife department, chaired by an avid crane hunter, eliminate these restrictions in 2012 and even extend the hunting hours.

Between 2001 and 2014 at least nineteen whooping cranes were shot and killed, including at least fifteen from the experimental eastern population. Likewise, at least three of the forty birds experimentally released in Louisiana in 2011 had been shot and killed by 2013, and in early 2014 both members of a nearly mature pair that had been building a "practice" nest were shot by an unknown vandal. The female was killed, and the male seriously wounded and later died.

Among the Aransas–Wood Buffalo flock, Texas hunters are known to have killed several whooping cranes during waterfowl hunting seasons, including one as recently as 2013. Probably others are killed each year, but most perpetrators are never caught. Most deaths in the keystone Wood Buffalo–Aransas flock (roughly 10 percent annually, or about twenty-five to thirty deaths of fledged juveniles, immatures, and adults per year) go undetected.

With regard to unhunted sandhill cranes, observations on a protected population of Florida sandhills indicate that, among those individuals that were banded as postjuveniles, about 25 percent survived for at least seven to eight additional years. About 10 percent of them were still alive nine to ten years after banding. These observations would suggest that, like whooping cranes, an approximate 85–90 percent survival rate might occur in protected postjuvenile sandhill crane populations.

Another important aspect of crane biology about which little is known concerns their maximum potential lifespan and the length of their potential reproductive life. It is well known that, at least in captivity, cranes are among the longest-lived of all birds. There are many instances of cranes known to have survived more than forty years in captivity, and some have reached ages of more than fifty years. There is even one case of a captive male

Siberian crane that was captured as an adult of unknown age in 1905 and was thought to be seventy-eight years old when he died. Until his late seventies he was still reproductively active, fathering three offspring at an estimated age of seventy-five! Another male white-naped crane at the International Crane Foundation was one of their best semen sources (for artificial insemination) when he was more than fifty years old. Pairs of white-naped and demoiselle cranes produced young when the parents were both at least sixty years old.

What is known of crane mortality rates in the wild would suggest that only a few birds are likely to survive beyond about twenty-five to thirty years under natural conditions, and thus it is highly unlikely that any wild cranes die of old age. Some banded sandhill cranes are known to have survived more than thirty years, even in hunted populations, and at least two color-banded whooping cranes in the Wood Buffalo–Aransas flock had reached thirty-two years of age by 2014 (Karine Gil-Weir, personal communication).

Of the fifteen currently accepted species of cranes in the world, three are currently (2014) classified as endangered and one as critically endangered by the International Union for Conservation of Nature and Natural Resources (IUCN). The Siberian crane is listed as critically endangered. The endangered species include the whooping crane, red-crowned crane, and gray crowned crane. Seven other species (black crowned, wattled, blue, white-naped, sarus, hooded, and black-necked) are classified as "vulnerable." Thus, over half of the world's crane species can be regarded as vulnerable or endangered, and very few can be classified as secure (see Table 5.1 at end of the species accounts).

Humans have attempted to preserve the rarest species of cranes in various ways, such as establishing sanctuaries in locations critical to their breeding or wintering and trying to protect them from hunting along their migratory routes. However, the problems are compounded by the long and frequently international routes that the birds take, often requiring the cooperation of several different nations for protection of habitats along the route. Some of these nations are more developed than others, and they have differing degrees of conservation orientation. Even in the more highly developed ones, it is ultimately up to the individual to recognize and refrain from shooting or disturbing these sensitive birds. Two of the world's rarest cranes, the whooping crane and the Siberian crane, provide examples of the problems of protecting such ecologically sensitive and vulnerable species from extinction. Only after nearly a century of total protection and intensive conservation activities, the whooping crane is making a slow but sustained comeback from what appeared to be certain extinction in the late 1930s.

For comparison, the first serious conservation efforts on behalf of the Siberian crane began in Russia and China at a time when fewer than 200 birds were thought to exist. After two years of intensive searching by Chinese biologists, the discovery in 1980 of a wintering flock of about 100 Siberian cranes on the lower Yangtze River in Jiangxi Province of eastern China was of great importance. Since then, protection along the migration route and wintering sites has improved, and the number of Siberian cranes wintering in China has increased to more than 3,000, bringing hope that this "lily of birds" can soon be officially removed from the list of critically endangered species.

When we are considering the costs and benefits of saving endangered species, it might be worth remembering that cranes are among the oldest of living bird groups, and the sandhill crane in particular is perhaps the oldest known currently existing bird species, based on the finding in Nebraska of a fossil humerus indistinguishable from that of the modern sandhill and judged to be about 9 million years old. Cranes were already on the scene when the earliest primates were small, hesitant, and shrew-like creatures that might well have cowered in fear of being eaten by early cranes. Cranes witnessed the genesis of many of the major river systems of the world and the formation of the tundras, prairies, and savannas that many of them now call home. Indeed, a few million years ago the cranes of eastern Africa were perhaps startled when some hairy-backed creatures from the nearby forests wandered out onto the expanding savannas and awkwardly began to harvest the very seeds and insects that they themselves had so efficiently been consuming for millions of years.

The winds of change have since repeatedly come and gone. The cranes of Europe ignored the human repression and Black Death of the Middle Ages, those of Asia have witnessed one horde of human invaders after another cross the central Asian steppes in vain dreams of glory, and the North American cranes have survived the plunder of a continent's natural resources in a millisecond of geological time. During the past century humans have managed to put most of the world's cranes at risk, at the very time that we might do well to listen to their ethereal calls, which drift out over space and time in a haunting and somehow omniscient cry that carries both the authority of ancient wisdom and the urgency of current reality.

Cranes learned long ago of the need for social living in an indifferent or hostile world, of the value of prolonged and intense parental care, and of concern for the safety of the flock in the face of danger. They have seen mountain ranges rise and crumble, have watched entire civilizations rise and fall, and have observed great climatic changes that sometimes brought other animal groups to extinction. Yet each year they dance with an exuberance that gives joy to anyone with the eyes to see it or even the imagination to visualize it. They seasonally cross entire continents with a precision that makes our best instruments seem inadequate, and they fly with a breathtaking beauty that must make every pilot more than a little envious.

Humans have assigned themselves the unique privilege of determining which of the world's endangered plants and animals are "worth" saving and which are not. In making such decisions, we must be able to look beyond the obvious. Cranes will never allow themselves to be domesticated, nor will they ever provide humankind with a source of unlimited food or eggs. They are here in part to remind us that there should always exist a few wild places on earth where only very special animals can survive. Such animals carry with them unspoken messages from those remote and wonderful places that only they can visit easily. Most people have never seen the Himalayas, nor will most of us have the good fortune to seek out black-necked cranes on the Tibetan Plateau. Yet perhaps it is enough to know that the mountains are there and that somewhere amidst those mountains there is a wonderful species of crane whose home is still largely a mystery and whose life is still essentially untouched by human influence.

FIGURE 2.1. *Sandhill crane, adult leaping*

Two

The North American Cranes

THE SANDHILL CRANE

A Brief History of the Species

THE SANDHILL CRANE FIRST OFFICIALLY entered the world of ornithology in 1750 when George Edwards, in his *Natural History of Uncommon Birds,* illustrated a "Brown and Ash Colour'd Crane" from the vicinity of Hudson Bay, Canada. A few years later Linnaeus classified it with the herons in giving it its first formal Latin name, *Ardea canadensis.* Scientists knew it by this name until 1819, when it was transposed into the crane genus *Grus,* and *Grus canadensis* is still the Latin name borne by the sandhill crane. However, many early ornithologists, including no less a personage than John J. Audubon, believed the species to represent simply an immature plumage phase of the whooping crane.

In 1794, E. A. Meyer described a new variety of crane from Florida, which he believed to represent a new species and which he named *Grus pratensis* (the Latin name *pratensis* refers to its savanna-like habitat). The American naturalist William Bartram's brief account of a "Savanna Crane" was the basis for naming the species. Bartram had encountered the bird in Florida and reported that it "made excellent soup." The Florida sandhill crane, as this race is now known, currently ranges across much of peninsular Florida and extends north into southern Georgia in the vicinity of Okefenokee Swamp. It formerly also nested in extreme southern Louisiana but has long been extirpated from that state.

Among the largest of the races of sandhill cranes by adult weight, the Florida sandhill consists of an entirely nonmigratory population. This population is especially associated with the original wet "prairies"

FIGURE 2.2. *Sandhill crane, adult brooding chick on back*

MAP 2.1. (FACING PAGE) *North American breeding ranges of lesser (vertical hatching), Canadian (horizontal hatching), and greater (diagonal hatching) sandhill cranes and residential ranges of Mississippi and Florida (cross-hatching). Lighter stippling indicates migratory staging areas, and denser stippling indicates major wintering areas of migratory races. The inset (lower right) shows the central Platte Valley of Nebraska, with major spring crane concentration areas stippled. Arrows indicate approximate fall migration routes; spring routes are essentially the same (modified from Johnsgard 1991).*

of central and southern Florida, where stands of sawgrasses once grew over vast areas, interrupted by scattered saw palmettos and cabbage palms and by clumped hammocks of pines and hardwoods on somewhat drier substrates. Perhaps 4,000 Florida sandhill cranes currently exist in that state. They are most numerous in the Kissimmee Prairie region of central Florida, although drainage and housing developments have increasingly infringed on their breeding habitats. On the other hand, the establishment of large areas of improved pasturelands and associated present-day grazing practices have provided increased foraging opportunities for Florida sandhills. Thus, although suitable breeding localities may locally be declining for these birds, their overall habitat conditions are somewhat improved over earlier times, and their numbers are probably increasing locally.

In 1905, Outram Bangs and W. R. Zappey reported that sandhill cranes breeding on the Isle of Pines (Isla de la Juvatud), south of Cuba, are slightly darker than those from Florida, and the birds are also somewhat smaller and shorter. These authors designated this population as a new species, *Grus nesiotes* (the name meaning "an islander"), but suggested that it should probably be regarded eventually as a new subspecies of *canadensis,* as indeed it now is. Even at the time of its discovery, this population was probably not very large, although it was also widely distributed across Cuba. Probably the densest populations occurred on the Isle of Pines, and in 1990 that island was judged to still support a remnant population of about 20 birds. A similar number also still existed in Cuba's Zapata swamp area, and about a dozen survived in the vicinity of Pinar del Rio. The Cuban sandhill crane is regarded now as a highly endangered race. Its population in 1990 was known to consist of only 54 individuals, but by the early 2000s was thought to be in excess of 500 individuals.

In 1925, James Peters concluded that sandhill cranes breeding in the western and northern United States were separable from those in Florida, as well as from the much smaller arctic-breeding cranes, and suggested the name *Grus canadensis tabida* for this race. The name *tabida* means "shrinking" or "wasting away" and presumably referred to its

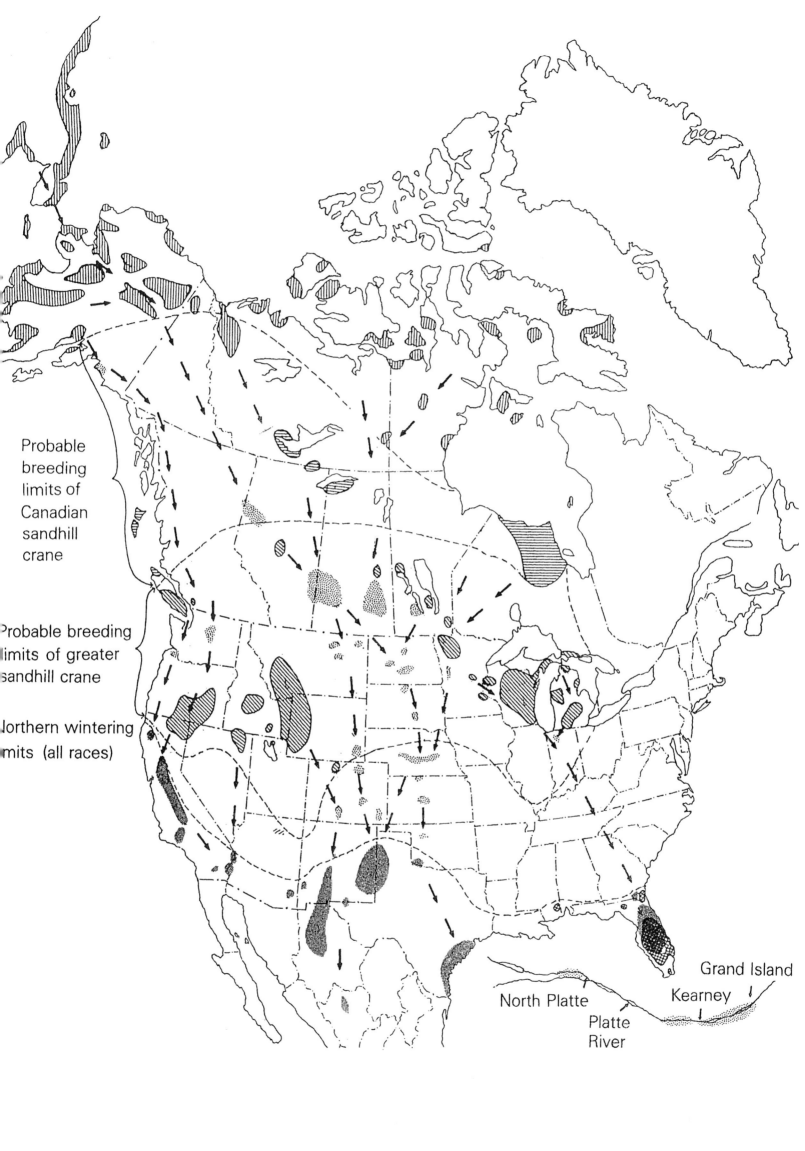

Probable
breeding
limits of
Canadian
sandhill
crane

Probable breeding
limits of greater
sandhill crane

Northern wintering
limits (all races)

Grand Island

North Platte

Kearney

Platte
River

FIGURE 2.3. *Sandhill crane, adults fighting*

then-shrinking population and habitats. More recent observations have shown that at least four geographically separate populations fall within the limits of this race, whose vernacular name is the greater sandhill crane.

One of these is the eastern or Great Lakes population, which consisted in the mid-1980s of about 16,000 birds nesting from Michigan and Wisconsin west through the northern half of Minnesota and into southwestern Ontario and southeastern Manitoba. In less than three decades this population has responded to conservation efforts, increasing over fourfold in numbers, to about 80,000. Birds of this population that nest from eastern Minnesota to Michigan mostly migrate southeastwardly to winter in Florida, with nearly all of the birds stopping for a time during fall migration at the Jasper-Pulaski Fish and Wildlife Area in northern Indiana. Those from northwestern Minnesota and adjacent Canada fly almost directly south to winter along the coast of Texas. Still others from the eastern population now winter west as far as Louisiana.

A second population breeds in the Rocky Mountains, mostly from Montana and eastern Idaho south through western Wyoming and into northern Colorado. This large population component of greater sandhills consisted of 17,000–20,000 individuals in the early 2000s. These birds winter mainly along the Rio Grande of New Mexico, especially at Bosque del Apache National Wildlife Refuge, with some occasionally reaching northern Mexico. This population has been relatively stable in recent years.

A third small population of 2,000–3,000 greater sandhills nests in northeastern Nevada and adjoining southern Idaho and winters along the lower Colorado River. What little is known of its population trends indicates that it has the lowest recruitment rate (4.8 percent) of any migratory sandhill population.

FIGURE 2.4. *Sandhill crane, adult uttering guard call*

Finally, in southern and southeastern Oregon and adjoining northeastern California there is a breeding population of several thousand greater sandhills that winters not far to the south in the Central Valley of California, along with the more abundant lessers. Winter surveys there during 2007–8 and 2008–9 indicated that the percentage of greater sandhills wintering in the Sacramento–San Joaquin delta region comprised about 20 percent of the total sandhills that could be field-identified. The greaters were found to have much smaller winter home ranges, stronger fidelity to wintering sites, and moved between wintering sites less frequently than did the lessers. Mid-winter surveys in the Pacific Flyway in 2007–8 and 2008–9 indicated 20,000–27,000 sandhill cranes in total. By comparison, flyway count estimates done during the 1980s were typically of only about 10,000 birds, so sandhill numbers in the Pacific Flyway have evidently increased substantially, even as winter habitats in the Central Valley delta region have declined.

In 1966 an intermediate-sized "Canadian" race breeding between the ranges of the temperate grassland- and forest-breeding greater sandhill crane and the arctic tundra-breeding lesser sandhill crane was described by Lawrence Walkinshaw and was called *Grus canadensis rowani*. Named after an illustrious Canadian ornithologist, William Rowan, this Canadian race of sandhill cranes is poorly studied. Its breeding grounds are scattered widely in boreal forest bogs and other subarctic wetland habitats across central and southern Canada from central British Columbia to eastern Ontario. The birds from Manitoba and Ontario winter along the coast of Texas together with some greater sandhill cranes. However, little is known of the movements of the more westerly populations, which also winter with greater sandhill cranes of the Rocky Mountain and Pacific flocks. Because of the difficulties of separating Canadian sandhill cranes from greaters at the larger extreme, and from lessers at the smaller end of their size range, little can be said with certainty of the population size of this ill-defined, transitional race, which is closer genetically to lessers than to greaters.

The recognition of the Canadian race of sandhill crane left only the small arctic tundra-breeding forms of sandhills as "lessers." This subspecies *(Grus c. canadensis)* is easily the most abundant of all of the races of sandhill cranes, with population estimates over the past decade ranging from about 300,000 to 600,000 birds. Visual and photographic surveys during late March in Nebraska's Platte Valley offer the best opportunities for estimating the much larger, mid-continental population of this

race, inasmuch as during that brief period this relatively small area supports more than 90 percent of the world's lesser sandhills (plus a few greaters and probably most of the Canadian sandhills).

In 1985 a total spring population estimate of 515,000 cranes was made for the Platte Valley, the vast majority of which were lesser sandhill cranes. This is one of the highest estimates ever made for this population of the lesser sandhill and perhaps is overly optimistic, but it does appear that the lesser sandhill has been at least holding its own, if not increasing in numbers, in spite of extensive hunting pressure. Annual spring survey total estimates in the central Platte Valley (from Grand Island west to Overton) by Karine Gil-Weir and Felipe Chavez-Ramirez between 1998 and 2010 have ranged from 200,000 to about 450,000, averaging out at about 300,000 birds during the third week of March. Many of these birds are headed for arctic breeding grounds scattered from eastern Alaska to northeastern Canada. Other populations, totaling perhaps 200,000 birds, stage farther west along the central Platte and North Platte valleys to about as far west as North Platte National Wildlife Refuge and consist mostly or entirely of cranes headed for breeding grounds in western Alaska and northeastern Siberia.

Besides this primary or "mid-continental" population of lesser sandhill cranes that winters in the southwestern Great Plains from southeastern Arizona to Texas, an entirely separate Pacific Coast population of about 25,000 birds winters mainly in the Central Valley of California and breeds along the southwestern coast of Alaska, from Cook Inlet to the Alaska Peninsula and Bristol Bay.

In 1972 John Aldrich described a small residential population of sandhill cranes that is native to southeastern Mississippi as a separate race, *Grus canadensis pulla*. First discovered nesting in Mississippi in 1938, when perhaps as many as 100 birds existed, the

FIGURE 2.6. *Sandhill crane, pair in flight*

Mississippi sandhill crane population is now essentially limited to a single county (Jackson) in Mississippi, although it may once have also occurred in Louisiana and Alabama. By 1975 it was thought to consist of only 10–15 breeding pairs in a total population of 30–50 individuals. At that time a special Mississippi Sandhill Crane National Wildlife Refuge was established, which ultimately grew to include more than 15,000 acres.

The Mississippi population is still the most endangered of all the races of North American cranes. Its wet savanna habitat has been seriously affected by drainage and conversion to pine plantations. Housing developments and various highway construction activities have exacerbated the problems facing this tiny population of currently only 100–110 birds, including the construction of a section of interstate highway through the heart of its breeding range. Breeding success has evidently also been hampered as a result of reduced genetic diversity, and recently there are no more than 30 breeding pairs, which are unable to sustain the population without supplements from captive-raised stock.

Although many ornithologists have studied cranes at various times, one person whose life has fallen completely under the spell of sandhill cranes is Lawrence Walkinshaw. A Michigan dentist and dedicated bird watcher, Walkinshaw first observed migrating sandhill cranes in 1921. In 1930 he encountered them on their Michigan breeding grounds and became fully captivated. He subsequently spent fifteen years studying sandhills from the Alaska tundra to the Isle of Pines and traveled some 70,000 miles while preparing his 1949 monograph, *The Sandhill Cranes*. No sooner had he completed that book than he began preparations for a monograph on all the cranes of the world. Retiring from his dental practice in 1968, he devoted most of his time during the next few years to the writing of his *Cranes of the World,* which was based on observations in the wild of nearly all the world's cranes. This book was published in 1973 and, together with his earlier one on the sandhill cranes, still provides much basic information for crane biologists.

Seasons of the Sandhill Crane

A CONGRUENCE OF CRANES

There is a river in the heart of North America that annually gathers together the watery largess of melting Rocky Mountain snowfields and glaciers and spills wildly down the eastern slopes of Colorado and Wyoming. Reaching the plains, it quickly loses its momentum and begins to spread out and flow slowly across Nebraska from west to east. As it does so, it cuts a sinuous tracery through the native prairies that has been followed for millennia by both men and animals. The river is the Platte.

There is a season in the heart of North America that is an unpredictable day-to-day battle between bitter winds carrying dense curtains of snow out of Canada and the high plains, turning the prairies into ice sculptures, and contrasting southern breezes that equally rapidly thaw out the native tall grasses and caress them gently. The season is sweetened each dawn by the compelling music of western meadowlarks, northern cardinals, and greater prairie-chickens, and the sky is neatly punctuated throughout the day with skeins of migrating waterfowl. The season is spring.

FIGURE 2.8. (OVERLEAF)
Sandhill cranes on a snowy roost, Platte River, Nebraska

There is a bird in the heart of North America that is perhaps even older than the river and far more wary than the waterfowl or prairie-chickens. It is as gray as the clouds of winter, as softly beautiful and graceful as the flower heads of Indian grass and big bluestem, and its penetrating bugle-like notes are as distinctive and memorable as the barking of a coyote or the song of a western meadowlark. The bird is the sandhill crane.

There is a magical time that occurs each year in the heart of North America, when the river and the season and the bird all come into brief conjunction. The cranes begin to arrive in Nebraska's Platte Valley about the end of February as the Platte begins to become ice-free. They funnel into the valley from wintering areas as far away as northern Mexico, but primarily from eastern New Mexico and adjoining Texas, where a variety of shallow alkaline lakes have offered them safety through the coldest months. These areas are all at least 600 miles from the Platte, the equivalent of a twelve-hour nonstop flight at 50 miles per hour. Some of the birds do stop briefly en route, but probably the majority makes the flight in a single day. They achieve their maximum air speed with the aid of south winds and fly in uniformly spaced gooselike formations, with their wings slightly swept back for optimum flight efficiency. As they reach the Platte near sunset, the formations begin to break up, and the birds start to circle above the river, looking for safe nighttime roosting sites. The occasional calls of the migrating birds gradually build into a deafening crescendo of crane music. Individual flock members try to maintain voice contact with parents, mates, and offspring as they begin to pour into roost sites on the river, and the darkening sky becomes a maelstrom of circling and descending birds. There are no words adequate to describe the voice of the sandhill crane; it has an authenticity that reflects millions of years of history, merged with a contemporary insistence that demands one's immediate attention. It carries across both miles of space and over eons of time, linking those lucky enough to hear it with both the distant past and the present, and humankind with the natural world.

Data from twenty-eight radio-tagged birds studied by Gary Krapu indicated that the daily distance moved away from the Platte River averaged 2.6 miles, with a maximum distance of 3.5 miles. On average, birds traveled 6.0 miles per day, and moved 5.4 times per day. A crane's average stay in the valley was 26–32 days, and their average home range was 14 square miles. Individual birds used an average of 7.3 miles of river channel, with 70 percent of the roosting use done on river sections at least 500 feet wide.

The vast majority of the sandhill cranes using the Platte Valley in spring are lesser sandhill cranes, the smallest of all the races of sandhills and the one with the longest annual migration, from the American Southwest to the arctic tundra of North America and northeastern Siberia. Although small, these cranes have the relatively longest wings of all sandhill populations. These birds have the longest migrations, extending from southeastern Arizona to northeastern Siberia, or well over 4,000 miles. These birds stage the farthest west in the Platte Valley in spring, with major roosts just west of the North Platte Valley at the western end of Lake McConaughy in the Clear Creek Wildlife Management Area and at North Platte National Wildlife Refuge near Scottsbluff. At the time of their arrival in Nebraska the birds weigh about six and a half pounds, and they stand about four feet tall. Like all other sandhill crane races, they are grayish in plumage, but the crown of birds at least a year old is bare and the skin is bright red. Many of the older breeders still carry some faded

FIGURE 2.10. (OVERLEAF)
Immature bald eagle attacking a sandhill crane, Platte River, Nebraska

brownish and unmolted feathers left over from the prior breeding season, especially among their upper wing coverts.

An uncertain percentage (possibly up to 20 percent) of the sandhill cranes in the central Platte Valley are slightly larger birds, with adults averaging perhaps eight and a half pounds and with proportionately longer bills. These birds, Canadian sandhill cranes, are headed toward subarctic nesting areas in Ontario and the other provinces west to British Columbia, to muskeg or boggy openings in the vast coniferous forest that covers the heart of Canada, and tend to be most common in the middle sections of the central Platte.

A very few of the cranes, probably no more than 5 percent, represent greater sandhill cranes, the largest of the migratory races of sandhills. These tall and distinctively long-billed cranes often weigh ten pounds or more. These large birds have notably stronger and lower-pitched calls than do the smallest lessers. The greater sandhills passing through the eastern edge of the central Platte Valley probably head for nesting areas in Manitoba or northwestern Minnesota, but a very few stop in Nebraska and rarely also in the Dakotas to breed. However, most greater sandhill cranes migrate either well to the west along the Rocky Mountains or east, from the Great Lakes states southward along the Mississippi Flyway to the Gulf Coast and Florida.

Counting all races, the sandhill cranes in the Platte Valley build up to a total of perhaps 450,000–550,000 birds by late March, which is probably close to 90 percent of the species' entire population. This number includes essentially all of the lesser sandhill cranes occurring east of the Rocky Mountains and is not only the largest concentration of sandhill cranes in North America, but easily the largest crane concentration in the world. (The other extremely widespread crane species, the Eurasian crane, also had an overall world population of approaching 500,000 birds in the early 2000s.)

The Platte Valley and the adjoining shallow marshes of the "Rainwater Basin" immediately to the south also host up to several million snow geese and at least a quarter-million greater white-fronted geese. Hundreds of thousands of various-sized Canada geese, tens of thousands of cackling geese, and thousands of Ross's geese are part of the mix. Millions of wild ducks, especially northern pintails and mallards, also migrate through the region in March. The overall migratory waterfowl numbers passing through annually total an estimated 7–9 million birds, making the Platte Valley one of the most spectacular concentrations of migratory birds to be found anywhere in the world.

In addition, several hundred bald eagles regularly winter along the Platte and North Platte rivers, concentrating in locations having open water, especially around reservoirs and power plants. While the eagles normally feed mostly on dead or dying fish, they occasionally fly over and harass the flocks of ducks and geese to determine if any crippled or partially disabled birds might be present and provide fairly easy prey. They pay little attention to the sandhill cranes, whose sharp beaks are likely to pose a serious threat to an eagle, and rarely does the sight of an eagle put a crane flock to flight. Young eagles are essentially ignored. However, adult bald eagles at times will attack disabled and grounded cranes and will very rarely even attack a flying bird. At times an immature eagle will land on a sandbar where sandhill cranes are already roosting. Then the cranes are likely to approach the eagle slowly and try to evict it.

The origins of the long-term love affair between the sandhill cranes and the Platte River are lost in prehistory. The oldest known evidence suggesting its antiquity is a fossil humerus, or upper arm bone, found in Miocene deposits of western Nebraska that date from about 9 million years ago. It has a structure virtually identical to that of modern sandhill cranes and other *Grus* species. If it were an ancestral sandhill crane, it would represent not only the oldest sandhill crane fossil ever discovered, but also the oldest fossil attributable to any modern species of bird. At that time in Nebraska's preglacial history, the landscape was evidently a grassland somewhat similar to today's, but having an associated mammalian fauna more like that of present-day East Africa than of North America, with rhinos and horses instead of bison and domestic cattle.

More definite evidence of long-term sandhill crane use of the Platte comes from the writings of various early explorers such as John Thompson, who in the spring of 1834 reported seeing sandhill cranes gathered on the Platte. A later hunter described his attempts to stalk a large flock of sandhill cranes that he saw near Grand Island during the fall of 1841. These were among the earliest explorers and immigrants to use the Platte as a convenient overland route leading into the western wilderness. By the mid-1800s the Platte Valley of Nebraska Territory was to become the primary route leading to Utah and the Oregon Territory. During that time tens of thousands of people followed the Mormon and Oregon trails beside the Platte on their way to new lives and fresh frontiers. Doubtless the cranes and waterfowl of the Platte provided important sources of food along the way.

At this time, even though the Platte was generally placid, it was still a surprisingly treacherous river for much of its length, famously being both "too thick to drink and too thin to plough." Its generally shallow, muddy, and wide channels could easily hide quicksand-like bottoms, and its annual spring floods could easily carry away both men and their horses or livestock. Its innumerable channels were constantly adding to and subtracting from the land, producing new sandbars and islands as rapidly as other ones were erased. Its banks were kept almost wholly free of trees by the spring floods and ice floes, and especially by the lightning-set fires that periodically raged over the prairies.

It is hard to know just what the attraction of the Platte River was to sandhill and whooping cranes in presettlement days, but probably its wide channels and vegetation-free islands provided ideal protection from prairie wolves and coyotes, while the adjacent wet meadows certainly offered protein-rich foods in the form of seeds and invertebrates. In the century and a half since the first white explorers described these flocks, the river has changed greatly. Most obviously, about three-fourths of its volume has been lost as irrigation projects have diverted its flows. The once-raging spring floods that carried mountain meltwaters down the Platte to the Missouri River have since largely been replaced by dried or isolated summer channels. Its once-grassy or shrubby shorelines, now protected from uncontrolled prairie fires, have grown up to gallery forests lining the riverbanks. Finally, its innumerable islands have become shrub- and tree-covered as the annual ice-scouring effects of early spring flooding have been progressively diminished.

With the loss of many of the Platte's historic channels, there has been an ever-increasing crowding of the birds into the few remaining acceptable roosting sites. These sites are now limited to a stretch of less than 100 miles of river mostly between Kearney and Grand Island

FIGURE 2.11. (OVERLEAF)
Sandhill cranes leaving the roost at sunrise along Nebraska's Platte River

along the middle reaches of the Platte in east-central Nebraska. As a result, a population that was once distributed along at least 200 miles of river is now concentrated into fewer than twenty major roost sites over a distance of about 80 miles, most of which are not on protected land and are subject to varying degrees of human disturbance. The two best-protected roosts, south of Gibbon and Alda, sometimes reach peak numbers of about 80,000 birds in late March. By the third week of April they are nearly all gone.

In 1974 the Lillian Annette Rowe Sanctuary was established as a result of a serendipitous bequest to the National Audubon Society by a New Jersey woman educator, which paid for the purchase of the sanctuary's initial 750 acres of prime crane habitat. It is located on Elm Island Road, a few miles southeast of the I-80 Gibbon exit (279), or about fifteen miles southeast of Kearney. More land has since been acquired, and a modern visitor center, the Iain Nicolson Audubon Center, was built in 2003 through the generosity of Iain's widow, Margery Nicolson. The sanctuary now owns or has easements on about 2,000 acres of crane habitat, including several miles of river shoreline. It has become a major destination for crane-watching and associated nature education in Nebraska (rowe.audubon.org). It celebrated its fortieth anniversary in 2014.

The Crane Trust (previously the Platte River Whooping Crane Habitat Maintenance Trust) was established in 1978. Its headquarters are located along the Platte River about three miles south of the I-80 Alda exit (305), or about ten miles southwest of Grand Island. It actively seeks to protect, restore, and maintain roughly 10,000 acres of vital crane habitat along the Platte River, including prime wet meadows and shoreline habitat—and the largest continuous stretch of tall- and mixed-grass prairie left in Nebraska. In fulfilling its conservation mission, the Crane Trust (www.cranetrust.org) also conducts a variety of research, including research focused on whooping and sandhill cranes (and their habitats), while operating the Crane Trust Nature and Visitor Center at the I-80 Alda exit (305) about six miles west of Grand Island. The Crane Trust's Nature and Visitor Center controls access to several miles of nature trails with year-round birding, hiking, and exploration along the Platte River. Both facilities offer access to riverside blinds from March to early April, from which people can watch the dawn and dusk crane spectacles in relative comfort and, more importantly, without unduly disturbing the birds.

The Rowe Sanctuary was initially funded by a single bequest, while the Crane Trust came about as the result of an environmental settlement in federal court. As part of that settlement, a fund of more than 7 million dollars was established for the Crane Trust to use for mitigating critical habitat losses for whooping cranes and other migratory birds caused by the building of Grayrocks Dam on a tributary of the North Platte River in Wyoming.

Today the central Platte River consists of no more than 30 percent of its historic flows, and its width has been reduced by at least 80 percent, from the combined effects of eight dams on the North Platte tributary and twenty on the South Platte and from the extraction of water from the massive below-ground Ogallala (or High Plains) Aquifer that underlies much of western Nebraska and emerges locally as springs and creeks to provide much of the Platte's downstream water supply.

The other primary source of the central Platte's water, the South Platte, has already been seriously dewatered and is often dry. Thus, in spite of the existence of these two important sanctuaries, the historic ties between the cranes and the Platte River are not guaranteed in perpetuity, and the conflicting needs of wildlife and the potential human exploitation of the Platte's water are likely to be brought into ever-sharper focus in the future.

If the Platte has become so seriously degraded in recent decades, what then is it that draws the cranes back to it each year? The Platte still offers nighttime protection in the form of scattered sandbars and islands, though in ever-fewer sites. Perhaps more importantly, the once-vast wet meadows have largely been replaced by cornfields, in which the birds can feed daily for as long as five or six weeks, eating unharvested corn left over from the previous summer. In this way they can quickly build up their fat reserves to a maximum, adding about a pound of fat to their total body weight and putting them into ideal condition for their long remaining journey to the arctic. They must arrive on the nesting grounds in prime physiological readiness to breed, for there will be very little to eat during the first few weeks on the tundra.

Each day while the cranes are in the Platte Valley, they leave their river roosts shortly after sunrise, as pairs, families, and small flocks spread out both north and south from the river to forage in nearby cornfields. The majority of their time is spent in cornfields, where over 95 percent of the food consumed is waste corn. Soybean fields are also available but ignored, as birds seem to be able to extract very little nutrition from consuming soybeans. Progressively more soybean and fewer corn crops are being raised in the Platte Valley, as water supplies have slowly become diminished. Gary Krapu has estimated that by about 2010 there was only about half the waste corn available in the central Platte Valley as there was in the 1970s, when he judged that no more than about 30 percent of the available waste corn was being consumed by the cranes. Part of this reduction in corn availability is a reflection of improvements in farming efficiency and changes in crop selection. Now, with the much larger goose populations competing for the available corn supply, it is an increasingly difficult talk for the cranes to acquire as much fat as they will need for completing their remaining migration and enduring the stresses of breeding.

In earlier years the birds foraged almost exclusively south of Interstate 80, where the human population is lower, but more recently they have increasingly moved north of the highway and thus closer to cities such as Kearney, Gibbon, Sheldon, and Grand Island. The birds have also moved westward, with nearly 100,000 concentrating in the vicinity of North Platte as of 2014, and several thousand more staging as far west as the North Platte National Wildlife Refuge near the Wyoming border.

Besides foraging in cornfields, the sandhills also feed in the few remaining wet meadows, where invertebrates still provide their best sources of high-protein foods. Each evening they return to traditional roost sites, each of which holds about 10,000–70,000 birds, located in the least-disturbed portions of the river, well away from bridges and easy human access. To these roosts vast numbers of cranes return every night near sunset after they have finished their daytime foraging activities. The sunrise and sunset flights of tens of thousands of cranes provide a sight that overwhelms the senses, the din of the birds almost making one dizzy and the sight of the vast wheeling flocks overhead seeming at times like a scene from fantasy or science fiction. The cranes tend to return to the same roosts night after night and to use the same roosts for multiple years.

FIGURE 2.13. (OVERLEAF)
Mixed flock of snow and Ross's geese, Platte Valley, Nebraska

At almost any time while on their roosts or especially while foraging, "dancing" behavior may suddenly begin. This consists of bows, jumps, tossing of vegetation, and wing-flapping activities that are not limited by age or sex. Dancing may quickly spread through a small group of birds and may just as suddenly end. Sometimes it is started by a sudden, possibly frightening stimulus, and under such circumstances the bounding movements of the birds may quickly change to actual flight, but at other times no apparent stimulus is evident. Although crane dancing vaguely resembles some primitive forms of human dancing and as such has been long believed to represent courtship, in fact it may have relatively little to do with initial pair-selection.

Cranes basically pair-bond permanently, with mate-switching infrequent and usually associated with a previous failed breeding experience. Or a female may find a potential mate holding a more desirable breeding territory than its current mate and chose to switch partners, in a manner not unfamiliar to humans. As a result, pair-forming courtship is needed only infrequently among cranes. Instead, various pair-facilitating activities by adults, such as "unison calling," serve periodically to reinforce existing pair bonds. In sandhill cranes, unison calling is done simultaneously by both members of a pair, the female usually uttering about two calls per male call and not throwing her head so far backward during the call as does the male. These sex differences during unison calling probably help to reinforce sexual identity and thus help to avoid same-sex pairings. Acoustic work on various crane species has proven that pair members can readily recognize one another by their voice characteristics alone; their harmonic-rich calls offer great potential for individual variability.

By early April, after depositing a substantial fat reserve, many of the sandhill cranes begin to leave the Platte Valley after staying individually up to about a month and gaining roughly 10–15 percent additional body weight (about twelve ounces). They begin their migration by gradually gaining great height, wheeling about in massive flocks that slowly gain altitude, their broad wings riding the updrafts produced by the warming April sun. Even before they leave, the birds have spent hours during sunny days under the thermals that develop below cumulus clouds. In such flocks they slowly circle above the Platte Valley, drifting gradually with the prevailing wind. Perhaps they are simply reveling in the sheer joy of such low-energy flying, or possibly they use these high-altitude maneuvers as reconnaissance flights to scan the river and commit its topographic features to the collective memories of the flock members. This procedure may be especially important for the younger and more inexperienced birds, which must eventually learn all of the species' most secure migratory stopping points along their remaining several-thousand-mile journeys.

Radio-telemetry studies of 153 cranes trapped in the Platte and North Platte valleys by Gary Krapu and others showed that they settled on breeding grounds in Siberian Russia (20 percent), the United States (23 percent), and Canada (57 percent). Of the cranes nesting in the United States, 3 percent settled in Minnesota, and 20 percent in Alaska. Three percent spent the summer on arctic islands in Alaska (Nunivak Island) and Canada (Richards, Banks, and Victoria islands). Of the Canadian breeding cranes, the birds scattered from British Columbia in the west to Quebec in the east, but the largest numbers settled in Nunavut (15 percent), followed by Northwest Territories (14 percent). Based on their chosen breeding grounds and fall staging areas, four geographically defined breeding affiliation groups were

FIGURE 2.14. (PREVIOUS PAGE)
Sandhill cranes gliding toward a roost on the Platte River, Nebraska

defined by Krapu for Platte Valley migrants: east-central Canada–Minnesota, west-central Canada–Alaska, western Alaska–Siberia, and northern Canada–Nunavut. All of the 153 cranes that were tracked to breeding sites the second year after tagging settled less than 5.0 miles from the sites occupied the previous year, and 38 percent settled less than 0.6 mile from the site used the previous year.

A Teton Summer

In some parts of the northern Rocky Mountain region, such as the vicinity of Grand Teton National Park, a thriving population of greater sandhill cranes nests each year. These birds are part of a Rocky Mountain population extending from southern Alberta to central Utah and northwestern Colorado. The Teton birds are already establishing nesting territories by late April and early May, long before the lesser sandhills have reached their arctic breeding grounds. Here, along the Snake River, the birds share their habitats with another large and very rare species, the trumpeter swan, as well as with a wide variety of other ecologically important wildlife, including grizzly bears, gray wolves, and beavers. Indeed, the trumpeter swans and sandhill cranes are both closely associated ecologically with beavers, for the dam-building activities of these animals provide small, stable impoundments that offer ideal nesting sites for swans and the cranes.

As soon as their nesting habitats become snow-free, the greater sandhills of the Rocky Mountain region begin to seek out suitable nesting territories. Ideally these must have not only excellent nesting locations but also nearby foraging areas where the soil is soft enough for them to dig up spring plants for their edible roots and where some high-protein foods are also available. The cranes are not averse to eating the eggs or chicks of smaller marsh-nesting birds that they happen to come upon, such as those of rails or red-winged blackbirds, and they may even eat the eggs of ducks as large as teal. There are a limited number of ideal wetland territories in this essentially semiarid environment, except where beaver activity has provided an abundance of ponds. Pairs sometimes fight fiercely for ownership of prime territories. Probably most of these fights involve the males of the respective pairs, although their mates take great interest in the contests, occasionally trumpeting encouragements and perhaps getting in an occasional peck or two. The fights may even attract others, setting off a general frenzy of activity.

Fights by cranes are similar to normal crane "dancing," which provides evidence for the view that such dances represent a variably ritualized or stereotyped version of aggressive behavior, including a jumping and simultaneous kicking, an occasional ground-pecking movement or tossing up of vegetation, and bowing or head-tilting movements that expose to its opponent the brilliantly red crown skin of the displaying bird. In fact the crown skin represents an excellent and conspicuous external clue to the internal state of the bird; relaxed sandhill cranes can retract the skin so that it barely extends back to the eye, but extremely excited birds can pull it back to the rear of the crown as it becomes engorged with blood. The aggression of cranes can also be directed toward other animals that perhaps represent a threat to their eggs or young, such as skunks. At times they have even been observed to stand up to such large animals as deer or moose when these huge animals have wandered too close to their nest.

FIGURE 2.15. (OVERLEAF)
Greater sandhill crane pair and nest, with falling snow, Yellowstone National Park, Wyoming

Sandhill cranes do their best to hide both their nests and themselves during the breeding season. They achieve this in part by their inconspicuous gray adult plumages, and even this color is effectively improved in its camouflage value by the birds' habit of staining their body feathers with mud and rotting vegetation prior to the start of nesting. This "painting behavior" has only infrequently been observed in wild individuals, inasmuch as they become extremely secretive just prior to nesting. Evidently it is done at odd times when the birds are not otherwise engaged in foraging or other activities. The birds dredge such materials from pond bottoms with their bills and spread it over their plumage, causing the feathers to become variably brownish from the soil and organic pigments. Gradually their body feathers become much the same color as the dead vegetation of their nesting environment, although the upper neck, which the bird cannot reach, remains unstained.

Just as mates are retained year after year for so long as both pair members remain alive, nesting territories are also reoccupied on a yearly basis by established pairs. Based on a sample of forty-five known-age greater and Florida sandhills, it has been found that initial breeding attempts most often occur at three years of age. However, these first nesting efforts are usually failures, and some birds may not even attempt to breed until they are five years of age. Pair bonding usually begins during the latter part of the crane's second year of life. Because of transitory associations, the subadult crane is, on average, associated with five different potential mates before breeding successfully. However, after pair bonds are firmly established a pair might remain together for ten years or more, depending on the survival of both its members.

In the Florida study, remating occurred fairly rapidly after the death of a mate, especially among males, which required from 5 to about 77 days to remate in four instances. However, one female required 132 days to remate, and another had still not remated 271 days after her mate's disappearance. In this same study it was found that almost half of the sandhill cranes (mostly of the Florida race) that were banded during or after their third year of life had been associated with more than one mate during varied periods of observation (ranging up to as much as eleven years).

Nest construction may require a week or more. Both sexes participate, although observations by Christy and George Happ (personal communication) in Alaska suggest that the male initiates it. Like trumpeter swans, sandhills slowly accumulate material on the nest as the bird stands or sits on it, reaches out, and pulls or throws material to the site. This pile is not lined in the least with feathers. Instead, the eggs are simply laid directly in the shallow nest bowl. Sandhill and whooping cranes almost invariably lay two eggs, which are deposited at intervals of about two days. Incubation of the first egg begins immediately after it is laid. This is in marked contrast to swans and geese, which do not begin incubation until their large clutches are complete. This is an important distinction, for in species that begin incubation immediately, the eggs will hatch in the same sequence in which they were laid and at roughly comparable intervals. However, if the female delays starting her incubation until the clutch is complete, all of the eggs can hatch almost simultaneously, and the entire brood can leave the nest at the same time. This simultaneous hatching is probably especially advantageous for those bird species, such as geese and ducks, that usually have large clutch sizes and precocial young, but it may not matter so much for cranes, having only two eggs and thus with no more than two offspring to look after.

FIGURE 2.16. (PREVIOUS PAGE) *Adult greater sandhill crane tending its two-egg clutch, with one egg pipped, Teton River, Idaho*

FIGURE 2.17. (OVERLEAF) *Male greater sandhill crane tending a day-old chick, Grand Teton National Park, Wyoming*

Fertilization occurs in the days prior to the laying of the first egg, mostly during the immediately previous week. During her egg-laying period, the female usually does not leave the nest at all, but neither is the male likely to visit it. However, as soon as the second egg has been laid, the male is likely to approach the nest and gently ease his mate off it so that he can begin incubating and she can go off to forage. From that point on, the pair takes turns incubating, with each parent staying on for several hours while the other forages or stands guard, watching for possible danger. Often the female will take over in late afternoon and remain on the nest all night, with the male roosting nearby.

For thirty long days of incubation, the life of the crane pair is centered on the nest. Meantime, other signs of spring and early summer are everywhere to be seen or heard. The dawn drumroll of a displaying ruffed grouse softly penetrates the stillness of the dense evergreen woods, scarlet gilia flowers begin to blossom at the edges of woodlands, attracting bees and especially calliope hummingbirds, and in more open sunlit areas early summer flowers begin to add dashes of color to the grayish green sagebrush-dominated upland flats. Here and there a mule deer doe delicately moves through the woods, and cow moose lead their newborn calves through beaver ponds, searching out beds of water lilies, one of their favorite foods. Cow elk have moved up from the open woodland and sagebrush flats by June, where they spent the winter, into cool mountain meadows, where they each give birth to their single young calves in isolation. Within a few weeks of their births, their mothers bring the young calves together. There they form a calf "pool" that can be collectively guarded by one or two of the females, while the others can take time to feed and generally recuperate from the stresses of calving. Grizzly bears take a heavy toll on newly born elk calves and perhaps occasionally come upon crane nests in the process of their methodical searches for calves. No doubt coyotes and foxes also find a few crane nests, and possibly do gray wolves as well.

During the hatching period the female crane sits tight on the nest, while the male stands close guard nearby. The hatching period of sandhill cranes is a critical time, as it is for all birds. As much as twenty-four hours may elapse from the time of initial eggshell cracking by the embryo until the baby bird finally kicks free of the shell, which is done without any assistance from the parent bird. During this time the female sits even more closely than before, only occasionally standing up to look at the hatching egg or sometimes move it gently with her bill tip.

After breaking free of the shell, the chick will lie for a time wet and helpless in the nest, resting from its ordeal and waiting for its wet down to dry out. During that time it slowly transforms from an almost shapeless mass into a beautiful creature covered with golden-coppery down, with a paler buffy ring around the eye. The fluid that initially swells the legs and toes becomes absorbed into the body, and within a few hours after escaping its shell the chick may begin to try standing on its feet. It huddles under the female's breast feathers for a time, but soon is peering out at the world or perhaps even trying to climb up on its mother's back.

Shortly after each chick has hatched, the parent bird picks up the empty shell and associated membrane and either discards them near the nest or, more commonly, eats them. She may also break the shell into tiny fragments and hold them up in front of the chick's bill, stimulating it to nibble them.

FIGURE 2.18. (PREVIOUS PAGE) *Greater sandhill crane chick nibbling on shooting star (Dodecatheon) flowers, northwestern Wyoming*

FIGURE 2.19. (FACING PAGE) *Greater sandhill crane chick among lupines, northwestern Wyoming*

Because of the approximately two-day difference in the ages of the chicks, the first-hatched chick is already adept at walking and swimming while the younger one is still being continuously brooded by their mother. This age difference, although seemingly minor, may be of great importance in crane breeding biology if the older chick seriously harasses its younger sibling. Authorities differ on the importance of this; in more than ten years of close observation, Christy and George Happ (personal communication) saw virtually no cases of sibling aggression, although on only one occasion did both chicks survive to fledging.

Sibling aggressive behavior between the chicks is a rather puzzling aspect of crane biology, since natural selection should favor behavioral patterns that maximize the survival of both young. Unlike many birds in which the young must strongly compete for a limited food supply, at least after the first few days when they are being fed almost entirely by their parents, the chicks soon become able to find and ingest a variety of food items on their own, including highly agile prey such as grasshoppers and even flying dragonflies. Nevertheless, innate sibling aggression might help account for the small, two-egg clutch size that is typical of all cranes except for the African crowned cranes, inasmuch as larger numbers of chicks would probably tend to increase aggression to a greater degree than already exists and make it more difficult for the parents to keep their chicks separated.

As the first-hatched chick begins to gain strength and starts to wander about increasingly far from the nest, the male parent usually steps in to take over its care. This arrangement, physically separating the two chicks from one another, greatly reduces opportunities for fighting between them, and each parent takes on the responsibilities for caring for a single offspring. Each chick closely follows behind one of the parents, while the latter searches out choice food items, such as insects. When food is found, the parent picks the item up and holds it at the chick's eye level, waiting for the youngster to take the morsel after first dissecting the larger items. Soon the chick is finding prey by itself.

When the second chick is able to leave the nest, the tending parent encourages it to follow, and shortly thereafter the family has completely abandoned the nest site. The families tend to move gradually into heavier cover, where they can rarely be observed. Here they will spend the approximately two-month period required for the young to gain the power of flight. During that time the weight of the young will increase from the few ounces at hatching to nearly six pounds, and they will stand nearly as tall as their parents. However, their high-pitched "baby voices," cinnamon-tinted juvenile feathers, and fully feathered crowns allow for ready recognition of juveniles through most of their first year of life.

An Arctic Diaspora

As the cranes of the Rocky Mountain region are busy with their nests in May, those that left their spring staging areas in the Great Plains in April have begun the last leg of their spring migration. Their tundra breeding grounds are still snow-covered and icebound through much of May, and thus the birds must wait in subarctic areas for the breeding grounds to become accessible. Those headed for western Alaska and Siberia fly northwest through Yukon Territory, past Whitehorse and the Pelly Mountains, following an ancient geologic

FIGURE 2.20. (PREVIOUS PAGE)
Bull moose in an autumn beaver pond, Grand Teton National Park, Wyoming

fault called the Tintina Trench that extends nearly 600 miles, from the British Columbia border near Teslin to approximately Woodchopper Creek along the upper reaches of the Yukon River in western Alaska. As they continue through central Alaska in late April to early May, most of the cranes follow the Tanana River valley, bordering the northern edge of the Alaska Range. The cranes migrating through interior Alaska often roost on river overflow ice of the Tanana River, or on the ice of ponds and lakes, as they wait for the tundra of western Alaska to become accessible to them. When the weather allows, they move westward and on into the lower Yukon-Kuskokwim drainage and the associated lowland tundra breeding areas along the Bering Sea.

The northernmost mid-continent cranes headed for mostly tundra breeding grounds in northern Alaska (the west-central Canada–Alaska breeding affiliation) fly north along Canada's McKenzie River, and probably many turn west only after they have passed the McKenzie Mountains.

Other lesser sandhills arriving from Pacific Coast wintering grounds are simultaneously passing north along the southeastern Alaska coast. These birds stage briefly along such traditional locations as the Stikine River delta, the Gustavus Flats near Glacier Bay, and the eastern Copper River delta. These flocks are headed for breeding areas around Cook Inlet, along the north coast of the Alaska Peninsula, or on the lowland tundra of adjoining Bristol Bay. Their fall migration will take them along the British Columbia coast to wintering areas as far south as California's Central Valley.

Along the mild and snow-free Copper River delta on Alaska's southern coast, the cranes reach their peak numbers in the first week of May. These tidal flats of the Copper River, enormously rich in invertebrate life, serve as a final staging area for uncounted millions of arctic-nesting shorebirds, a role comparable to that of the Platte River for lesser sandhill cranes. Shorebird flocks numbering in the tens or hundreds of thousands frequently build up in this delta in mid-May, when there may be as many as a quarter-million shorebirds feeding in a single square mile of tidal flats. Shortly after mid-May the shorebirds make a rapid and spectacular departure, headed in a northwesterly direction for breeding grounds in western Alaska and probably also northeastern Siberia.

How many cranes also continue from Alaska's Yukon-Kuskokwim delta across the Bering Sea to nesting grounds in arctic Russia is still uncertain, but Gary Krapu has estimated the Siberian breeding component at about 120,000 birds. This population is evidently still increasing, and its range expanding, with at least some nesting now occurring as far west as the Kolyma River, about 900 miles west of the Bering Sea. These cranes later return east through Denali Park in early September and through Delta Junction in late September.

Banding data indicate that cranes nesting in eastern Siberia migrate across the Bering Strait and winter from Arizona to Texas at least 4,000 miles away, and perhaps close to 5,000 miles for birds wintering in Arizona and recently expanding approximately as far west as Siberia's Yana River (longitude 140° west). This Asian–North American route is the longest known migration of any crane species. There they encounter and overlap with the major breeding grounds of the Siberian crane. In that area, the sandhills nest at a density of about five pairs per 100 square kilometers (about 40 square miles), and the Siberians occur as somewhat smaller densities. If, instead, the birds simply flew south to central China, as do the Siberian cranes, the sandhills could reduce their total migration route by about half. They would thereby also avoid the dangerous Bering Strait crossing, which is frequently stormy and often fogbound for much of the year.

By late May, the lesser sandhills are on the final leg of their spring journey, breaking out beyond the limit of trees in western Alaska and into the trackless wilderness of lowland coastal tundra that centers on the deltas of the Yukon and Kuskokwim rivers. This is the greatest breeding ground for waterfowl, cranes, and shorebirds in all of North America, and about a quarter-million cranes, or perhaps half of the world's total sandhill crane population, will scatter out to breed in the lowland tundras of western Alaska and adjacent Russia. It is an environment having almost as much water as land, with an endless maze of lakes, streams, ponds, and marshes present during the brief summer. This complex interplay of water and permafrost-bound land provides a variety of seasonal wetland habitats ranging in size from tiny ponds to large lakes as well as coastal beaches.

The lesser sandhill crane is one of the most conspicuous species nesting on the vast tundra flats of the Yukon-Kuskokwim delta. Here at least two-thirds of Alaska's breeding sandhill cranes spend the brief summer to nest and raise their young. Lesser sandhills, like the greater sandhills farther south, are highly territorial, with their nests widely scattered and usually well hidden, averaging considerably less than a nest per square mile.

In the Canadian high-arctic Banks Island population of lesser sandhills, the cranes have been observed to forage regularly on lemmings, using a special head-lowered peering posture that enables the bird to look down lemming burrows for its prey or perhaps hear them better. At times the lemmings are captured in their burrows or, if necessary, chased about above ground until captured. Then they are shaken and stabbed to death and finally torn to pieces.

The problems of nesting in arctic tundra are somewhat different from those faced by the cranes nesting in the Rocky Mountains, with the much shorter available breeding season being the most important factor. Snow or freezing rain is possible almost any time, and even during the warmest months freezing rain may mercilessly pelt the land, threatening to chill adults, their eggs, or their young. Perhaps because of this, newly hatched lesser sandhills have considerably more luxuriant downy coats than do the sandhill cranes breeding in the southern United States. Much under-the-wing brooding of newly hatched chicks is also typical of arctic-nesting sandhills. On one occasion a parent has been observed carrying a day-old chick on its back while standing and foraging, the only time such behavior has ever been observed in cranes.

Very young chicks stay close to their parents, especially to their mothers, who spend much time with the head close to the ground, pointing out food morsels to their chicks or even feeding them directly. At this time the male is more likely to be involved in vigilance behavior and territorial defense. As each chick matures, it gradually strays farther and farther from its parents during foraging and becomes increasingly less dependent on them for food. At least in Florida sandhills, by the time a juvenile is 180 days old, it is essentially independent of its parents for food but still not fully grown, and remains dependent on them for protection and learning to cope with the environment for nearly all of its first year of life.

Lesser sandhill cranes have also apparently been able to adapt to the much shorter breeding season as a result of their considerably smaller overall body size. Although this has not influenced the length of their incubation period, the newly hatched young require somewhat less time to fledge than do the larger cranes breeding farther south. This short-ened fledging period of about sixty days may be a combined result of their lighter body weights at fledging and the nearly twenty-four-hour daylight conditions that permit them to forage almost continuously from the time they hatch until they are ready to begin their fall migration. Gary Krapu and others (2005) have noted that the high-arctic sandhills are now arriving on their nesting grounds to begin nesting about ten days earlier than they did twenty-five years ago, which, with a milder fall climate, gives them about twenty more days to complete their breeding cycle.

George and Christy Happ of Fairbanks, Alaska, have closely observed and extensively documented a pair of sandhills that have nested annually on their property for more than a decade (personal communication). From 2002 through 2013 at least one chick hatched in all but three years, and in four years both chicks hatched. Of the thirteen or fourteen total eggs that hatched, seven young fledged, but never more than one per season. However, the Happs found no evidence of sibling rivalry during those four years when twins were present.

Lesser sandhill cranes fledge when they are about several weeks younger than is typical of greater sandhill cranes, and they are thus vulnerable to jaegers, gulls, arctic and red foxes, and other predators for significantly shorter periods. After fledging the young must be phys-ically ready to migrate within a matter of a few weeks. The Happs have observed that, once the young fledge, in as few as fifty-four days but usually at about sixty days, they are given flight training almost daily, depending on rain, fog, and light level. Both parents take part in these training exercises, which no doubt also allows the youngsters to learn the area's local landmarks. In western and central Alaska the young have fledged by early August. They are ready to leave their breeding areas in late August or early September, little more than 100 days after the spring arrival of their parents.

Radio-telemetry studies by Gary Krapu and his colleagues (2011) determined that cranes of the four geographic breeding affiliations had slightly differing breeding timeta-bles. Those of the western Alaska–Siberia breeding affiliation had an average arrival date of May 17, remained an average of 108 days, and had an average departure date of September 3. Cranes of the northern Canada–Nunavut affiliation had an average arrival date of May 25, remained an average of 107 days, and had an average departure date of September 8. Those of the west-central Canada–Alaska affiliation had an average arrival date of April 30, remained an average of 113 days, and had an average departure date of August 20. Those of the east-central Canada–Minnesota affiliation had an average arrival date of April 23, remained an average of 127 days, and had an average departure date of August 30. In north-central Alaska, George and Christy Happ have observed a range of 118–131 days of summer occupation over a nine-year time span (personal communication).

An Autumnal Hegira

By the end of August the day lengths are already noticeably diminishing, and snow begins to accumulate on the protected northern slopes of the low Kuskokwim and Askinuk Mountains that rise above the coastal tundra. The shorebirds and most waterfowl have by then already

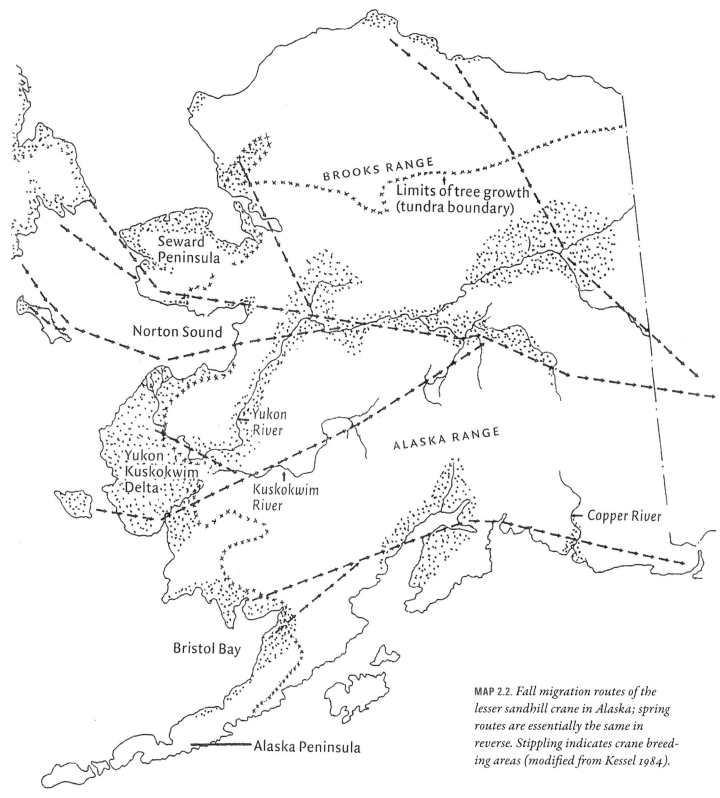

BROOKS RANGE

Limits of tree growth
(tundra boundary)

Seward
Peninsula

Norton Sound

Yukon
River

ALASKA RANGE

Yukon
Kuskokwim
Delta

Kuskokwim
River

Copper River

Bristol Bay

Alaska Peninsula

MAP 2.2. *Fall migration routes of the
lesser sandhill crane in Alaska; spring
routes are essentially the same in
reverse. Stippling indicates crane breeding areas (modified from Kessel 1984).*

left the Yukon-Kuskokwim delta, with many of the shorebirds undertaking phenomenally long migrations to southern South America or, as in the case of the bristle-thighed curlew, have begun possibly nonstop trips to the South Pacific islands. Some of the waterfowl migrate to the Alaska Peninsula to complete postbreeding molts in food-rich coastal waters, while others, such as the spectacled eiders, move out to sea to spend their entire winter in scattered areas of open water.

The cranes soon begin to leave, heading east across the Kuskokwim Mountains and up the Kuskokwim River, where they will join the equally large flocks of cranes coming from Alaska's Norton Sound and those that nested in northeastern Siberia.

As the birds move east along the north side of the Alaska Range in early September, thousands enter Denali National Park and fly past the brooding and majestic presence of Mount McKinley. Typically the birds migrate at a height of about 1,000 feet above ground level during the fall migration period. This altitude is somewhat lower than is typical during the spring migration, when flight altitudes of 3,000–5,000 feet above ground are common and at times reach at least 7,500 feet. Perhaps one reason for this seasonal difference is that recently fledged young birds may be less able to reach such great heights very easily, and the greater heights used in spring may be to avoid the sometimes severe air turbulence occurring closer to ground, which is more prevalent during spring than fall.

Many flocks stop and spend a few days resting and feeding along the McKinley River bars, a habitat that is much like the Platte River. Even more will rest for a week or so on the Minto Flats, along the lower Tanana River, and at Creamer's Field Migratory Waterfowl Refuge on the outskirts of Fairbanks. Sometimes the cranes have to fly in fog or snow and must remain close to the ground, risking collisions with elevated structures such as electrical lines or communication towers. At other times strong headwinds, poor visibility, or heavy rains completely halt their migration. The birds also make a regular stopover farther upstream on the Tanana River near Delta Junction.

As the cranes pass through interior Alaska, they pass scattered groups of caribou that are also engaged in migrations, the animals gradually moving back south out of their tundra calving grounds into heavier winter cover. These animals are soon to face the rigors of the fall rutting season and the even greater stresses of an Alaskan winter. In somewhat heavier cover than that used by the caribou and cranes, moose are also putting on fat for the winter, although they do not have the additional pressures of migration to contend with. Likewise, grizzly bears spend all of their rapidly diminishing daylight hours in their search for food prior to hibernating. They are able to consume almost any sort of plant or animal food they encounter, including even carrion and insects, but relish the abundant fall crop of wild berries that give sparks of cold color to the Alaska landscape during this colorful if brief autumnal period.

Most crane migration is done during daylight hours, with the birds stopping to rest each night, although in fine weather flights may continue well past sunset, especially on moonlit nights. The daylight period is shorter during the fall migration through Alaska than during spring, and thus the birds are more likely to encounter darkness on the longer legs of their journey.

Entering Yukon Territory, as many as 150,000–200,000 lesser sandhills swing southeast and follow a major geological fault zone known as the Tintina Trench (which parallels the North Klondike Highway 2 northwest of Whitehorse), their numbers peaking in mid-September. Eventually in northeastern British Columbia they break out of the Canadian Rockies and pass into the western Great Plains. From there they make a nearly straight-line southeastern flight through the Peace River area of central Alberta. They then fly on into south-central and southwestern Saskatchewan, spreading widely across the region from the South Saskatchewan River on the west to Quill Lakes on the east. Here they arrive in mid- to late September, as the grain fields are being harvested and the native prairies and marshes are rich in natural foods. Based on the radio-tagging data of Gary Krapu and others, they are

FIGURE 2.21. (OVERLEAF) *Gray and black pelage types in a mated pair of gray wolves, Denali National Park, Alaska*

likely to stay in that region from about four to seven weeks and then move rather quickly to wintering grounds. A substantial number of birds from the eastern Canada–Minnesota and northern Canada–Nunavut breeding affiliations similarly stop for a time to forage in western North Dakota, and those breeding in eastern Canada and Minnesota also often likewise stop in Manitoba's Whitewater–Oak Lake area and the Souris River valley.

During their stay in Saskatchewan, the sandhills begin to encounter small family groups of whooping cranes, which have also begun their fall migration out of the Wood Buffalo Park nesting area about 600 miles to the northwest. Many of the whooping crane pairs are by then leading single offspring, already almost as large as their parents, but distinctly rust-colored on their heads and upperparts. Great flocks of lesser snow geese and other arctic-breeding geese also use this same region before hurrying southward to escape winter.

Many of these geese turn toward the southwest and head for wintering areas in California via the Great Salt Lake region of Utah, while some will go directly south to the Rio Grande Valley of New Mexico. Still others follow a route very similar to that of the lesser sandhills, moving on a broad front southeast into the Dakotas and then down the central and southern Great Plains into wintering areas of interior Texas or along the Gulf Coast. During the warmer winters of recent years tens of thousands of snow geese have overwintered much farther north, from Oklahoma and Kansas north to along the Missouri River as far as southeastern Nebraska, southwestern Iowa, and the central Platte Valley. So far only a few thousand lesser sandhills have similarly chosen to survive a Nebraska winter. During the two recent years when this has occurred (2011–12 and 2012–13), there was no apparent mortality associated with the winter weather. Given the generally milder recent winters and the benefits of having substantially shorter spring and fall migrations, it is likely that overwintering in the Platte Valley will gradually become more common.

Although the lesser sandhills and whoopers use the plains of western and southern Saskatchewan simultaneously, there is little or no direct competition between them, as the whoopers tend to use wetland areas while the sandhills are feeding in natural prairies and grain fields. Both, however, must accumulate the important fat energy reserves to be used in making the last major leg of their fall migration, just as was the case during their stopover in the Platte Valley on the way north in spring. During this early autumn period the birds are likely to encounter crane hunters, inasmuch as sandhill crane hunting has been legal in Canada since 1959 and in the United States since 1961.

Many of the effects of recreational hunting on the population ecology of lesser sandhill cranes are unfortunately still only poorly understood, such as the effect of the loss of one or both parents on the chances for survival of their juvenile offspring. Fortunately, a relatively high percentage of the cranes that are killed are inexperienced and relatively unwary young of the year, the loss of which is not so serious as the destruction of paired and reproductively active adults. The killing of about 40,000 sandhill cranes annually also places whooping cranes using the same migration routes in jeopardy of being mistakenly shot.

Although it is known that, like all cranes, lesser sandhills mate quasi-permanently, it is not yet clear just when the cranes of this race normally mature and initially reproduce in the wild, how rapidly they change mates following the death of a partner or "divorce," or what their typical longevity might be under both hunted and protected conditions. Only a very small number of lesser sandhills (probably under 2,000) have been banded with standard metal bands, and even fewer (probably under 200) have been radio-tagged or color-banded. As a result, management of hunted populations of lesser sandhill cranes has been as much a matter of guesswork as of informed judgment.

It is a testimony to the innate wariness of the birds and their adaptability to changing conditions that the North American lesser sandhill crane has apparently not yet been seriously impacted by the advent of legalized hunting, although these annual hunting-related losses probably so far account for about 5–10 percent of its total population. An unknown amount of additional mortality unrelated to hunting also occurs, such as fatal diseases and accidental deaths from sources such as collisions with wind turbines or with overhead wires or electrical lines.

Yet apparently all of these hunting and nonhunting losses collectively still represent less than the lesser sandhill's average annual recruitment rates of around 7–11 percent, and the population is certainly maintaining its numbers, if not actually increasing. It is, however, surprising to most non-North Americans to learn that slow-flying cranes, strongly symbolic of longevity and good fortune throughout much of the Orient and fully protected almost everywhere else, are treated in North America as highly attractive targets for shotguns.

After spending several weeks foraging on the grain-rich Canadian prairies, the sandhills begin to leave in early October. Some of them turn to go southward through eastern Montana and follow the eastern foothills of the Rockies to wintering areas in southern New Mexico and adjacent Mexico, but most will continue southeastwardly through central North Dakota, stopping again for a time in the Dakota grain fields and shallow marshes. From that point on they have a nearly direct flight southward, crossing the Platte Valley of Nebraska. Few of the birds stop there, owing to its heavy concentration of waterfowl hunters. Instead, their destination is the arid grasslands and saline playas of eastern New Mexico and northwestern Texas, where they will spend the entire winter. The whoopers follow a similar route, but rather than going to western Texas they head directly for the Gulf Coast and to the safety of Aransas National Wildlife Refuge.

Gary Krapu and his colleagues (2011) used radio-tags on 153 lesser sandhills to determine that cranes of the four geographic breeding affiliations that they identified fly to different wintering areas. Cranes breeding in the western Alaska–Siberia region mostly winter in western Texas, but about a fourth of them winter in central New Mexico, southeastern Arizona, or northern Mexico. About twenty saline lakes in western Texas provide the most important wintering habitats for these birds. Those from the northern Canada–Nunavut region winter in western Texas, and those from the west-central Canada–Alaska region primarily winter in western, central, and coastal Texas. Cranes from the east-central Canada–Minnesota region winter in coastal, east-central, or western Texas or at more northerly locations in Oklahoma or Kansas. On average, birds from all four breeding affiliations arrived at their wintering grounds in the date range October 17–27 and departed March 2–9. Their average residence on wintering areas ranged from 128 to 144 days.

The greater sandhill cranes of the Rocky Mountains, whose young are fledged in late August or September, also begin to funnel southward during October. The birds of the northern Rockies pass south along the western slope of the Colorado Rockies until they

FIGURE 2.23. (OVERLEAF) *Snow geese at dawn leaving roost fly above greater sandhills, Bosque del Apache NWR, New Mexico*

reach the drainage of the upper Rio Grande in southern Colorado. From there they pass straight south along the Rio Grande of New Mexico, with some birds continuing on as far as Chihuahua and Zacatecas, Mexico. Although most of the Rio Grande's crane habitats have been lost, a few important suitable wintering sites remain, of which the most important is Bosque del Apache National Wildlife Refuge, about fifty miles south of Albuquerque.

This refuge is beautifully situated at the foot of the arid Magdalena Mountains, which shimmer pastel tones in the clear desert light. The area has probably been a haven to wildlife since prehistoric times, with aboriginal ruins dating back to AD 1300. Scattered ponds and diked wetlands provide perfect roosting sites for the cranes and also offer protection to snow and Ross's geese, Canada geese, and other waterfowl. In addition, cornfields planted for wildlife use allow both the cranes and the geese to spend their time in relative safety, although some goose and deer hunting is allowed. Snow geese have responded to effective management efforts, and upward of 50,000 of these beautiful birds have been attracted to Bosque del Apache refuge in recent years. Many tiny Ross's geese are present as well and are nearly hidden among the masses of larger snow geese and cranes.

A few hundred miles to the east, in the dry Staked Plains of the New Mexico–Texas border country, lesser sandhill cranes are also arriving on their wintering grounds in late October. In refuges such as Bitter Lake National Wildlife Refuge, New Mexico, and Muleshoe National Wildlife Refuge, Texas, the birds pour into the shallow, highly alkaline playa lakes that are scattered over this desolate landscape. There the birds must rely on waste grain from croplands and native vegetation, such as grama grasses, to get them through the bleak winter months. Still farther east, in the lower Rio Grande Valley and along the Gulf Coast, sorghum and rice are the major agricultural crops and provide important winter foods for the cranes. In New Mexico as agricultural practices shifted during the 1970s and 1980s from sorghum production to alfalfa, many of the cranes that once wintered in the Bitter Lake region have moved east to winter in western Texas, where sorghum production has remained high.

In eastern New Mexico the shallow Pecos River passes slowly southward in its narrow U-shaped valley, and shallow areas of seepage provide marshes that conform to the outlines of now-ancient channels of this river. These alkaline marshes, fed also from underground springs that give rise to a creek called Lost River, form the lifeblood of Bitter Lake refuge. This isolated and starkly beautiful refuge is rimmed on most sides by low mountains and is characterized by barren salt flats, gypsum sinks, scattered temporary ponds, and impoundments. Rare freshwater springs seeping from underground aquifers offer critical life-sustaining water to the plants and animals of eastern New Mexico and western Texas, although groundwater pumping has caused increasingly severe declines in the southern parts of the High Plains (Oglala) Aquifer.

Other than migratory geese and smaller waterfowl, the wintering birds of Bitter Lake and Muleshoe refuges are primarily lesser sandhill cranes. As they arrive they are finishing an epic journey that has spanned an entire continent in only about two months, from arctic tundra to desert wilderness, one they have reenacted annually for millions of years. Their pattern for survival has been fixed in an endless seasonal repetition of tundra, mountains, and plains and cycles of annual birth, death, and rebirth. In remote and safe places

FIGURE 2.24. (PREVIOUS PAGE) *Greater sandhills in the early-morning light at Bosque del Apache NWR, New Mexico* like Muleshoe National Wildlife Refuge the birds can finally rest and recuperate during the short winter days. And thus they will be ready for another spring flight northward, when the arc of the sun again turns to give warmth and light to the northern lands and renew life to a frigid landscape.

Recent Sandhill Crane Populations

The most common crane in the world is the North American sandhill crane. In the first edition (1991) of this book its total numbers were estimated as follows: lesser sandhill 500,000, Canadian sandhill a few thousand, greater sandhill 35,000–40,000, Florida sandhill about 4,000, and the Mississippi and Cuban sandhills about 50 birds each. The summary in Table 5.1 shows that nearly all of these races have undergone varying amounts of population increases since the early 1990s.

The most numerous of these races, the lesser, has two population components. A relatively small number (perhaps about 5 percent of the lesser's total population) nests south of the Alaska Range along the Gulf of Alaska and winters in the Central Valley of California. The major population component consists of the "mid-continent" assemblage of lesser sandhills that breed on arctic tundra from the Kolymskaya Plains of northeastern Siberia eastward to coastal Alaska and northern Canada, east to James Bay and western Hudson Bay, and on Banks Island and western Baffin Island north almost to latitude 75° north. Many of these lesser sandhills winter some 4,000 miles or more to the south of their northwestern breeding limits in widely scattered wetlands of southeastern Arizona, New Mexico, Texas, and northern Mexico, south to about the Tropic of Cancer along Mexico's Gulf Coast.

However, during the spring flight north nearly the entire mid-continent population, including arctic-breeding lessers, subarctic breeding Canadians, and some greaters from central and southern Canada, stage during late March and early April in the Platte Valley, where its nocturnal roost sizes can be readily counted from ground or air.

Recent ground and air surveys from the late 1980s through 2012 show maximum estimated spring numbers in Nebraska's Platte Valley rather consistently ranging from about 300,000 to 500,000 birds. Counting that many cranes accurately is extremely difficult and open to many sources of variability. However, if these counts provide a reliable index, it would appear that the mid-continental sandhill population has undergone a slight increase since the 1980s or early 1990s, with a few recent estimates (when corrected for probable sampling errors) exceeding 600,000 birds. Owing to unusually early springs during the past few years, recent late-March counts on the Platte have been too late to catch the peak of the migration. By then some cranes had already moved into the Dakotas, casting doubt on the survey's long-term utility.

The cranes are not alone in their spring use of the Platte Valley. Since the 1990s, up to several million white geese (snow geese and a rapidly increasing percentage of Ross's geese) have moved from their traditional spring route along the Missouri Valley west into this fertile valley, supplementing the million or more Canada geese, cackling geese, and greater white-fronted geese that have traditionally used the region as a spring staging area. The cold-hardy

FIGURE 2.25. (OVERLEAF)
Greater sandhills, ducks, and snow geese on a foggy morning at Bosque del Apache NWR, New Mexico

FIGURE 2.27. *Winter panorama of greater sandhills at sunrise, Bosque del Apache NWR, New Mexico*

FIGURE 2.26. (PREVIOUS PAGE) *Greater sandhill cranes dancing and foraging, Bosque del Apache NWR, New Mexico*

snow geese typically reach peak numbers in early March, at least two weeks before the cranes attain maximum numbers, getting an early start on consuming the waste corn that has been the crane's primary spring "fuel" ever since the advent of the region's corn-growing culture that developed after World War II.

Corn-based agriculture mushroomed with the development of center-pivot irrigation a few decades later, using ever-increasing amounts of water diverted directly from the Platte or pumped from its closely associated water table. As a result, groundwater levels declined an average of nearly six feet in the Central Platte Natural Resources District between 1999 and 2006. Not only did groundwater levels decline seriously at this time, but also after an extended drought and increased upstream surface-water diversions, the Platte River proved to be exhaustible. During that period the Platte's largest impoundment, Lake McConaughy, also sank to historic low levels, and for several weeks during the summers of 2002 through 2006 the Platte completely dried up over a stretch of about sixty miles from Grand Island to Columbus, killing uncountable thousands of fish and other aquatic life. Some dried channels of the Platte then appeared silvery when viewed from above, owing to the bodies of countless dead fish defining them.

As a part of a long-negotiated and much-delayed federal relicensing agreement for the operation of Kingsley Dam, the dam's operators (Central Nebraska Public Power and Irrigation District) agreed in 1998 to set aside 10 percent of Lake McConaughy's storable inflows as an Environmental Account. This water would be released for maintaining wetland

habitats of the central Platte Valley as needed. In essence, the broader Platte recovery plan, formalized in 1997 by the Department of Interior and the three affected states (Nebraska, Wyoming, and Colorado), would fulfill the basic requirements of the Endangered Species Act; thus protecting the whooping cranes and three other federally listed species.

The agreement's primary function would add and restore up to 30,000 acres of wetland habitats in the central Platte Valley. The resulting initial thirteen-year recovery plan (the Platte River Recovery Implementation Program, or PRRIP) that was begun in 2008, committing $157 million in federal support and $30 million each from Wyoming and Colorado. The program has thus far (2015) been fully supported by all of the participating parties, resulting in the acquisition of over 10,000 wetland acres in the central Platte Valley and the development of management programs for whooping cranes, piping plovers, and least terns. However, if Nebraska or any the other parties should decide to withdraw from the agreement, the future of the Platte Valley as a primary spring staging area for migrating cranes and waterfowl will be put at great risk, as will the broader water-based agricultural economy of the central Platte Valley.

While center-pivot irrigation in the Platte Valley has produced at least tenfold more corn than did previous dryland agriculture, the resulting progressive dewatering of the Platte has had disastrous effects on the ecology of both the river and its associated subirrigated wet meadows. Yet even with the present-day near-monoculture of corn in the Platte Valley, cranes have had increasing difficulties in finding sufficient leftover waste grain each spring for accumulating enough body fat to carry them thousands of miles to their tundra breeding grounds. Harvesting technology has progressively improved as crop production has increased, gradually reducing the percentage of corn remaining unharvested. For arctic-bound cranes, the combination of fewer wet meadows (their primary source of invertebrate foods, a primary protein source) and diminished supplies of their primary carbohydrate food base means that there will be decreased chances of surviving the spring migration and successfully completing the next breeding season.

The gradual increase in spring snow goose populations in the Platte Valley has added to the goose populations already present, and competition between cranes and geese for limited corn supplies has increased the problems of depositing fat during the cranes' stopover period. Late-March body weights of both lesser and greater sandhill cranes weighed during 1978 and 1979 were found by Gary Krapu and others (2005) to be significantly greater than those weighed in 1996. Reaching the arctic breeding grounds with a fat base inadequate to carry the birds through the early stresses of reproduction could seriously impact their productivity.

Increased stress in finding enough spring food is not the only danger the cranes now face. Recreational crane hunting has become increasingly more popular in the Great Plains since it was initiated as an "experimental" hunting season in Texas and New Mexico in 1961. Legal crane hunting in the Great Plains now occurs in Colorado, Kansas, Montana, New Mexico, North Dakota, South Dakota, Texas, and Wyoming as well as in Alaska, Mexico, and Canada. It also has been legal in several Rocky Mountain states in recent years, where a small percentage of the sandhill population consists of lesser sandhills. The popularity of crane hunting has gradually increased since hunting was initiated, with Nebraska the only Central Flyway state lacking a legal hunting season. The lack of a Nebraska crane-hunting season is the result of the importance of the Platte Valley as critical habitat for whooping cranes.

By the 1970s legal sandhill crane hunting seasons had been widely established throughout the states and Canadian provinces of the Central Flyway. Estimated annual legal sandhill crane "harvests" (the official euphemism for legal kills) by US and Canadian hunters during the late 1970s and early 1980s averaged about 14,000 birds in the Great Plains. There has been a gradual increase in kills since then. For example, from 1975 to 1984 an average of 12,000 birds were killed in the Central Flyway. Texas, Saskatchewan, and North Dakota collectively contributed three-fourths of the total mean crane kill in the Central Flyway of more than 29,000 birds between 1998 and 2003.

Data for the annual mid-continent sandhill cranes, along with population trend and kill trend estimates from 1982 onward, have been analyzed by K. L. Kruse and others (2008, 2010). They judged that the population rose from 1982 to 2008 by an average of 0.5 percent annually, while the annual kill increased at a rate of 2.6 percent. During that period, aerial March surveys of cranes on the Platte Valley have varied from about 200,000 birds in 2006 to nearly 500,000 in 2008, but when a photo-correction factor was applied to adjust for undetected birds, a theoretical maximum peak of about 700,000 birds was calculated.

Sandhill hunting also is legal in Alaska and Mexico. Data for 1998–2003 in Mexico suggests that 2,000–3,000 cranes are killed there annually. The 1975–2001 average retrieved kill for Alaska was less than 1,000 birds. The average 1998–2003 kill in Saskatchewan and Manitoba was nearly 9,000 birds and was tentatively estimated at 9,074 for the 2011–12 season by Kruse and others (2012). Adding in the Canadian and Alaskan numbers to those for the Central Flyway states, it is likely that well over 30,000 sandhill cranes were being legally shot in Alaska, Canada, and the Central Flyway states by the early 2000s. Kruse and others (2010) calculated that the total mid-continent sandhill crane kill had reached a peak of about 40,000 birds by 2010.

Assuming that the mid-continent sandhill crane population now has about 500,000 birds in spring and there is a 9 percent recruitment rate, about 45,000 young cranes should enter the population each fall. In that case, about 90 percent of the potential annual population increases are being killed by hunters, with the rest caused by basic mortality factors such as predation, disease, and accidents. Since nonhunted sandhill crane populations, such as the Florida race, have a known mortality rate of at least 10 percent, one would expect an additional loss of 36,000 birds from such sources every year.

The recent population stability in this population is not so much a biological conundrum as it is a mystery why the US and Canadian wildlife administrators assess the so-called "recreational" benefits of killing sandhill cranes (and the substantial revenues accrued from selling federal hunting permits) above valuing them for their simple aesthetic and crane-viewing values, as is generally recognized throughout nearly all the rest of the civilized world.

In the Platte Valley of Nebraska alone, the estimated economic benefits of spring sandhill crane migration tourism amounts to an estimated $11–40 million annually, depending on how it is calculated, all achieved without endangering the lives of any birds or humans, damaging the property of anyone, or even scaring the living daylights of every human and other creature within hearing range. By comparison, the federal migratory bird stamp, required of all hunters of such species, sells for $15 and raises about $25 million annually.

Considering all the other states that now benefit from crane and general bird watchers (there are now crane-based festivals in several states and provinces) and their associated incomes from these activities, all the blood money acquired by the Fish and Wildlife Service from stamp sales seems like a paltry sum that might be better generated by charging admission to national wildlife refuges. In 2011 46.5 million people visited national wildlife refuges, with 75 percent of the visitors engaging in nonconsumptive activities such as birding and hiking and generating $2.4 billion in economic activities (Carver and Caudill 2013). Only 7 percent of this estimated income was derived from hunting, which is increasingly allowed on national wildlife refuges, a trend illustrating an obvious nomenclatural oxymoron that only the federal government does not appear to find troubling. Even charging only one dollar per person-visit to the refuges would produce three times as much revenue as is now being generated by the sale of migratory bird-hunting stamps, which allow US hunters to annually kill some 15 million ducks, 3 million geese, 40,000 cranes, 20,000 swans, and an uncertain number of other less popular or less sporting targets, including coots, rails, woodcocks, and snipes.

The greater sandhill crane had done relatively better than the lesser sandhill crane in recent decades. It consists of four major populations, plus a small one that has only recently been recognized as distinct. The eastern (Great Lakes) population has increased from estimated fall population totals of about 13,000–14,000 in the early 1980s to about 80,000 birds by 2014. This population has increased greatly in recent decades and has expanded its range into Iowa, Illinois, Ohio, Pennsylvania, New Jersey, New York, Massachusetts, Vermont, and Maine as well as to eastern Ontario and southwestern Quebec. Between 2000 and 2010 there were at least twenty-three nests in Maine, Massachusetts, and Vermont, and at least six pairs were territorial in Maine during 2010. Most of these birds migrate to wintering grounds in southern Georgia and Florida. Some greater sandhill cranes from Ontario, Manitoba, Minnesota, and Michigan have begun to winter along the Gulf Coast in Louisiana, and in recent years large numbers have also wintered in Kentucky and Tennessee.

One major reason for the expansion of the eastern population of greater sandhills has been its notably high recruitment rate. Counts of over 12,000 cranes made on fall staging areas in Michigan from 2003 to 2010 revealed a mean fall recruitment rate of 11.2 percent. The mean brood size among 407 pairs leading young averaged 1.3 young per pair, and 29 percent of these successful pairs were leading two young! This high level of productivity is occurring in a virtually unhunted population.

The eastern US population of greater sandhill cranes was exposed to legal hunting for the first time in 2011, when Kentucky established a limited hunting season. Only some 50 birds were killed during the first season, increasing to 96 during the 2013 season. Tennessee decided to join the hunting scene in 2013, by issuing 400 permits and killing or wounding 352 cranes. Hiwassee National Wildlife Refuge in Meigs County, Tennessee, attracts up to about 23,000 migrating sandhill cranes each autumn, as well as some whooping cranes, and is closed to hunting.

Kentucky and Tennessee both lie directly in the migration route of the newly established migratory whooping crane flock that migrates from Wisconsin to Florida, and crane hunting in these two states poses a serious threat to whooping cranes. Indeed, a pair of whooping cranes was shot in Kentucky in November of 2011, but the culprit remained unknown in spite of a $15,000 posted reward. Other states along the route of migrating whooping cranes of the eastern flock have also considered opening a hunting season on greater sandhill cranes, but so far their better angels have prevailed

A relatively isolated population of greater sandhills breeds in northwestern Minnesota and adjacent parts of Canada and consists of perhaps 10,000–15,000 birds. These birds migrate directly south to winter on the coast of Texas, where they mingle with smaller cranes from northern Canada and are exposed to significant sport hunting. Minnesota began a limited month-long crane-hunting season on this population in 2010, with fewer than 1,000 birds being killed during each of the first two seasons. The number of hunting permits purchased had declined significantly by 2012, perhaps in part because of strong public opposition to the hunt.

The Rocky Mountain population of greater sandhills was estimated at 20,000–21,500 in the early 1990s by Roderick Drewien and others (1995) and was judged by them then to be stable or slightly declining. From 1997 through 2001 this population has remained stable, with fall populations in the range of about 18,000–22,000 birds. These birds have a major fall stopover in the San Luis Valley of Colorado, and wintering mostly occurs in western New Mexico and southeastern Arizona, plus some in northern Mexico. Annual fall recruitment rates over twenty-one years averaged 8.1 percent, and survival rates ranged from 91 to 95 percent during that period.

Arizona began a hunting season on the Rocky Mountain population in 1981 and was later successively joined by New Mexico, Utah, Montana, and Idaho. Drewien, Brown, and Kendall (1995) concluded from recruitment and mortality data that the population could not sustain any increased harvests. The average retrieved kill from 1990 to 1999 was 457 birds. However, by 2001 about 800–900 cranes were annually being killed in these five states, and a peak kill of 1,392 was estimated for the 2009 season.

In addition, there is a relatively small population of greater sandhills that breeds in northeastern Nevada and southwestern Idaho and winters along Arizona's lower Colorado River and Gila River and in California's Imperial Valley, especially concentrating in Cibola and Salton Sea national wildlife refuges. From 2000 to 2012 winter counts have ranged from 1,215 to 3,876 birds, and the population appears to be stable. There is also a somewhat larger (6,000–7,000) population of greaters breeding from southern British Columbia south to northeastern California and wintering in California's Central and Imperial valleys, where they mix with sandhills from northern British Columbia and southern Alaska.

The resident Florida race of the sandhill crane is thought to be a stable population. Since the late 1970s its population has remained fairly constant at about 4,000 birds, all in Florida except for a population in the Okefenokee Swamp in Georgia. Studies by Stephen Nesbitt (1992) indicate that these birds may attempt to breed when males are as young as two years and females at three. The modal age for first successful reproduction was five years, and mean individual productivity was 0.35 young per breeding pair annually. In a related Florida study, 105 nesting attempts produced 34 fledged chicks, and over two decades there were 26 mate changes among the studied pairs. Rapid re-pairing occurred after death or divorce, and abandoned territories were quickly filled, sometimes in only a few days. Some territorial boundaries remained almost unchanged over nearly twenty years of observation (Nesbitt and Wenner 1987; Nesbitt et al. 2001; Nesbitt and Schwikert 2014).

There is a long breeding season of up to nine months in Florida, and bobcats and snakes are probably important predators. As many as three renesting efforts have been observed, even after chicks have survived as long at 16 days, with an average renesting interval of 19.5 days. The average clutch size of 210 nests was 1.78 eggs, and the average postfledging brood size was 1.27 young. These are among the highest brood sizes reported for any sandhill crane population. Yearly percentages of juveniles in the population ranged from 6.7 to 17.8 percent over seven years, the recruitment rate averaging 11.9 percent. Adult annual survival was estimated as 86.7 percent. A similar study in Georgia indicated a mean adult survival rate of 89 percent, with females having somewhat better survival rates than males, and adults higher than subadults (Bennett and Bennett 1990).

All told, these statistics would indicate that Florida should have an expanding crane population. However, the population is seemingly limited by habitat fragmentation and loss. Florida's resident cranes are unhunted and have nonetheless adapted very well to even suburban situations, and are often remarkably tolerant of nearby human activities.

Both the Mississippi and Cuban races of sandhill cranes may be the last surviving remnants of a single population that once extended from Florida to Cuba and west along the

Gulf Coast to at least Mississippi. The Mississippi race is now limited to about 110 birds in a single national wildlife refuge of 19,400 acres, of which only about 12,500 are suitable for cranes. The total refuge population has always had poor reproduction, perhaps because of low genetic diversity, and didn't rise above 100 birds until the late 1980s. In more recent years the population reached a maximum of about 130 birds, but it never has had more than about 25 breeding pairs. Captive-bred birds have supplemented breeding efforts, since the wild stock has been unable to maintain itself.

The Cuban sandhill crane is also a remnant population with limited remaining habitats, and in recent decades its numbers have declined. According to Curt Meine and George Archibald, the surviving birds are limited to thirteen Cuba locations, scattered from Pinar De Rio on the west to the Cauto River delta in the east as well as on the Isla de Juventud (Isle of Pines) and some small offshore islands. Their habitats include savannas, grasslands, wetlands, and swamps. The total population may have consisted of about 650 birds by the early 2000s and is thought to be increasing as a result of recent Cuban conservation efforts.

THE WHOOPING CRANE

A Brief History of the Species

If any single bird species symbolizes the North American conservation movement of this century and the closeness many wildlife species came to extinction, it is the whooping crane. Probably never very common, the whooping crane population numbered perhaps a couple of thousand birds at the time of European settlement, but its breeding range probably extended broadly across the grasslands and marshes of interior North America. In 1722 the English naturalist Mark Catesby visited South Carolina and obtained the skin of a whooping crane from a Native American, providing the first known record of the species in the ornithological literature. Catesby recognized it as a previously undiscovered species and named it *Grus americana alba*. However, it was not until more than a century later that the United States National Museum finally obtained a whooping crane skin for its own collection.

The whooping crane was probably never common; some estimates have judged its pre-settlement population at even less than 2,000 birds. Following the Civil War and the opening of the Midwest to settlement, the whooping crane was increasingly encountered, and its breeding and wintering habitats were progressively altered and finally destroyed. The last three decades of the nineteenth century were especially disastrous for the birds, for during that period not only were they killed by market hunters, but also egg collectors and taxidermists became aware of the great value of whooping crane eggs and skins to museums and other collectors.

It has been suggested that perhaps as much as 90 percent of the entire whooping crane population was destroyed during that relatively brief period, when the rich grasslands of the upper Great Plains of the northern states and prairie provinces were also being converted to farms. Thus, nesting in Illinois was eliminated by 1880, and during the next ten years the birds

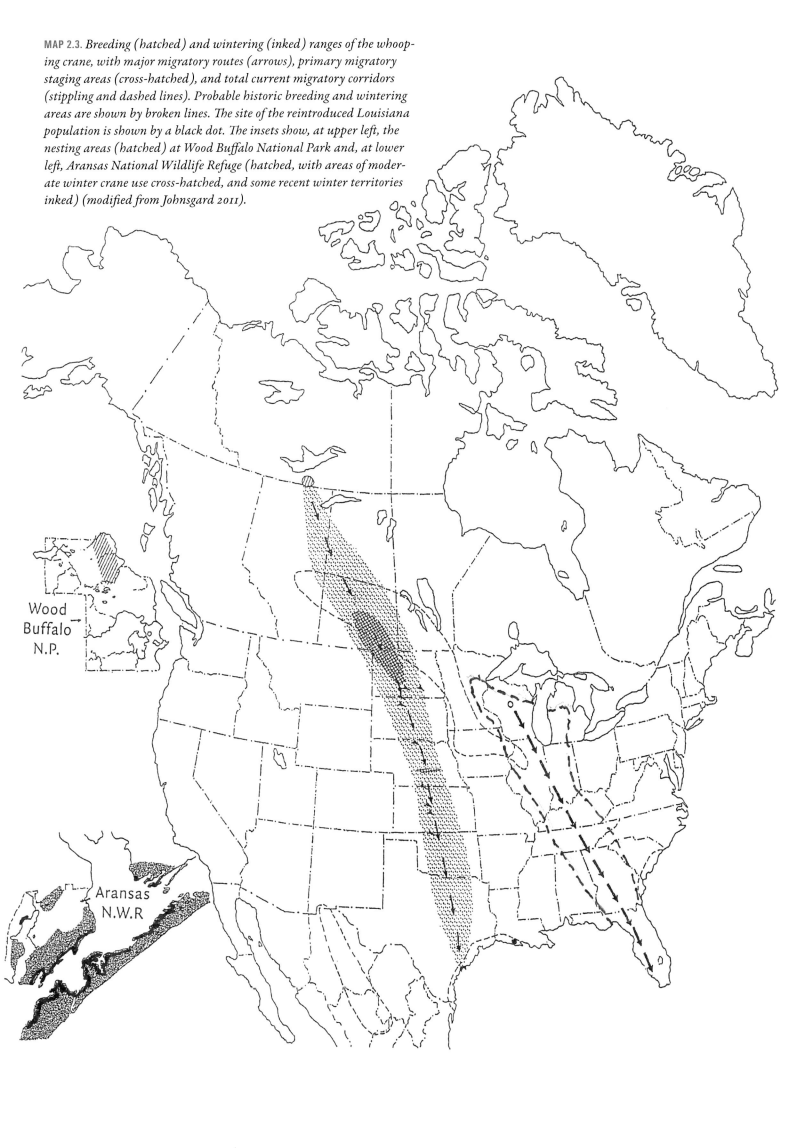

MAP 2.3. *Breeding (hatched) and wintering (inked) ranges of the whooping crane, with major migratory routes (arrows), primary migratory staging areas (cross-hatched), and total current migratory corridors (stippling and dashed lines). Probable historic breeding and wintering areas are shown by broken lines. The site of the reintroduced Louisiana population is shown by a black dot. The insets show, at upper left, the nesting areas (hatched) at Wood Buffalo National Park and, at lower left, Aransas National Wildlife Refuge (hatched, with areas of moderate winter crane use cross-hatched, and some recent winter territories inked) (modified from Johnsgard 2011).*

Wood
Buffalo
N.P.

Aransas
N.W.R

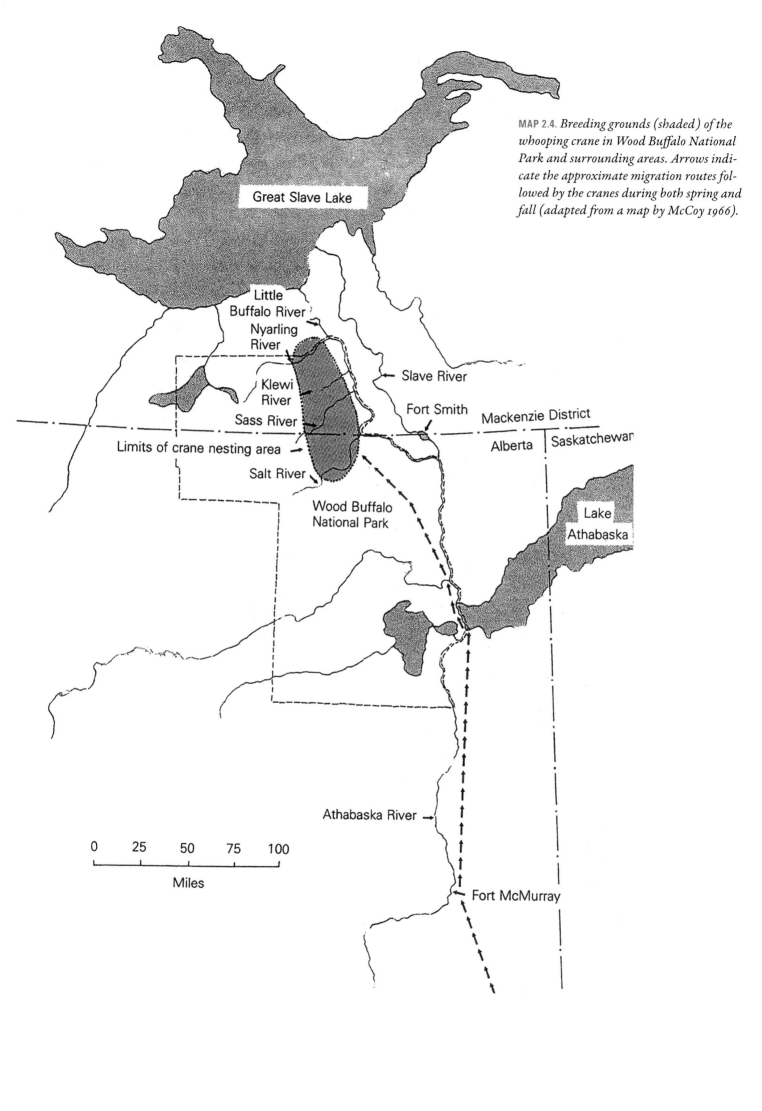

Great Slave Lake

Little
Buffalo River
Nyarling
River

Klewi
River

Sass River

Limits of crane nesting area

Salt River

Wood Buffalo
National Park

Slave River

Fort Smith

Mackenzie District

Alberta | Saskatchewan

Lake
Athabaska

Athabaska River

Fort McMurray

0   25   50   75   100

Miles

MAP 2.4. *Breeding grounds (shaded) of the
whooping crane in Wood Buffalo National
Park and surrounding areas. Arrows indicate the approximate migration routes followed by the cranes during both spring and
fall (adapted from a map by McCoy 1966).*

FIGURE 2.28. *Whooping crane, adult preening*

were lost as breeders in Minnesota and North Dakota. During the 1890s the birds were also eliminated from Iowa, which represented the last known breeding record for the United States. However, in adjacent southern Canada the birds persisted longer, with a nesting pair discovered as late as 1922 at Muddy Lake, Saskatchewan. The nestling chick of this pair was collected for a Canadian museum, and thus ended the last known nesting site of the species in North America.

During this period it was known that a population of whooping cranes still existed in the coastal marshes of southern Louisiana. These birds certainly represented wintering birds from the Great Plains or farther north and apparently also included a resident population of unknown size. During the late 1920s the US Army Corps of Engineers extended the Intracoastal Waterway to Grand Lake, Louisiana, thus making accessible the vast areas of coastal marshes to hunters and the adjoining tallgrass prairies to farmers, who quickly set about converting the area to rice culture. By 1940 the Louisiana whooping crane population had declined to only six individuals, less than half of the previous year's total. During the 1940s the Louisiana population slowly declined from six birds to only a single individual in 1948, and it too had finally disappeared by 1951.

During the 1930s it became apparent that the major remaining whooping crane population consisted of birds wintering in coastal Texas in the Blackjack Peninsula area (between Aransas and San Antonio bays) of Aransas County. Their breeding grounds were judged to be somewhere north of the US boundaries, most probably somewhere in the vast and largely unexplored regions of northern Canada.

A critical moment in the history of the whooping crane's survival occurred during the late 1930s when the Bureau of Biological Survey (later to become the US Fish and Wildlife Service) purchased a substantial portion of the Blackjack Peninsula for habitat preservation. In December of 1937, President Franklin D. Roosevelt signed an executive order creating the Aransas Migratory Waterfowl Refuge (later renamed

FIGURE 2.30. *Whooping crane, pair dancing*

the Aransas National Wildlife Refuge), protecting over 47,000 acres of land on Blackjack Peninsula. The area's bargain-basement purchase (at about ten dollars per acre) unfortunately excluded control of grazing rights and mineral rights, both of which would later cause serious problems in refuge management. In addition, shooting rights by a hunting club extended to the refuge's boundaries, threatening the safety of any cranes straying beyond the refuge. To make matters worse, in 1940 the Army Corps of Engineers began to dredge a channel for the expanding Gulf Intracoastal Waterway, cutting a 300-foot-wide ditch and associated right-of-way through a previously isolated part of the refuge. This waterway reduced the cranes' wintering habitat by nearly 1,500 acres, gradually eliminating at least 11 percent of the species' wintering habitat.

During the area's initial fall and winter survey of 1938–39 the refuge manager counted only fourteen whooping cranes, including two juveniles, causing him to estimate that a total of no more than eighteen birds might be present. In the following fall five pairs returned with young, two of the pairs with twins, and five other adults were also present, for a total of twenty-two birds.

FIGURE 2.31. *Whooping crane, adult incubating*

In 1940 oil drilling began just outside the refuge's boundary, and the Army Air Corps took over nearby Matagorda Island for military use. This 56,000-acre barrier island, along with nearby San José Island, was an important foraging area for the cranes and had been recommended for inclusion in the refuge, but the federal budget hadn't permitted its purchase.

During the fall of 1941 only fourteen adult whooping cranes and two young returned to Aransas, a total that marks a historic population low point for the species, although six additional birds were then still surviving in Louisiana. By 1959 the Aransas flock had increased by twenty birds, reaching a grand total of thirty-four, but this number represented an average population gain of only two birds annually. By the end of the next decade (1959–60), the Aransas flock still hovered precariously at only thirty-three birds, but by the fall of 1969–70 it had gained another twenty-three birds, totaling fifty-six.

By 1979–80 the total was 76, and by 1989–90 the flock had experienced a burst of breeding success and had reached 146. At the turn of the twenty-first century the autumn refuge total was 188 birds, and by the fall of 2008 the Aransas flock had reached a record high count of 283 cranes.

During the past century the Aransas refuge has had more than its share of disappointments. Oil drilling, illegal shooting, and other disturbances along the Intracoastal Waterway became serious problems during the 1940s and still persist. During World War II Matagorda Island was used as a practice bombing range by the Air Force, causing an unknown amount of disturbance and damage to the cranes. It was not until 1955, a year after the crane's nesting grounds in Wood Buffalo National Park were finally discovered, that the Air Force agreed not to undertake nighttime bombing practice on Matagorda Island, which would have caused a major wildlife disturbance. In 1973 the Aransas National Wildlife Refuge finally acquired management jurisdiction over half of Matagorda Island, increasing the refuge's

FIGURE 2.32. *Whooping crane,
adult standing in water*

FIGURE 2.33. *Whooping crane, adult landing*

effective management control to more than 115,000 acres. In 1995 that part of Matagorda Island was combined with a State of Texas Natural Area to be managed jointly for conserving rare and endangered birds and supporting migratory bird management.

Other problems also have persisted at Aransas. Heavy grazing by 2,500 or more cattle on the refuge impacted grassland-dependent birds such as the Attwater's prairie-chicken, and it eventually was extirpated from the area. Since then, grazing has been terminated, and the prairie conditions have improved, although invasive growth by scrub (shinnery) oak is a significant problem. Periodic hurricanes have also ravaged the area. In August of 1965 a major hurricane slammed into Matagorda Island, illuminating the region's vulnerability to such storms, although these have so far occurred when the cranes were not present on the refuge.

By the late 1940s, with the whooping crane's migratory population persistently remaining at about thirty birds, it became increasingly apparent that it would be important to locate and protect its breeding grounds. In 1945 the US Fish and Wildlife Service and the National Audubon Society thus established a whooping crane project, agreeing to a joint sponsorship of field studies, research on crane biology, and especially a hunt for the whooping crane's breeding grounds. Fred Bard Jr., of the provincial museum in Regina, Saskatchewan, initially took up this almost impossible task. Bard used historical migration and breeding records to narrow his field of search to various parts of eastern Alberta and Saskatchewan. His fieldwork began in the spring of 1945, when he and Robert H. Smith, a Fish and Wildlife Service biologist assigned to the project, hunted fruitlessly

FIGURE 2.34. (FACING PAGE) *Adult whooping crane resting in grass on a marshy island, Grays Lake NWR, Idaho*

through many of these areas. During the next breeding season the search was taken up by a well-known ornithologist, O. S. Pettingill Jr. He similarly searched out potential breeding areas in Manitoba, Alberta, and Saskatchewan, partly with the assistance of Robert Smith, but again to no avail.

When Pettingill had to return to his teaching responsibilities that fall, a biologist from the National Audubon Society was named to replace him. This dedicated and indefatigable man, Robert Porter Allen, had already done important work on roseate spoonbill conservation and was a perfect choice for such a daunting task. During the 1946–47 winter, Allen studied winter territoriality in the whoopers at Aransas and also made important observations on foods and foraging behavior, and habitats used by the cranes. The next spring he set off for Canada to look for possible nesting areas in Manitoba, Saskatchewan, and Alberta with the help of Robert Smith.

Like the previous searches, this too proved unsuccessful, and it became increasingly evident that the birds must be nesting farther north than anyone had previously suspected. Interestingly, as early as 1864 two nests had been discovered in Mackenzie District of Northwest Territories, one near Fort Resolution and the other on the Salt River. Both of these had been found in aspen parkland habitat, which was judged by Allen to be the most probable nesting habitat of Canada. These two nests were among the first ever discovered for the species, and therefore Allen and Smith had briefly scanned the general area south of Great Slave Lake from the air in 1947. This effort also failed, perhaps because bad weather had caused greatly reduced visibility in the most promising area.

In 1948 Allen decided that the vast wilderness to the north of Great Slave Lake must be searched. Yet, after extensive aerial surveys of coastal and interior areas, not a trace of the whoopers could be found that summer. Thus four years of searches had all been fruitless. In frustration, Allen turned to writing up his data on the species, which were published by the National Audubon Society as a special research report (Allen 1952).

Ironically, the first real clue to the location of the species' nesting grounds also emerged in 1952, when Robert Smith found two whooping cranes during July in an area of wilderness near Great Slave Lake, southern Mackenzie District. However, a second flight over the same area in August revealed no cranes. Another possible sighting of a single bird was made the next year in the same general vicinity, and during the fall of that year a flock of eight migrating birds was seen along the Slave River, just south of Great Slave Lake. Thus, a pattern involving the Slave River as a migratory pathway for breeding birds, if not for nesting itself, seemed to be emerging. By then, wintering counts indicated that some two dozen whooping cranes existed, suggesting a very slight upturn in their total numbers, but with no real results evident from the winter protection afforded by the Aransas refuge.

The critical breakthrough was finally made in 1954 by William Fuller, a Canadian Wildlife Service mammalogist stationed at Fort Smith on the Slave River. Fuller was doing a survey of mammals such as bison in the Fort Smith region when he received a radio message on June 30 that three probable whooping cranes (including one juvenile) had been seen in nearby Wood Buffalo National Park.

This vast wilderness park of more than 11 million acres had been established in the region along the Alberta-Mackenzie District boundary, largely to protect the woodland race of the bison. On his way by helicopter to visit a reported fire in an inaccessible boundary area of the park, Fuller scanned the area where the cranes had been reported earlier that day, finding two adult whooping cranes. Later in the flight an additional lone adult was found some distance away near the Nyarling River. This news was quickly reported to Canadian wildlife authorities and to Robert Allen, who immediately began to arrange with Canadian and US agencies for a detailed search of the area to be conducted the following year.

Thus, by 1955, the stage was finally set for the discovery of the nesting grounds, which ironically proved to be within an already protected area, namely Wood Buffalo National Park. At long last, Robert Allen and Fuller's assistant, Ray Stewart, were able to reach the nesting grounds, and on May 18 Stewart and Fuller located seven whooping cranes, two of which were observed standing beside their nests. After a great deal of difficulty, on June 23 Allen reached a nesting territory by helicopter and on foot, where he was at last rewarded with a sight of the breeding pair flushing directly in front of him.

After nearly a decade of effort, the greatest wildlife search in North American history was finally successfully completed (Allen 1956). In his notes he wrote, "It has taken us 31 days and a lot of grief, but let it be known that at 2 p.m. on this 23rd day of June, we are on the ground with the Whooping Cranes! We have finally made it!" Later aerial observations that summer indicated that at least eleven adults were present in the general vicinity of northern Wood Buffalo National Park in the area between the Sass and Nyarling rivers, these birds representing about six pairs and their six young. Four of the breeding pairs were found in the Sass River area, and two additional pairs plus several more apparent nonbreeders were in the Klewi River area. All told, the Wood Buffalo area seemingly accounted for nearly the entire North American breeding population of whooping cranes, although Allen believed that the region to the north of Great Slave Lake might at times be used by wandering nonbreeders.

During the fall of 1955 some twenty-eight whooping cranes returned to Aransas, including eight juveniles, the highest number recorded since the establishment of the refuge. At last the hinge of fate had apparently turned. The birds continued a painfully slow ascent in numbers, so that by 1965 there were forty-four birds recorded at Aransas, and by 1975 there were fifty-seven.

More encouragingly, the original flock of whooping cranes wintering at Aransas reached a record total of almost 150 birds by the winter of 1989–90, including some 32 breeding pairs and about 20 juveniles. By the spring of 1990 the total whooper population included 141 birds in the main Wood Buffalo–Aransas flock, 13 in the declining Grays Lake–Bosque flock, and more than 50 additional individuals in captivity, the majority of which are at the International Crane Foundation in Wisconsin. During the fall of 1990 a total of 155 whoopers left Wood Buffalo National Park, including 14 juveniles produced as a result of 32 initiated nests.

At Aransas, the wintering whooping cranes were then not nearly so secure as their increasing numbers (155 in the winter of 1990–91) might have suggested. Important coastal pond areas used by the cranes for foraging had eroded at a rate of up to about three feet per year, largely as a result of wave action caused mainly by heavy boat traffic through the adjacent Intracoastal Waterway. Similarly, the deposition of sediment spoils associated with dredging activities by the US Army Corps of Engineers has affected critical crane wintering habitat, reducing it by as much as 1,150 acres in the past half century. In the process of such dredging, the Corps may well have been violating the Endangered Species Act. Legal action against the Corps by the National Audubon Society has since forced it to agree to reassess the biological effects of its dredging.

Clearly, constant vigilance will be required if the species is to continue to prosper and remain a primary symbol of North American bird conservation efforts. Difficult economic and ecological choices are ahead, such as whether the Intracoastal Waterway should be relocated well outside the limits of Aransas Refuge, whether the refuge's shoreline can somehow be stabilized to resist further erosion, or whether some other less costly solution to the problem of habitat loss and environmental degradation can be found. And as the total population increases, the question of providing enough suitable wintering habitat for the birds must be addressed.

Like the critical role of the endangered Platte River in the present and future well-being of sandhill cranes, whooping cranes cannot long survive without the security and winter foraging sites provided by areas such as Aransas, which is under increasing threats from development and human population pressures. However, without the establishment of Aransas National Wildlife Refuge at a critical time, the species would almost certainly have been added together with the passenger pigeon, Carolina parakeet, Eskimo curlew, and probably the ivory-billed woodpecker to the dismal list of twentieth-century North American bird extinctions.

The Year of the Whooping Crane

THE WINTER SEASON

For nearly half the entire year, from about early November until mid-April, the primary flock of whooping cranes occupies traditional winter quarters along a very small part of the Texas coastline at Aransas National Wildlife Refuge. There the birds spread out as pairs and family groups, which maintain exclusive foraging territories. These territories along estuarine fringes are established soon after fall arrival and are maintained until just prior to spring departure. At the edges of these territories the birds may threaten or even fight with one another. Within the territories the birds forage on a wide diversity of animal and plant materials, but their primary foods consist of blue crabs, marine worms, pistol shrimp, mud shrimp, crayfish, and other crabs. The most important of these foods are the blue crabs and, to a lesser degree, mud shrimp and other crustaceans, which are abundant and easily captured. Other animal materials are probably taken as they are available, but terrestrial plant foods such as the small tomato-like berries of wolfberry are normally of far less importance in the winter diet than is the case with sandhill cranes.

On the average, about 400 acres of salt flats, ponds, and estuaries make up a single winter territory, which typically includes various salt-flat ponds and beach frontage along one or more of the inside bays. The male of the pair takes primary responsibility for defending the territory and also serves as the leader in making any movements to various areas within the territory. Occasionally two pairs in adjacent territories may gradually approach one another during foraging, calling in a challenging manner as they reach the edges of their territories. Such signaling is likely to suffice, and usually the birds gradually move apart again. Exceptions to the code of territorial behavior may occur if the owners of adjoining territories are closely related, in which case an unusual degree of tolerance may be typical.

Robert Allen (1952) once observed two males approaching each other at the very edges of their territories where these came into contact, finally facing one another while only about a yard apart. They then dropped their black primary wing feathers, raised their ornamental wing plumes (the innermost secondary feathers), pointed their bills skyward, and emitted their trumpeting calls. Nearby paired females soon joined in, but the juvenile offspring of both pairs paid no apparent attention to the proceedings. After a short circling walk, with their heads held low, as if foraging, the adult males again came close together. This time each made short bowing movements and finally stood with their bills held so low that they nearly reached between their legs, and their crimson crowns were almost touching. Eventually the pairs separated and moved back into their respective territories.

This observation provides several insights into the social behavior and signals of cranes and deserves some additional comment. First, it illustrates that much of the aggressive signaling of cranes consists of slow, often rather stately movements that emphasize the head (and especially the bare crown), the highly contrastingly colored black primary feathers, and the long, ornamental tertial wing feathers. Calling by one or both members of the pair may supplement these visual aspects of threat display and probably provides a kind of emotional bonding as well as a united front for the pair when they are confronted with territorial intruders. Lowering of the head and drooping or partial spreading of the wings are also evident in the very preliminary stages of "dancing," which thus may be seen as a more complex and apparently more elaborately "ritualized" version of what is essentially aggressive behavior.

Allen thought that the whooping crane's dance must have "an emotional basis" and that as such it probably serves to strengthen the sexual bond between the pair. However, he also believed that at times it might additionally represent a kind of generalized emotional and physical outlet, or even possibly be a means of relaxing. He also observed that such dancing (in sandhill cranes at least) seems almost involuntary in its onset and saw no evidence that sandhill cranes engaging in such dances during spring migration were paired. He thought that perhaps these spring dancing activities might serve as a generalized prenuptial display, readying the birds physiologically and psychologically for the release of actual courtship dancing when they arrive on the nesting grounds. Recent observations of color-banded whooping cranes have also indicated that dancing behavior is more frequent in subadults than in adults, suggesting that dancing in that species may indeed play a significant role in pair bonding.

George Archibald, who danced on a daily basis with a captive but unmated female whooper named "Tex," provided a famous example of the biological significance of dancing in whooping cranes (personal communication). George even slept beside her, huddled in a down sleeping bag through cold Wisconsin nights, to stimulate her to lay eggs. With the help of some sperm from a donor male whooper, this technique proved successful, and George eventually became the proud godfather of a baby whooper, which he appropriately named "Gee-whiz."

FIGURE 2.35. (OVERLEAF)
Whooping cranes taking flight, Aransas NWR, Texas

If crane dancing has an aggressive origin, could it possibly serve as a means of effective pair bonding? Evidently it can, just as the "triumph ceremonies" engaged in by nearly all species of geese and swans in their pair-bonding behavior are believed to be derived from redirected aggressive tendencies. Thus, by channeling potentially dangerous aggressive responses to another bird (who might represent a potential mate) into a harmless "dance," it may be possible to reduce the danger of actual fighting breaking out between them and furthermore provide a kind of mutual social stimulation. In addition, the "unison call" that is uttered by the pair when they are excited, such as in the situation described by Allen, provides an equally important device for mutual stimulation and coordination, and indeed is probably far more important in pair bonding than is dancing behavior.

Whooping cranes undergo annual wing molt in which the primary and secondary flight feathers are molted synchronously, resulting in a flightless period of 38–46 days. In a Florida study (Folk et al. 2008b) 70 percent of the birds studied molted their flight feathers for the first time at three years of age, 20 percent at two years, and 10 percent at four years. The birds never molted their flight feathers every year; the average duration of holding a set of flight feathers was 2.5 years. In Florida the flight feathers were molted from April 10 to June 23, and the other body feathers were molted later, from June 24 to October 23.

The Spring Migration

By the second week of April, the warm southeasterly winds coming out of the Gulf of Mexico have already driven the sandhill cranes north to the Platte Valley of Nebraska, if not beyond, and many of the migratory shorebirds have also left the coast of Texas to cross the Great Plains toward their rendezvous with far-off arctic nesting grounds in Alaska and Siberia. During March the whooping cranes spend an increasing amount of time on land, especially on higher sites, where perhaps they show a gradually increasing tendency to take flight. But there is still no coalescence into spring flocks; instead the pairs and family groups tend to remain distinct, with territorial boundaries being maintained. Then one day, often with a south wind and clear skies, each family somehow makes the fateful decision to leave, and with that they take off, circle about to gain a thousand feet or more of altitude, and finally head north without hesitation.

The usual spring migration flock consists of only two or three birds, a pair and their single surviving juvenile of the previous year. However, a surprising number of whooping cranes migrate north as single birds. Groups of up to ten birds are at times seen in spring; color-banding analyses (Karine Gil-Weir, personal communication) suggest that these are likely to be multigenerational family groups consisting of up to at least four generations migrating together. When flying in groups of three or more birds, the typical migrating flock pattern is more regularly V-shaped than that of sandhill cranes. The older birds take the lead, and the younger ones tag along behind, thereby gaining the benefits of reduced wind pressure and enhanced wind flow from the bird in front, relying on the lead bird to make decisions on stopping places. It has been estimated that the energy-saving benefits of such formation-flying may amount to as much as a 20 percent reduction in energy costs for large birds like cranes and geese.

Although cranes are normally rather slow-flying birds, while on migration they remain in tight formation and assume a distinctly streamlined wing conformation, using a combination of alternating thermal-aided ascents and long glide-path descents to save energy and gain speed. Robert Allen accurately judged that a typical cruising air speed for whooping cranes is forty-five miles per hour, which with the aid of moderate tail winds would produce ground speeds in excess of fifty miles per hour. Since the birds regularly choose following winds for migration, ground speeds are likely to be greater than observed air speeds.

The trip north from Aransas to the Platte Valley of Nebraska is done over a several-day period, especially for pairs that are leading young. Historically, the Platte Valley has been the most important single spring stopover area for whooping cranes, the birds remaining in the region for several days. In earlier times the birds roosted on the river at night and fed on frog and toad egg masses that they found in the numerous remaining buffalo wallows. The whoopers also seemed to favor the open areas of buffalo grass, turning over the cattle chips and feeding on the beetles that they found underneath. At least in early years, some of the birds remained in the Platte Valley until about the first of May, or after all the other larger spring migrants had already left except for the American white pelican.

In recent years, dewatering of the Platte River in Nebraska for irrigation and other purposes has reduced its attractiveness to whooping cranes, but it was still sufficiently important that it was one of the first sites to be designated as "critical habitat" for whooping cranes after the passage of the Endangered Species Act. In the early 1970s the US Fish and Wildlife Service tried to establish a national wildlife refuge of about 15,000 acres of prime Platte River habitat, but it alienated and infuriated local landowners by trying to obtain the land through condemnation rather than fair purchase offers. As a result, these efforts failed miserably, and it was feared that no real protection would ever be provided in the Platte Valley.

However, in 1974 the National Audubon Society used an unexpected but highly serendipitous bequest of a New Jersey professor, Lillian Annette Rowe, to purchase 750 acres of habitat for a nature sanctuary along the Platte's major channel southwest of Gibbon in prime crane habitat. The total protected area, through later purchases and conservation easements, has since been expanded to nearly 20,000 acres.

In 1979 the Platte River Whooping Crane Critical Habitat Maintenance Trust (renamed the Crane Trust in 2012) was established as part of the habitat loss mitigation settlement associated with the building of the Grayrocks Dam in Wyoming on a North Platte tributary. One of the trust's properties, a 2,000-acre Mormon Island preserve, consists of diverse wet meadows, shallow river channels with sandbars, variably vegetated islands, and riverine woodland vegetation and represents one of the best of the few remaining Platte River wetlands still usable by whooping cranes. Collectively the Crane Trust now manages or helps manage about 10,000 acres of crane habitat in the Platte Valley. Restoration of river stretches through brush removal and disking from Grand Island to Kearney by the Crane Trust, Rowe Sanctuary, and Nature Conservancy have opened new channels and made barren many previously overgrown sand bars and islands, providing both additional crane roosting habitat and ideal nesting sites for least terns and piping plovers.

In 2007 the Platte River Recovery Implementation Program (PRRIP) was established on the basis of joint agreements by Colorado, Wyoming, Nebraska, and the federal

FIGURE 2.36. (OVERLEAF) *Six whooping cranes migrating over western North Dakota*

government; it has invested about $150 million over a multiyear restoration of the central Platte River for the benefit of four endangered and threatened species, including the whooping crane. By 2012 the PRRIP had gained management control of more than 10,000 acres of crane wetland habitat in the central Platte Valley, through purchase, leases, sponsorship agreements, or perpetual easements. It has also participated in a Platte and North Platte River restoration project through chemical control of invasive and channel-blocking plants such as the tall reed grass *Phragmites*. Through 2012 the program had spent over $53 million in habitat acquisition, wetland rehabilitation, monitoring, and research.

Through the efforts of the Audubon Society, the Crane Trust, the Nature Conservancy, and the PRRIP, habitat acquisition and wetland improvement programs along the central Platte have vastly improved its wildlife values. Whooping cranes have been using this part of the Platte Valley with increasing frequency, usually arriving about the time that most sandhills have departed and remaining anywhere from a day to a week or more, but more often no longer than a day or two.

After leaving Nebraska, the birds continue on their slightly west-of-north bearing, crossing the central Dakotas, making a diagonal crossing from southeastern to northwestern Saskatchewan, and entering northeastern Alberta in the general vicinity of Fort McMurray. By then they have left the grasslands and croplands of the Great Plains, crossed the mixed hardwood-conifer forests of central Saskatchewan and Alberta, and entered the great boreal forest region that stretches from the Pacific coast of Canada to the Atlantic.

The cranes soon become swallowed up in that enormous wilderness, somehow finding their way to their traditional breeding grounds at Wood Buffalo Park. Quite possibly they encounter the Athabaska River or its tributaries shortly after entering Alberta, follow it north to Lake Athabaska, and then simply follow the Slave River to reach their nesting grounds in northern Wood Buffalo Park. Young birds remain with their parents until they arrive at the breeding grounds, after which the family bonds are temporarily broken. Considering that some of the cranes in the population are known to survive beyond thirty years, memory of landmarks encountered during previous migrations must play an important role in the species' migratory traditions.

THE BREEDING GROUNDS

The final spring destination of the birds is a subarctic muskeg-like area of glaciated potholes, with innumerable ponds and small lakes varying in size from less than an acre to about sixty acres. All of these are quite shallow and are separated from one another by low, sandy ridges that support a dense growth of birches, willows, black spruce, and tamaracks. The ponds in turn have edges that are densely covered with bulrushes, cattails, sedges, and all of the other shoreline plants of the region. Because of the fairly recent glacial action (the area lies at the southern boundary of the Precambrian Shield, a vast area of scoured-off ancient rock that covers much of arctic Canada), the surface clay soils have limestone-derived glacial till materials that are quite high in calcium rather than being distinctly acidic. The cranes use those ponds that are slightly on the alkaline side, ignoring or avoiding nearby ponds that are somewhat more acidic and less rich in invertebrates. In addition, the birds use only those sites that are shallow enough to allow for easy foraging by wading.

Sharing the whooping crane's nesting habitat are such lake- or marsh-adapted birds as the sora, Wilson's snipe, American bittern, red-winged blackbird, and Pacific loon, brush-nesting sparrows such as the song sparrow and Lincoln's sparrow, and a variety of ground-nesting ducks, including the mallard and green-winged teal. On slightly drier sites lesser yellowlegs and least sandpipers nest, and American kestrels, dark-eyed juncos, chipping sparrows, and northern flickers all find suitable nest sites in more wooded upland habitats. Gray wolves are common in the region, and red foxes and lynxes also occur, as do black bears and wolverines. Bald eagles, golden eagles, and ravens are also present. Of these, ravens may be the most significant egg predators, although whooping cranes can protect their nests quite effectively against most avian and mammalian threats.

Although the region does not receive much annual precipitation, drainage is poor, and higher than normal precipitation early in the nesting season may cause nest flooding, delayed nesting, and lowered overall breeding success. On the other hand, below-average precipitation allows the nesting season to proceed normally, although the adults and young may have to travel farther from the nest site to forage. Regardless of the weather, there are always enough potholes of varying depths to allow for adequate foraging. The most important foods for the cranes are immature stages of dragonflies, caddisflies, mayflies, and other insects, plus some fresh-water crustaceans. Some terrestrial foods such as berries are also eaten, but much of the protein needed by the growing chicks must come from aquatic sources.

Probably because of the great food needs of adults and young, breeding territories of whooping cranes are extremely large. Eighteen breeding territories averaged nearly 1,900 acres each, but with considerable individual variation. Substantial seemingly unused areas often existed between adjoining nesting territories, at least in the case of the larger territories. Territories are typically used by the same pair for many years and probably are vacated only with the death of both adults during the same year. However, the same nest site is rarely if ever used in successive years, although the birds may nest in the same marsh. Because of the low population density, there are few actual contacts with or territorial conflicts between adjoining territorial pairs, although resident birds will attack and frighten off any intruding cranes, whether these are single individuals or pairs.

As in other cranes, pair bonds in whooping cranes are essentially permanent and potentially lifelong. Although apparent pair-bonding behavior has been observed in two-year-old birds, it is likely that they usually begin nesting as five- to six-year-olds, by which time the birds probably are sufficiently experienced to establish and defend suitable nesting territories successfully. The youngest whooping crane so far known to have nested in the wild at Wood Buffalo was three years old, and the oldest was seven years old when it first nested.

In spite of such delayed sexual maturity and permanent pair bonding, new mates can sometimes be taken fairly rapidly when the situation requires. Thus, when one of the adults (probably a male) of a wintering pair was lost in January to unknown causes, the surviving bird had taken on a new mate within a period of only three weeks. Likewise, during a lifetime of at least thirty-five years, one male ("Crip") was known to have had a total of five different mates, three of which were provided to him under captive conditions. After

FIGURE 2.37. (OVERLEAF)
Migrant whooping cranes arriving at Wood Buffalo National Park, Alberta

his first wild mate was shot in March 1948, Crip was observed with a new mate within a month. Since copulations are rarely if ever observed on the wintering grounds, it is apparent that this behavior must play little or no role in pair-bond formation. In one of the few descriptions of copulatory behavior (Lewis 1993), it would seem to be very similar to that of other cranes species and is said to occur at any time of day, but is most frequent at daybreak. Observations on the breeding of nonmigratory whooping cranes in Florida (Folk et al. 2005) indicate that copulations can begin as early as sixty-two days prior to incubation and are mostly likely to occur between early morning and early afternoon hours. The only known case of extra-pair copulation was observed in Florida, when a female whose chick had been predated three days earlier copulated with a lone male.

Nests are usually built along the margins of lakes or marshes, among rushes and sedges growing in water from about eight to eighteen inches in depth. During the period when breeding still occurred in the Great Plains, nests were also found on the tops of muskrat houses and on damp prairie sites near water. The nests are huge, ranging from two to five feet in diameter, and rising eight to nineteen inches above the surrounding water level. However, changing water levels can greatly alter both the surrounding water depth and the height of the nest above water.

Eggs are laid at intervals of two days, and the vast majority of nests have two eggs present in completed clutches. Less than 10 percent of the incubated nests have only a single egg present (some of these possibly resulting from egg losses), and even more rarely (in about 1–2 percent of the nests) three eggs have been found. Although renesting is known to occur fairly commonly in greater sandhill cranes to the south, where there is more available time for breeding, only a few cases of apparent renesting have been found in whooping cranes following nest abandonment or other causes of nest loss.

Both sexes assist in incubation, with the male perhaps incubating somewhat more during the day and the female doing more nighttime sitting. The nonincubating bird always remains alert and fairly near the nest, ready to sound an alarm and to ward off any intruders, whether they be small or potentially serious threats to the sitting bird and the eggs. Video surveillance studies in Florida found that, at nests that failed, pairs exchanged incubation duties infrequently and did not share in these duties equally, whereas in successful nests the mean incubation bout lasted 32.5 minutes and the mean duration that the nest was left untended by either parent was only 1.5 minutes.

Incubation requires thirty-three or thirty-four days in the wild, and somewhat less under conditions of artificial incubation. The second-laid egg normally hatches two or three days after the first, since incubation begins immediately after the first egg is laid. Only a few cases of attempted renesting following nest loss have been observed among birds at Wood Buffalo Park, but this occurs commonly among hand-raised birds whose first clutch of eggs has been removed.

Newly hatched whooping cranes are very similar in color to the golden-garbed chicks of the sandhills, although they are substantially larger and average about five ounces. The chicks are able to swim about almost immediately after hatching, but are brooded frequently by the parents, especially during the cool nights and often unsettled weather that is typical of late June and early July in northern Canada. Typically the family leaves the nest site when the younger chick is two days old. During the first three weeks or so after hatching, the family remains within a mile or so of the nest. By the time they are three weeks old, the chicks weigh about four times what they did at hatching, and by six weeks they are almost sixteen times their hatching weight. Their six-weeks weight is again doubled by the time they are ten weeks old. Fledging typically occurs at eighty to ninety days, so a minimum of about four months is needed too complete a breeding cycle, placing a northern limit on potential breeding habitat for the species.

The birds move around to feed at a substantial pace following hatching and evidently never return to their nest site. They hide in dense vegetation when necessary, although the white plumage of the adults and the rusty color of the chicks make it difficult to remain completely invisible. In a study of chick mortality between 1997 and 1999, radio transmitters were attached to eighteen chicks from twenty-two pairs that had hatched both eggs. Five of the chicks fledged, five died from the effects of stress, exposure, or head trauma, and four were lost to unknown causes (three of which had lost their transmitters). Of the other four chicks, it was believed that two were taken by red foxes and one by a raven, and one died of pneumonia. Among the twins it was the younger chick that was most at risk, in part because of injuries caused by aggression from its older sibling. Yet, of the five chicks that fledged, two were the second-hatched chicks, showing the biological value of having two-egg clutches.

The young and gangly cranes fledge by about the middle of August. Until they can fly well, they are highly susceptible to predation by wolves and perhaps other predators such as foxes and eagles. When the young have reached 100 days old, they are capable of sustained flight. Even after they fledge, they continue to be fed by their parents, especially by the female. However, by the time they have fledged, it is almost time to begin the arduous and dangerous fall migration southward, one of the most stressful periods of their young lives.

THE LONG JOURNEY SOUTH

As September passes, the first signs of autumn are all too evident in northern Alberta. The golden fires of the aspens and birches soon flare and are quickly gone, and frost touches everything with ever-sharper fingers.

On their first day of autumn migration, whoopers often fly about 300 miles southeast to northwestern Saskatchewan. On the next day they often fly on to their fall staging area in west-central Saskatchewan, within a triangular region broadly outlined by Meadow Lake, Regina, and Swift Current.

The fall migration of the whooping cranes is done more as a series of waves than as a single coordinated movement. Thus, it is likely that single birds and unsuccessful pairs begin to move south early, to be followed later by family groups. Some immature or nonbreeding birds even appear in Saskatchewan by early September, while successful pairs are still tending unfledged young in Wood Buffalo Park.

The flight south is the reverse of the northward route, although stopover times along the way are likely to be rather different. Rather than staging at the Platte, the birds are much more likely to make the grain fields and prairie marshes of western Saskatchewan their most important single fall staging area. This stopover pattern is also typical of lesser and Canadian

FIGURE 2.38. (OVERLEAF)
Whooping cranes dancing during autumn migration, Saskatchewan

sandhill cranes, whose routes pass through this part of Canada and whose fall stopover periods overlap with those of the whooping cranes.

By late September, family groups are starting to leave the Wood Buffalo Park area and may join some of the whooping cranes that are still in Saskatchewan. Some whooping cranes are likely to stay in the Canadian provinces well into October and rarely as late as November, but by mid-October they are starting to show up in North Dakota and even as far south as Nebraska and Kansas. Typically the birds pass through Nebraska's Platte Valley between October 10 and 25 and may begin appearing on the Texas coast by late October or early November.

Fall migration thus consists of three general phases. The first of these is a rather rapid and direct flight of two or three days to Saskatchewan, a distance of more than 600 miles. The second phase consists of foraging and resting in a rather diffuse region of about 25,000 square miles of Saskatchewan south of Saskatoon, where they may remain for as long as twenty-four days. Like the spring staging of sandhill cranes in the Platte Valley, this period is probably of great importance to the cranes in storing needed fat reserves. The final phase consists of a fairly rapid series of fairly long flights from the staging grounds of Saskatchewan to the Aransas wintering grounds.

In recent years it has become possible to follow the migration of individual birds or family groups very accurately, inasmuch as some of the birds have been equipped with small radio transmitters that allow for tracking their every movement. For example, one family group was tracked all the way from Wood Buffalo Park to Aransas during the fall of 1981 (Kuyt 1987, 1992). The family left the park on October 4 and flew 175 miles to the Fort McMurray area of Alberta, where they remained for five days. On October 9 they flew another 270 miles to Reward, Saskatchewan, and there they spent eleven days in this traditional fall staging region.

Between October 20 and 27, the family covered 1,250 additional miles, or about half of their total migration route, from Saskatchewan to the Red River of Texas. They remained along the Red River until November 1, when they flew 230 miles to Rosebud, Texas. The next day they went an additional 178 miles to Tivoli, Texas, only some 18 miles from Aransas. They made the final short flight into Aransas the next morning, completing a total migration of about 2,400 miles in slightly more than a month.

The maximum straight-line flight distance covered during any single day of that migration was 470 miles. This distance represents a rather notable feat even for the adults, representing ten hours of continuous flying at an average ground speed of 47 miles per hour, but it is an especially remarkable feat for their young offspring, having almost certainly fledged less than a month previously. Available data indicate that about three-fourths of the young whoopers banded in Canada are likely to survive their first fall migration to Aransas.

During the following year a flock of five birds (a family of three plus two additional birds) made a maximum single-day flight of 510 miles in 10.8 hours, likewise averaging 47 miles per hour. A general analysis of telemetry data for the entire 2,450-mile migration route used by one family resulted in a calculated average ground speed of 27 miles per hour, with an average flying time of about six hours and twenty-eight minutes per day, excluding days of resting.

FIGURE 2.39. (PREVIOUS PAGE)
Six whooping cranes on autumn migration, Saskatchewan

FIGURE 2.40. (FACING PAGE)
A whooping crane flock pauses in its fall migration along a Saskatchewan river

FIGURE 2.41. (OVERLEAF, LEFT)
Adult whooping crane foraging for blue crabs, Aransas NWR, Texas

FIGURE 2.42. (OVERLEAF, RIGHT)
Juvenile whooping crane foraging on blue crab, Aransas NWR, Texas

According to Ernie Kuyt (1992), whooping cranes spend similar periods of time on their breeding grounds (164 days) and their wintering grounds (154 days). He also estimated that on a normal migration day whooping cranes average 7.5 hours of flight time, covering about 245 miles, and averaging 32 miles per hour. At times they can reach 60 miles per hour when wind-assisted. Favorable winds sometimes result in flights lasting 9–10 hours, and from 425 to 490 miles might be traveled in a single day.

A more recent effort to track migrating birds has been to attach radio transmitters to about sixty-five adult and young whooping cranes. In 2010 two radio-monitored cranes took thirty and thirty-one days to fly from Aransas to Wood Buffalo Park, and eleven birds took an average of thirty-five days to make the return trip that fall. The 2012 data showed that the total time spent migrating between wintering and summering areas was between fifteen and forty-six days, averaging twenty-seven days.

Radio-based data collected in Texas during the winter of 2011 showed the birds used a variety of distinct areas, including coastal salt and brackish marsh, agricultural and ranching areas, and the inland freshwater wetlands. The marked cranes provided more than 11,000 locations of use, of which approximately 65 percent were within the boundaries of the Aransas National Wildlife Refuge, and 22 percent were on nearby privately owned lands (based on various Internet sources). A new environmental factor that is now emerging and that might affect crane foraging habitat at Aransas is the incursion of the coastal wetlands by black mangroves, which are likely to greatly reduce winter foraging opportunities, resources that are already in short supply.

As of the spring of 2014, about forty of the sixty-five ratio-transmitter birds were still being tracked. Since individual transmitters are expected to have functional lifetimes of about three years, it is hoped that a great deal of information can be gathered on migration patterns, critical habitat, social interactions, individual survival, reproduction, and mortality factors before their batteries expire. The radio-marking program was terminated in 2014, leaving biologists with an anticipation of new data on all these topics appearing over the next several years.

Young whooping cranes exhibit a mottled mixture of juvenile tawny and first-year white feathers on arrival at Aransas and still lack bare crown skin. Perhaps by retaining these distinctive juvenile traits through their entire first year they are better able to maintain their strong parent-offspring bonds and less likely to stimulate any aggressive responses from their parents or other adult cranes.

The juvenile cranes still utter only high-pitched "baby voices" on their arrival at Aransas. By then they have lost their food-begging call but have acquired a flight-intention call and an alarm call. As their voices slowly change to the adult type and the last of their brownish juvenile feathers are molted, when they are nearly a year old, juveniles will begin to utter loud "guard calls" and "location calls." The guard call is usually uttered during the collective threat behavior of adults and young toward other crane families or toward other somewhat frightening stimuli. The location call is similar but more plaintive-sounding and is used to help locate other cranes when the birds are visually isolated from one another. However, the socially important "unison call" does not appear until the second or third year of a crane's life, when it begins to assume its primary pair-bonding functions.

The young cranes gradually gain a degree of independence from their parents during their first fall and winter, although they remain within their overall care and protection and follow them back north the following spring. Probably only when their parents have reached their nesting territory are the young birds, now nearly a year old, finally severed from their parents' care. From then on they are increasingly forced to survive on their own, but after the breeding season is over they are very likely to rejoin their parents for the fall migration. Research by Karine Gil-Weir and colleagues (2010, 2014) on the movements of color-banded birds has shown that up to as many as four generations of a family lineage may migrate together as unified social units. In this way information on traditional flight routes and desirable stopover points can be easily transmitted from older and more experienced birds to later generations.

Pair bonds in whooping cranes are probably established extremely slowly, through a delicate socialization that may begin at about two years of age. As in the sandhill crane, pair bonding is evidently a highly tentative process that may require about two years to complete. Thus, actual nesting attempts may not begin for as long as two years after sexual maturity is reached, or perhaps typically when females are approaching four years of age, although some females raised in captivity have nested and laid eggs when they were only three years old.

Of 132 young whooping cranes that had been color-banded at Wood Buffalo between 1977 and 1988, 67 formed nesting pairs. Banded females first produced hatchlings when between three and seven years old, and the percentage of mature females that successfully reproduced ranged annually from 56.6 to 60.6 percent (Gil-Weir et al. 2012). About 60 percent of 260 whooping crane eggs produced in Wood Buffalo Park over a several-year period produced hatched chicks, a surprisingly high incidence of hatching success.

Since 1983 there has been a significant increase in the number of whooping crane juveniles and subadults, and a corresponding increase in the breeding population. The breeding population at Wood Buffalo increased from fifteen to thirty-three nesting pairs between 1970 and 1991, and by 2014 there were at least seventy-two known nesting pairs. According to Ernie Kuyt's (1981a, 1981b) studies of tagged birds, home ranges of thirteen pairs averaged 4.1 square kilometers, or about 1.6 square miles. By 1993 several pairs were breeding south of the species' previously known nesting zone in the Alberta portion of Wood Buffalo National Park. By 2005 three pairs were breeding outside the limits of the park, complicating the need for protecting all usable breeding habitats.

In a 2005 study, Brian Johns and others reported that, of 136 banded juveniles, 103 (76 percent) returned to Wood Buffalo the following spring, and that at least 76 percent of first-time breeders nested within 20 kilometers (12 miles) of their natal sites. This high degree of site-fidelity is probably related to learning migration routes from parents or other close relatives and is most common in migratory species having long-term monogamy.

Collisions with power lines are apparently a very serious threat to migrating whooping cranes, accounting in one study for two of six deaths that were casually documented. So far, wind turbines have apparently killed none, but the vast majority of whooping crane deaths go unnoticed and undocumented. Current evidence indicates that about 80 percent of the mortality in the Wood Buffalo–Aransas flocks occurs during migration, an activity that occupies only 17–20 percent of time in their annual cycles.

FIGURE 2.43. (OVERLEAF) *A pair of whooping cranes with a juvenile, Aransas NWR, Texas*

At least thirty-nine whooping cranes were killed by gunshot between 1938 and 1948, when the species' survival was still hanging by a thread. From 1950 to 2006 at least eleven more were shot. The situation has not improved since then. In spite of a century of education, at least six whooping cranes from the Wood Buffalo–Aransas flock were shot in Texas between 1968 and 2014, and others have been killed elsewhere in several Central Flyway states or provinces where sandhill cranes can be hunted, including Kansas, South Dakota, and Saskatchewan. As of 2014, at least fifteen individuals of the experimental eastern population of whooping cranes had been shot and killed out of a population of no more than 125 birds, or more than 10 percent. The new and struggling Louisiana flock has also suffered several discouraging mortalities caused by gunshots, totaling at least 10 percent of the total by 2014.

Among adult whooping cranes the overall annual postjuvenile mortality rate is probably 10–15 percent per year, compared with an estimated long-term recruitment rate of about 12–14 percent. If accurate, these figures should allow for an annual rate of population increase of 1–3 percent. Assuming an annual mortality rate of 12 percent, of 100 cranes surviving their first year, about eight would likely survive to their twentieth birthday, and two might be lucky enough to reach thirty years of age. Karine Gil-Weir (2006) calculated that, based on several decades of data, the mean length of a generation among wild whooping cranes to be about thirteen years. In spite of these odds, a few wild whooping cranes are known to have survived more than thirty years (Karine Gil-Weir., personal communication). What a host of memories such rare birds might have!

For persons old enough to remember when the idea of ever seeing a wild whooping crane seemed little more than a fantasy, the presence of several hundred birds now alive in the wild is almost too good to be true. We owe this good fortune to the work of a great number of dedicated field biologists, aviculturists, and scientists, plus individuals and organizations who have helped to underwrite the purchase of critical habitats or to fund research needed to maintain a viable population of whooping cranes. Very few people are lucky enough to feel as if they have helped save a species from extinction; these are among the select few.

For anybody to be fortunate enough to see and hear a family of whooping cranes crossing the sky and headed for unknown destinations, their voices drifting down to earth from far above, can recognize it as nothing less than a gift from the gods.

Whooping Crane Restoration Efforts

THE SANDHILL CRANE CROSS-FOSTERING EXPERIMENT

During the 1960s a captive flock of whooping cranes was begun at the US Fish and Wildlife's Research Center in Patuxent, Maryland. This captive population was produced by the removal of single eggs from the clutches of wild pairs nesting in Wood Buffalo Park, incubating them, and rearing the young in captivity. It was hoped that basic biological information on whooping cranes could thereby be obtained and furthermore that offspring of these hand-reared birds might eventually be produced and released into the wild.

However, this flock has never become very large, in part because of high chick mortality, and in 1988 it contained only six reproductively active females. Partly to reduce the dangers

FIGURE 2.44. (PREVIOUS PAGE) *Whooping crane pair with a juvenile wearing leg bands and a radio telemetry transmitter, Aransas NWR, Texas*

of losing part or all of this flock to disease, a second captive flock was developed in Canada, starting in the early 1990s. In addition, half of the Patuxent flock of whooping cranes was sent to the International Crane Foundation in Wisconsin to protect this invaluable gene pool more effectively.

In the mid-1970s the Canadian Wildlife Service and the US Fish and Wildlife Service began an even more experimental program. It was designed both to increase the total whooping crane population and also to try to establish a second independent flock, with a migration route much shorter and less hazardous than the 2,500-mile route from Wood Buffalo National Park to Aransas National Wildlife Refuge.

Spearheaded by such people as Dr. Roderick Drewien, the idea was to remove one of the two eggs from as many whooping crane nests as possible and to hatch some of these for captive rearing and eventual breeding at Patuxent (Drewien and Kuyt 1979). Other eggs were to be quickly transported to Grays Lake National Wildlife Refuge in southeastern Idaho, where they were placed in the nests of greater sandhill cranes for hatching and foster rearing by these birds. The remaining whooping crane egg was to be left in each nest for its parents to raise normally. Although this seemingly reduced the potential productivity of the Wood Buffalo population, whooping cranes rarely succeed in raising two chicks, owing in part to the competition for food that occurs between the young. Thus, by having only a single chick to raise, the pair's productivity is not noticeably reduced and possibly even enhanced, owing to the greater care given by the parents to their single chick.

This innovative procedure posed a great number of risks, such as the danger of the whooping cranes abandoning their nests upon disturbance, the possible damage to the eggs in transit, and the danger that the sandhill cranes would fail to accept and rear their foster offspring. There was also the risk that the young whooping cranes would not respond appropriately to their alien "parents" or, even more ominously, might "imprint" on them and grow up thinking that they too were sandhill cranes, and thereby become unable to recognize and mate with their own species.

The egg-switching project was initiated in 1975. Both of the sandhill crane eggs were usually removed from an active nest and replaced with a single whooping crane egg. Sometimes only a single sandhill egg was removed, the second one being taken away prior to hatching. In addition to wild-taken eggs, some additional eggs were obtained from the captive flock of whooping cranes that had been gradually built up at the Patuxent Research Center in Laurel, Maryland.

From 1975 to 1977 a total of forty-five eggs from wild whooping cranes were transported to Grays Lake, and an additional sixteen eggs were sent there from the captive flock at Patuxent. The project was plagued by bad luck from the very beginning, with many losses of eggs and chicks to cold weather, nest flooding, and predation. The surviving young migrated with their foster parents to traditional greater sandhill crane wintering areas about 700 miles farther south, at Bosque del Apache National Wildlife Refuge in the Rio Grande Valley of New Mexico.

A total of 417 eggs were taken from wild whooping crane nests between 1967 and 1994 in order to establish a captive breeding flock and to carry out the egg-transplant experiment. During that period the original Wood Buffalo–Aransas flock continued to thrive, in spite

FIGURE 2.45. (OVERLEAF) *Greater sandhill cranes tending a foster whooping crane chick, Patuxent Wildlife Research Center, Maryland*

of these annual egg removals. Of 289 total whooping crane eggs transferred to Grays Lake, 209 hatched but only 85 chicks fledged, mostly as a result of coyote predation and unfavorable weather during the breeding season. Fledged young were most often lost as a result of collision with power lines or fences (62 percent of 72 deaths), with disease and predation accounting for most of the rest.

The Grays Lake–Bosque del Apache flock reached a maximum of thirty-three birds in 1985. However, thereafter it rather rapidly declined. By the spring of 1989 it numbered only thirteen individuals, and decision was then made to terminate the egg-transfer program. A major cause of the experiment's failure was that the cross-fostered birds failed to recognize themselves as whooping cranes and never attempted to mate with their own species. Evidence for this view was the fact that at least one whooper-sandhill hybrid was produced by a male whooping crane and a female sandhill. Of all the cross-fostered cranes that hatched and survived long enough to migrate to Bosque del Apache, the last survivor had disappeared by the spring of 2002.

RESTORATION EFFORTS IN FLORIDA

By 1989, when the cross-fostering experiment had been recognized as a failure, a decision was made to try establish a nonmigratory whooping crane flock in central Florida, where wild whooping cranes had existed (as winter migrants, but with no definite evidence of breeding) until the early 1900s. The site chosen was the Kissimmee Prairie, an area of about 800 square miles where Florida sandhill cranes were already thriving. After obtaining approval from state, federal, and provincial agencies, the first group of captive-reared cranes was released in Florida early in 1993. The young cranes had been hatched and reared in the Patuxent facilities of the US Fish and Wildlife Service and those of the International Crane Foundation at Baraboo, Wisconsin. A total of 14 juveniles were released in 1993, followed by 19 in 1994, 19 in 1995, and additional birds for almost a decade, until a total of 289 birds had been released by 2004. Initially they were placed in large well-fenced enclosures that were not predator-proof; during the first two years bobcats killed two-thirds of the released birds. Later, by using portable enclosures well away from known bobcat habitats, survival was greatly improved, with 69 percent of the birds surviving their first year. First-year survival remained about 50–70 percent thereafter, and an 83 percent survival occurred during the second and third years.

By 1996 some of the released birds were forming pair bonds, mating, and building nests. During the spring of 2000 three pairs attempted to nest, and one of the four-year-old pairs hatched two chicks successfully. In 2002 another pair of four-year-olds hatched and successfully fledged one youngster, its sibling having been snatched from the nest by a bald eagle shortly after hatching. The surviving chick, named Lucky by the people who had witnessed the eagle attack, lived long enough to see its parents nest again the following year and hatch Lucky II.

In 2003 a total of eight nests were built, and three chicks were fledged. By that spring there were 106 birds living independently in Florida, raising hopes that a breeding flock of twenty-three breeding pairs might be attained by 2020. By the spring of 2005 there were twelve nesting pairs present, which hatched a total of nine chicks, five of which survived at least to the summer of 2006. However, high mortality among older age classes and a very low level of breeding success eventually led to a decision to terminate additional infusions of new birds. As of early 2015 there were only eight whooping cranes still alive in Florida, and almost no reproductive success has occurred there in recent years.

Restoration Efforts in Louisiana

In 2011 ten hand-reared whooping cranes were introduced into the White Lake region of southwestern Louisiana, the start of a multiyear effort to try establish a resident flock in that state, from which whooping cranes had been o sixty years previously. Although a total of fifty birds were introduced, postrelease mortality was high, and by January 2014, the flock had been reduced to about three dozen birds. In February of 2014 teen-aged vandals shot and killed the female of a pair of three-year-old subadults that had been building a nest, the first such breeding evidence by the new flock. The male also suffered two broken wing bones and later died. By then at least five of Louisiana's introduced cranes had also been killed or wounded by firearms. The male's death represented the thirty-first documented loss of wild whooping cranes from gunshot since 2001, another statistic that provides a dismal commentary on the state of environmental education and conservation attitudes in America.

In the spring of 2014 another nesting pair produced and incubated two eggs, although the eggs were infertile. The pair laid again in 2015, providing the first breeding attempts by wild whooping cranes in Louisiana since 1939. About a dozen juveniles were added in December 2014, offering some hope for the future of this highly vulnerable flock. As of early 2015, forty birds were still alive in Louisiana, including three bonded pairs.

Operation Migration and the Eastern Migratory Flock

Beginning in the 1990s, an intensive effort began to establish a migratory flock of whooping cranes in eastern North America. Six years later, two whooping crane chicks were hatched from a wild but captive-raised pair at Necedah National Wildlife Refuge in central Wisconsin. This success represented the first breeding of wild whooping cranes south of Canada in more than a century. Necedah National Wildlife Refuge, located near the crane-rearing facilities of the International Crane Foundation at Baraboo, had been selected as the focal point for the development of a migratory whooping crane flock independent of the Aransas–Wood Buffalo flock.

The project's goal was to train the cranes to migrate to Florida wintering grounds, from which they would hopefully thereafter return independently to their natal home and, when mature, breed there. The success of this highly imaginative project would initially depend in large part on the skill of biologists in rearing cranes that would not imprint on their human caretakers and thereafter become socially and sexually attached to humans, rather than mating with other cranes. This danger was avoided by having their foster "parents" wear black-and-white crane-like costumes while rearing the chicks to fledging (Ellis et al. 1992, 2001; Duff 2014).

Social imprinting in cranes actually begins before hatching, so that the newly hatched chicks will quickly learn to recognize their parents and vice versa. To achieve this socialization, the eggs are exposed to the sound of an ultralight engine during the final twenty-four hours before hatching and the voice of the ultralight pilot's imitations of parental crane calls. The young birds also learn much about survival in nature from the wild sandhill cranes that live near them throughout the year. For example, they become increasingly wary of people in their yearling summer through their association with wild sandhills.

Prefledged birds are taught to follow the body of an ultralight plane without its wings, driven by a crane-costumed parent-figure. Success in learning the migration route also relies strongly on the ability of highly skilled ultralight pilots training the newly fledged birds to follow the aircraft in flight, over distances of more than a thousand miles to Florida wintering grounds. Accomplishing that, the ultimate hope was that the birds would survive winter and safely migrate back to Necedah on their own in spring, using their memories of the fall migration as a navigation guide.

This ultralight-led migration experiment was clearly an audacious and high-risk idea and was necessarily preceded by several years of experimentation with Canada geese and sandhill cranes, training them to follow an ultralight craft, which serves as a "lead bird." The ultralight must travel at the cranes' typical flapping-flight air speed of about 30–40 miles per hour and cover appropriate daily distances. Its pilot also must avoid accidental collisions with obstacles such as power lines, attacks by predators such as golden eagles, and somehow keep all the birds together as a single unit. The first motorized migration experiment was done with Canada geese in 1993, and the first motorized sandhill crane migrations were attempted in 1995. Attempts with whooping cranes began in 1997, initially by introducing them into groups of similarly imprinted sandhill cranes.

The success of this ambitious, stranger-than-fiction adventure required the skills and resources of an array of private and governmental organizations that together formed the Whooping Crane Eastern Partnership (WCEP). To test the migration route and also performance and coordination during the many complex parts of this effort, a trial migration was undertaken with sandhill cranes in 2000. Each year since, WCEP has successfully reared, trained, and flown a cohort of whooping cranes along a 1,200-mile route from Necedah National Wildlife Refuge in central Wisconsin to national wildlife refuges located along the Gulf coast of Florida.

The sponsoring nonprofit organization, Operation Migration, is headquartered in Port Perry, Ontario, and oversees the training of chicks and the ultralight migration. Typically four ultralight aircraft are used, three of them leading young while the fourth, a slightly faster ultralight called the "chase plane," recovers any birds that may stray from the flock. A fixed-wing plane also flies overhead and moves more swiftly ahead or behind as needed, should any of the young falter and have to land. Ground vehicles also follow below. Typically the birds fly at heights of about 350–1,000 feet and in good weather may cover up to a hundred miles or even more in a day. The entire journey south takes several weeks and often is held up for days or even weeks during periods of inclement weather.

In the spring of 2002 five young whooping cranes that had wintered in Florida made their way back to Necedah in less than ten days. By the spring of 2006 the new migratory

FIGURE 2.46. *Greater sandhill crane tending a foster-raised whooping crane, Bosque del Apache NWR, New Mexico*

flock had grown to sixty-four birds, to which twenty-four more young were added that fall. In February of 2007, disaster struck, with almost the entire cohort of young being killed during a severe storm and tidal surge that swept over the winter release pen at Chassahowitzka National Wildlife Refuge. In spite of this devastating loss, WCEP added another cohort of seventeen juveniles to the population in 2007. Since then, migration training efforts have been directed to leading the birds to winter at St. Marks National Wildlife Refuge, a more northern location somewhat less likely to be so severely affected by tropical storms.

The reintroduction efforts in the eastern population have included intensive monitoring efforts by the Fish and Wildlife Service and ICF. Detailed histories have been collected of the movements and social behavior of each bird. From these efforts, several lessons have become clear. One is that yearling cranes will return in spring to the general area where they had fledged, not the place where they were hatched. The young, after a single ultralight-led migration during their first autumn, are quite capable of retracing the migration on their own back to central Wisconsin. They do not follow the precise flight path that they experienced in fall, but rather follow a general flight corridor. Thus, they must not have to rely on specific local landmarks to find their way.

Weather events as the cranes are migrating north, such as strong west winds, sometimes set the birds off course, so they end up on the east side of Lake Michigan rather than returning to their release area. And those birds that, for one reason or another, have missed parts of the ultralight migration by being transported by land are more likely to become lost when they travel north on their own in the spring. WCEP personnel, however, have successfully retrieved some of these birds and moved them back to Wisconsin.

By 2010, after a decade of efforts, there had been many nesting attempts by the developing flock at Necedah, but nearly all the clutches there have been abandoned prior to hatching. The first hatching success there occurred in 2006, when a renesting pair hatched two chicks. One of these lived to mate and produce its first egg when only three years old. The same pair that produced the 2006 chicks also hatched a chick in 2009, as did a second pair. In 2010 seven chicks hatched, of which two young survived to fledging.

An alternate rearing technique, the so-called "Direct Autumn Release" (DAR) approach, has also been attempted. Keepers wear white costumes to disguise themselves and tend the young until they are twelve to fourteen weeks old. In late October they are released into the company of older cranes, from whom they could learn the migration route to and from wintering areas. By using this approach, perhaps the time-consuming ultralight learning technique can eventually be phased out as the population becomes increasingly self-sustaining. Of thirty-three young that had been released as DAR birds at Necedah National Wildlife Refuge in 2005–9, twenty-five survived their first migration and returned north, with eighteen returning to the core Wisconsin breeding area. The first nesting efforts by the DAR birds occurred in 2010.

As a result of the annual supplements from hand-reared whoopers, the reintroduced migratory population of whooping cranes in eastern North America gradually increased, reaching 115 birds by late 2011. In the spring of 2011 four chicks had hatched at Nacedah, but none survived the approximate eighty-day fledging period. In 2012 seven nests successfully hatched nine chicks, but only two of the young fledged. In 2013 there were eighteen nesting efforts at Necedah, but all the nests were abandoned soon after a major black fly emergence. Between 2005 and 2013 a total of twenty-two chicks hatched successfully, but only six fledged.

Many of the Nacedah breeding failures have been attributed to depredation by predatory black flies, whose bites result in severe trauma and blood loss. Black fly attacks on incubating adults may even cause them to abandon their efforts, and multiple bites are likely to kill the chicks. As of early 2014, all the young that have been successfully produced at Necedah have hatched after the black fly season is nearly over as a result of renesting efforts. Thus, future restoration efforts will focus on retarding the nesting cycle by removing early clutches from nesting pairs, in hopes that the pairs will renest and their chicks will thereby avoid the worst of the black flies.

In addition, it has been found that black fly larvae need clear water to breathe effectively, so by concentrating future restoration efforts in marshes that have suspended solids sufficient to clog larval breathing tubes, it might be possible to avoid this serious hazard to health. In an effort to determine if breeding conditions for whooping cranes might be better elsewhere in southern Wisconsin and to help spread out the population, young hand-reared cranes were introduced in 2011 at Horicon National Wildlife Refuge near Waupun. Young cranes have also been released at White River State Wildlife Area near Berlin. As of early 2014, three cohorts of whooping cranes had been introduced at White River, so initial breeding there might begin as soon as 2015, when the oldest cohort will have reached four years of age,

Another serious problem with the eastern migratory flock recovery program has been that of illegal shooting. As of early 2014, fifteen birds in the eastern flock had been killed, including two that were shot in Kentucky during November 2013. Only a few of the persons responsible have been caught, and the apprehended individuals have often been given discouragingly light fines. As an "experimental" flock, the eastern whooping cranes don't benefit from all of the legal protection provisions of the Endangered Species Act, and a person who harms or kills one can be sentenced only to the much lower penalties authorized by the Migratory Bird Treaty about a century ago. The estimated costs of raising, training, and teaching a single whooping crane to migrate were nearly $114,000 in 2011.

Recent Population Trends in the Wood Buffalo–Aransas Flock

With all the recent publicity associated with Operation Migration, the original Wood Buffalo–Aransas migratory flock of whooping cranes has been somewhat neglected by the media, but it too has made remarkable progress.

Based on winter counts at Aransas, the population increased from 146 birds in 1991–92 to 236 in the winter of 2006–7, averaging an impressive six birds per year. During the five-year period 2002–7 a remarkable total of 63 more birds were added to the total flock, and by the winter of 2006–7 there were 236 cranes present at Aransas. The 2007 and 2008 breeding seasons added 21 more immatures to the wintering flock, so the Aransas population had reached about 280 birds by the winter of 2008–9. Over the six-decade period from 1941 to

FIGURE 2.47. (OVERLEAF) *Adult and juvenile foster whooping cranes wading and foraging along Intracoastal Waterway, Aransas NWR, Texas*

2010 the Wood Buffalo–Aransas population increased by a cumulative average of 4.6 percent per year, and by 2014 it finally reached 300 birds.

Disaster struck this flock in the winter of 2008–9 with the onset of a prolonged drought in Texas. The major source of fresh water to Aransas National Wildlife Refuge is the Guadalupe River, which maintains the salinity of the coastal wetlands and allows for the survival of blue crabs, the whooping crane's major winter food. Increased drought-related diversions of this river water by Texas water authorities (the Texas Commission on Environmental Quality) resulted in an increased salinity of water around the Aransas refuge and decimated the local population of blue crabs. Other important estuarine prey, such as crabs, shrimp, and crayfish, might also have been impacted. The availability of the nutritious berries of wolfberry, a solanaceous forb also known as salt-flat cranberry and an important alternative food source, was also greatly reduced by the drought.

These near-starvation conditions contributed to the death of at least twenty-three whooping cranes during the winter of 2008–9, reducing the population to about 260 by the spring of 2009. A lawsuit filed in US District Court in 2010 by a Texas environmental group (the Aransas Project) resulted in a finding three years later to the effect that these water diversions violated the Endangered Species Act in failing to provide adequate water flows into Aransas Bay. In 2014 a three-judge panel of the Fifth District Court agreed with this decision. The finding resulted in the development of a Habitat Conservation Plan for Whooping Cranes, which should reduce the likelihood of a repeat of the 2008–9 disaster.

In 2011 the whoopers built a record high of seventy-five nests at Wood Buffalo Park and fledged about thirty-seven young, the offspring representing a 49 percent breeding success rate. The later 2011–12 winter survey of Aransas reported 245 whoopers within the coastal survey route, but an additional number of birds were also reported from scattered sites in several other inland counties and states north to Nebraska, owing to unusually warm winter weather and widespread drought. By adopting a new survey technique involving sampling rather than attempting a complete survey, the winter flock was statistically estimated at 272 birds. However, the actual population could have ranged from 198 to 324 birds, assuming 95 percent statistical confidence limits.

In 2012 a total of thirty-one families were counted at Wood Buffalo Park, including two sets of twins, producing a total of thirty-three young, and a 47 percent rearing success rate as of mid-August. Using the newer statistical sampling methods adopted the previous year, the 2012–13 wintering Aransas flock was calculated to be about 273 birds (with 95 percent confidence limits of 178–362 birds).

After the following breeding season, a total of seventy-four whooping crane nests were counted during a June 2013 survey at Wood Buffalo Park. Among these, eight nests were located beyond Wood Buffalo's boundaries, and several of these were seen for the first time. A total of twenty-eight fledglings were counted in mid-August, which had been produced by twenty-seven of the nesting pairs. In spite of this relatively poor breeding success, the 2013–14 winter surveys for the Aransas area resulted in a record high estimate of 304 whooping cranes. If accurate, this arithmetically unlikely estimate (the increase of thirty-one birds was three greater than the total number of fledged juveniles counted at Wood Buffalo Park) would represent a very welcome sign of recovery in the species' most important wild population.

In the spring of 2014 a record number of eighty-two pairs nested in Wood Buffalo Park, a total representing seven more than the previous record of seventy-five nests in 2011. From these, thirty of the pairs fledged thirty-two juveniles, with two of the pairs succeeding in raising twins. Compared with the prior twenty-year average breeding success rate of 0.48 fledged young raised per breeding pair, the 2013 and 2014 breeding success rates were 0.38 and 0.39 respectively.

The 2014–15 wintering population at Aransas was estimated at an all-time record high of 308 birds in March 2015, but with a substantial range of possible sampling error. This total included a record count of thirty-nine juveniles, or seven more fledglings than had been detected during the earlier Wood Buffalo breeding survey! The Whooping Crane Recovery Plan calls for an ultimate goal of 250 breeding pairs of cranes, which would require about 125,000 acres of coastal wintering wetlands in Texas, which currently sell for about $2,000 per acre. Only about 27 percent of these wetlands are now protected, and future rises in sea levels associated with global warming may inundate more than half of these in the future.

Can Whooping Cranes Survive in a Twenty-First-Century America?

On a more somber note, during the five-year period 2010–14 at least nineteen whooping cranes from all three major wild populations were shot and killed (totaling about 4 percent, or about 1 percent annually). Of fifty carcasses examined involving birds of the Wood Buffalo–Aransas flock between 1950 and 2010, at least nine had been shot. This total was second only to overhead line collisions among identified mortality causes during that period, which caused at least ten deaths.

In January 2013, a Texas man who was hunting waterfowl in a restricted zone near Aransas National Wildlife Refuge shot and killed a whooping crane. He was fined $5,000 and ordered to make a substantial community service restitution. In December 2014, a dead whooping crane was found near Aransas National Wildlife Refuge, but its cause of death could not be determined. Since 1968, five people have been charged with shooting and killing whooping cranes in Texas and were either found guilty or accepted plea agreements.

The loss of a single breeding crane in a population of only about eighty breeding pairs can have significant future effects on reproduction. Karine Gil-Weir (personal communication) has tracked the color-banded offspring of a single pair of whooping cranes that were banded in 1977. As of 2013, their descendants and descendants' mates had totaled at least fifty-two individuals. Of course, it is impossible to estimate the value of an individual's unique genes to a species' survival, but this example proves the genetic importance and reproductive value of every single breeding bird in a very small world population.

Considering the costs of the efforts in breeding and release programs for captive whooping cranes, of monitoring and protecting the wild flocks, of generating and maintaining captive stock, and of acquiring and protecting all their critical habitats from northern Canada to Texas, a fine of $50,000 for knowingly killing a whooping crane would seem far more appropriate than the recent one in Texas of $5,000, or of the unbelievably paltry fine of one dollar that was imposed on a person found guilty of killing a whooping crane from the eastern flock.

Cranes, like humans, are never separated from their environments, and it does little good to increase crane populations by techniques such as egg-swapping, captive-rearing, or other impressive technical feats if environmental factors impose population constraints, or if they can't be protected from the destructive effects of human behavior. Also like that for humans, the quality of life for cranes is inversely related to the amount of crowding and resource-sharing they must endure. Cranes survive best in remote and undisturbed surroundings, but the little that remains today is quickly disappearing.

Perhaps the conservation question to be posed should not be whether as a civilized society we can afford to maintain an environment that is expansive enough and with sufficient biological diversity to support a flock of wild whooping cranes, and thereby help sustain our own emotional needs for a source of ethereal beauty and mental sustenance, but rather whether we can afford not to.

One of the saddest and most iconic objects in the Smithsonian Institution's natural history museum is a mounted female passenger pigeon ("Martha"), the last living example of a species that probably was once the most abundant bird in North America. Martha died at more than twenty years of age in a Cincinnati zoo barely a century ago. Her demise occurred less than fifty years after a single migrating pigeon flock had been estimated as containing perhaps 3.5 billion birds, and more than a decade after all of her wild kin had already vanished from earth. Her bright red, still-shiny glass eyes reflect a world now totally changed from the America of the early twentieth century, and one that few still-living persons experienced.

If, by neglect or economic decisions, we should likewise allow all the wild whooping cranes to disappear, it is likely a few captives will likewise be able to live on in captivity several additional decades. By then their boreal Canadian homeland will probably have been entirely logged-over or mined, and the cranes' winter Aransas retreat might well have become the site of another massive oil spill. I doubt if any of the birds then still living could imagine what it would have been like to be a wild whooping crane.

As Baba Dioum, a Senegalese ecologist, said in a 1968 speech to the International Union for the Conservation of Nature, "In the end, we will protect only what we love, we will love only what we understand, we will understand only what we are taught." I fervently hope that, as responsible citizens, we can teach our countrymen the importance of preserving a few wild populations of cranes and their wetland habitats as emblematic symbols of our once unimaginably rich and varied but rapidly vanishing legacy of North America's natural world that we have inherited and are duty-bound to transmit to generations still to come.

FIGURE 2.48. (FACING PAGE)
Gray crowned crane pair taking flight from their roosting tree, Ngorongoro Conservation Area, Tanzania

THREE

The Other Cranes of the World

TIME PROCEEDS INEXORABLY ONWARD, and more than two decades have passed since the first edition of *Crane Music* was published. During that time more than a billion people have been added to the earth's rolls, and global warming has increasingly been recognized as a real threat to our planet's future. Although during that period a small percentage of Americans have become very rich through advances in technology, expanding markets, and globalization, wildlife in general has suffered. Continuing population growth and associated economic and ecological pressures have resulted in greatly increased wetland drainage and destruction of native grassland habitats. In addition, global climate changes are bringing on unforeseen massive ecological changes that will have serious effects on crane populations, especially in arctic and alpine regions, where the effects of climate change are occurring most rapidly.

Downward population trends in wildlife that are associated with these factors are especially apparent among native grassland and wetland-dependent birds; nearly all of North America's grassland-adapted birds are now in serious continental decline, and probably much the same is true elsewhere in the world. Nearly all of the world's fifteen species cranes are also strongly dependent on grasslands and wetlands; those that are generally the rarest and most in danger of extinction are the ones most strongly dependent on extensive wetlands. The whooping, Siberian, white-naped, wattled, and red-crowned cranes are all strongly wetland-dependent for breeding and are now among the world's most endangered species.

On the other hand, some relatively herbivorous and terrestrial species such as the sandhill, Eurasian, demoiselle, and blue cranes have learned to take advantage of agricultural technology by incorporating

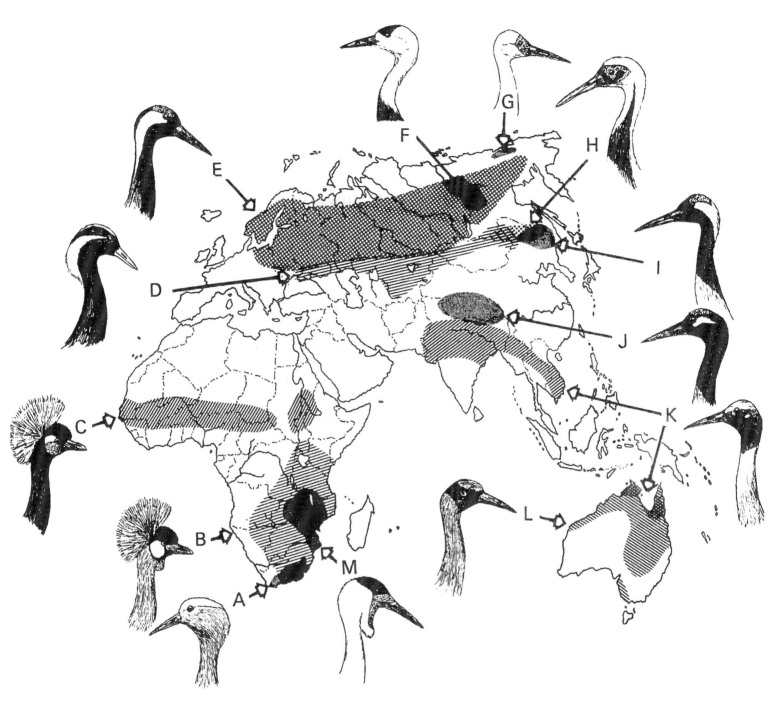

MAP 3.1. *Breeding ranges of the Old World cranes, including blue (A), gray-crowned (B), black-crowned (C), demoiselle (D), Eurasian (E), hooded (F), Siberian (G), white-naped (H), red-crowned (I), black-necked (J), sarus (K), Australian (L) and wattled (M) (adapted from Johnsgard 1991)*

into their diets of native plants various cultivated grains, such as com and wheat in Europe and rice in Asia. As a result, these species have exhibited local, regional, or even national population increases. Such foraging practices have often brought cranes into conflict with agricultural interests, resulting in economic conflicts and sometime draconian control measures.

An overview of the current status of the world's cranes is perhaps in order to bring up to date the accounts given in 1991 in *Crane Music*. Table 5.1 at the end of this section presents a variably updated summary of world crane distribution and status, which shows some significant differences from the similar table presented in *Crane Music*. Some of these differences are the likely result of more complete and more accurate surveys, such as the substantially increased population estimate of the black-necked crane and the Siberian crane.

In 2013 the Siberian crane was listed by the International Union for Conservation of Nature and Natural Resources (IUCN) as critically endangered, with a global population in the early 2000s of about 3,750, virtually all of which winter at China's Poyang Lake. The tiny central and western populations of the Siberian crane that bred near the Ob Valley of central Siberia and until recently wintered in India are also perhaps extinct. Surveys in 2008 of this crane on its breeding grounds found only ten breeding pairs, and only two of these had chicks. The relict population that wintered along the Caspian Sea may also be extirpated.

The Asian red-crowned crane was classified by the IUCN in 2013 as endangered, together with the North American whooping crane. Although the migratory Asian mainland population of the red-crowned crane is evidently declining, its sedentary Japanese population on the northern island of Hokkaido began slowly increasing in the early 1970s as the result of special protection of the birds' limited breeding areas and winter-feeding. Under these conditions, their numbers have increased sixty-fold, from little more than 50 birds in 1972 to nearly 3,000 by 2012. These magnificent birds have attracted an international audience from tourists and wildlife photographers, adding greatly to the local economy. Like the North American whooping crane's near brush with oblivion, this species' return from near-extinction is one of the greatest successes in Asian bird conservation. However, the Hokkaido population has now apparently reached a saturation point, and the red-crowned crane's mainland population is believed to be in slow decline. In the early 2,000s the red-crowned crane had a resident Japanese population of nearly 3,000 birds, plus wintering populations of about 1,000 birds on the Korean Peninsula, and 400–500 birds in China.

The gray crowned crane was additionally listed in 2013 by the IUCN as endangered, when its estimated recent population was judged to be as little as 30,000 birds, as compared with an estimate of more than 100,000 in 1991. Its classification has since changed to endangered status because of threats such as extensive habitat loss and the large-scale illegal removal of birds and eggs from the wild, resulting in very rapid declines during the past half-century.

The hooded crane's breeding grounds in eastern Siberia still remain to be well surveyed and its population accurately estimated. Birds that summer north and east of Lake Baikal fly south and winter along the Yangtze River of China. This western population is thought to consist of about 1,000 birds. A much larger group migrates south through Korea after breeding in far-eastern Russia and northern China (where some stop and overwinter) to winter on Japan's southern island of Kyushu. There, in very small, protected areas, the population has progressively increased, from about 260 in the mid-1900s to more than 10,000 by 2006. Like the red-crowned crane, these birds have responded strongly to wintering-ground protection and artificial feeding, but the overcrowded birds risk increased chances of disease outbreaks and conflicts with local farmers.

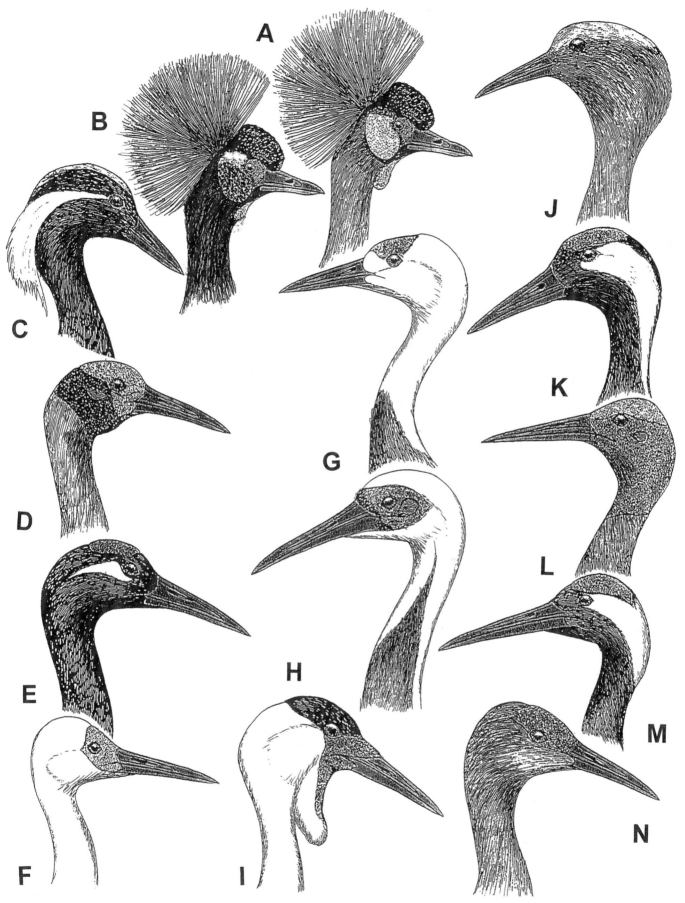

FIGURE 3.1. *Head profiles of the Old World cranes: gray crowned (A), black crowned (B), demoiselle (C), Australian (D), black-necked (E), Siberian (F), hooded (G), white-naped (H), wattled (I), blue (J), Eurasian (K), sarus (L), red-crowned (M), and sandhill (N)*

Substantially larger numbers of demoiselle and Eurasian cranes are now known to exist worldwide than had been previously believed. About half the world population of about a third of a million demoiselles winters in Gujarat, northern India, after having bred in the central Asian steppes. Other demoiselles winter in eastern India, after flying in from distant Mongolian breeding grounds and navigating over the towering Himalayan Mountains. The remoteness of their arid and little-populated breeding grounds offers the best hope for the continued abundance of these elegant cranes. By contrast, in Africa, the isolated Atlas Mountains population of the demoiselle crane has now vanished.

The widespread Eurasian crane's breeding habitats extend from western Europe and Scandinavia eastward across virtually all of Europe and Russia, giving it perhaps the broadest breeding range of all crane species and making it the second-most common of all cranes, numbering 300,000–400,000 birds by the early 2000s. In Europe these cranes have recently extended their breeding range south in Germany, where as many as 5,400 were breeding by 2006. Breeding now occurs locally in Great Britain, France, the Netherlands, the Czech Republic, and Hungary. By 2005 at least 160,000 cranes were wintering in France, Spain, and Portugal, while another 100,000 or more were migrating from the Baltic Sea through central Europe to wintering areas scattered from the Mediterranean coast of Africa south to Ethiopia and Sudan. Wintering areas in Europe have shifted to the north in recent years as climates have altered, with about 70,000 cranes wintering in France during 2000–2001 rather than in southern Spain, as compared with about 100 only two decades previously. Part of this recent range expansion of both breeding and wintering European ranges might also be attributed to effective international protection and to increased corn production, which Eurasian cranes have learned to exploit in the same manner as have sandhill cranes in North America.

Population estimates for the Australian crane have varied greatly in the past. Much of the confusion over the Australian crane's population stems from early and unverified statements to the effect that as many as 100,000 birds might have once been present. This estimate has recently been reduced by about 50 percent to 40,000–50,000 birds, most of which are centered in Queensland. In addition, there is a declining population of only 500–1,000 birds in Victoria and a small group in southern New Guinea. Australian cranes are everywhere dependent on seasonal wetlands for nesting. Because of widespread destruction of wetlands, reduced natural foods, and competition (as well as hybridization) with the larger sarus crane, the long-term future of the Australian crane is somewhat clouded.

The following species accounts are organized here in the taxonomic sequence suggested by the recent mitochondrial analysis of Krajewski, Sipiorski, and Anderson (2010).

BLACK CROWNED CRANE

(Balearica pavonina)

The crowned cranes, named for their tuft of golden head feathers, are the most distinctive of all living cranes, and the genus *Balearica* is usually separated from all other crane genera by its placement in a unique subfamily. Evidence from molecular biology suggests that divergence of the ancestral crowned cranes and the more typical cranes may have occurred as long ago as 10 million years, when very much like crowned cranes roamed the savannas of what is now Nebraska. The crowned crane lineage has retained a greater number of seemingly generalized ("primitive") traits than any of the other living cranes.

Early literature often treated the gray crowned crane of southern Africa as only racially distinct from the black crowned crane, but the most recent taxonomies regard them as a separate species, as they are treated here. Black crowned cranes occur in sub-Saharan Africa from Senegal, Sierra Leone, Nigeria, and northern Cameroon on the west eastward to the upper Nile Valley in Ethiopia.

The more western populations (the "West African black crowned crane," subspecies *pavonina*) differ slightly from those of eastern Africa. This western race is declining rapidly, but still occurs in the extensive sub-Saharan semidesert grassland region, known as the sahel, and in the Sudan-Guinea savannas, with records known from as far south as the Democratic Republic of Congo. The major remaining concentrations of the western race apparently are from Lake Chad, Mali, and Mauritania east to Senegambia. It has been extirpated from Sierra Leone and from nearly all of Nigeria, where ironically it is designated as the national bird. The western population was estimated to number about 13,000 birds in 2004.

The eastern race (the "Sudan black crowned crane," subspecies *ceciliae*) extends from about Khartoum south to Lake Turkana and east to the Ethiopian lakes. This race appears to have declined markedly, from 65,000 to 90,000 individuals in 1985 to 28,000–55,000 individuals in 2004, with the great majority occurring in Sudan and South Sudan (IUCN 2013).

Black crowned cranes differ only slightly from their gray-necked and more southerly relatives. Besides their generally darker body coloration, they also have a much smaller gular wattle, which apparently serves also as a vocal resonator. As a result, the calls of the black crowned crane are higher-pitched and less strongly resonated than those of the gray crowned crane, resulting in disyllabic notes of variable pitch. Birds of the eastern race of black crowned crane also tend to be somewhat smaller and darker than those from farther west, and they exhibit a smaller white area on the upper cheek than do most western birds. In both races the lower portion of the cheek is tinged with red.

Studies by Lawrence Walkinshaw on the black crowned cranes breeding in Nigeria indicate that the birds are highly territorial, with nesting territories ranging in size from 200 to more than 900 acres. Not only are other crowned cranes excluded from the nesting territories, but so are spur-winged geese, various ducks, and bustards. The cranes will also frighten away cattle that approach the nest too closely.

The nests of this species are fairly large platforms made from nearby wetland plants and are often surrounded by a narrow ring of open water. Like the gray crowned crane, these birds produce clutches that average three eggs, as compared with the two-egg clutches typical of *Grus* cranes. Eggs are laid at average intervals of slightly more than one day per egg. The incubation period lasts 26–31 (mean 28) days, with the period for the last-laid egg somewhat shorter than those for the earlier eggs in the clutch, resulting in a more clustered period of hatching. Most or all of the chicks hatch within a twenty-four-hour period, and by the second day after hatching the entire brood is able to leave the vicinity of the nest. The birds then tend to move into heavy cover, where they spend the next three or four months prior to fledging.

Fledging periods are evidently quite variable in crowned cranes. Some hand-reared West African birds did not fly until they were four months old, while other hand-reared East African young were nearly fledged when they were only two months old. Probably 60–100 days is a normal range of fledging periods in crowned cranes; food availability for the young probably influences fledging periods in these species.

GRAY CROWNED CRANE

(Balearica regulorum)

This species and the related black crowned crane constitute a group of four nonoverlapping populations that are now confined to Africa south of the Sahara. They are the only living descendants of a group of cranes that once ranged widely over the world, including North America, but were eventually replaced by more advanced types of cranes. Crowned cranes have relatively short, stout bills and legs; they lack elongated, decurved inner wing feathers and also the highly developed intrasternal tracheal (windpipe) structure that is so characteristic of the more advanced *Grus* cranes. Nevertheless, they are an extremely attractive group of birds, with distinctive golden yellow feathered crowns, white to golden wing coverts, and grayish white to pale blue eyes.

The crowned cranes are associated with open country, especially favoring grasslands in the vicinity of water. Unlike the other types of cranes, they prefer to roost in elevated locations, especially large trees. However, they also at times roost in shallow water in the manner of more typical cranes. They are quite social and outside the breeding season often occur in flocks of from a few dozen to as many as 150 birds. Like other cranes, they are strongly monogamous, and probably even during the nonbreeding season the nuclear social unit consists of the pair or family. Families remain intact for nine or ten months, after which the adults drive the young from their territory and prepare to nest again. At that time the young birds from the same general area tend to associate in flocks, spending much of their time foraging in fields. Crowned cranes consume a wide variety of foods, ranging from grass and grain seeds to insects, earthworms, and even crustaceans.

Like all other cranes, this species "dances," and these dances include lively leaps and bows as well as a ruffling of the long and ornamental feathers of the lower neck and breast. The wings are also often spread, exposing the beautiful contrasting upper wing coverts. The unison call of the pair is performed with the birds standing in a stationary position; as the calls are uttered, the red gular sac is inflated, and the head is turned slowly from side to side. The wings are not raised or moved during unison calling.

Gray crowned cranes range from South Africa north to extreme eastern Zaire, Uganda, and Kenya, with the northernmost birds separated by only a few hundred miles in northern Kenya from the eastern race of the black crowned crane. At least until recently, gray crowned

FIGURE 3.2. *Gray crowned crane, adult profile*

cranes were still relatively common in many areas, such as in Kenya and southern Uganda, where the population has been judged as dense as two to three birds per square mile. The breeding season is highly variable, with nesting in Uganda occurring throughout the year, while in Zambia the nesting records extend from December to April during the rainy season. Breeding during the wetter (summer) season is typical in Malawi, Zimbabwe, and South Africa, with the approximate peak of breeding there occurring in January. In South Africa they nest in open, shallow marshes, where relatively dense, tall stands of grasses and sedges are present and sufficiently high as to hide the incubating birds effectively.

Breeding territories range from 200 to 900 acres, depending on the local population density. Large platform-likes nests are constructed in fairly heavy wetland vegetation. From two to four eggs are laid, and incubation by both sexes lasts about 28 (26–31) days. Fledging periods range from 60 to 100 days. In spite of the relatively large clutch size of crowned cranes, typically only a single chick survives to fledging. Like demoiselle cranes, crowned cranes molt their major wing feathers gradually and so never become flightless during their molting period. This continuous flying ability might be of particular advantage to these tree-roosting birds.

As recently as the early 2000s there was an estimated world population of about 40,000–50,000 birds, with 17,000–20,000 individuals in Kenya, 13,000–20,000 individuals in Uganda, perhaps 5,000 birds in the Democratic Republic of Congo, and 4,000–5,000 birds in South Africa. At that time the gray crowned crane was still regarded as of "least concern" by the IUCN, but in 2009 it was reclassified to "vulnerable," and by 2013 it had again been reclassified as "endangered." It has been described as the crane with the world's most rapidly declining population rate, and in western Kenya, where it was once common, it has suffered from conversion of land to sugar cane, and wetlands to eucalyptus plantations. On the bright side, the Zambian population on the Kafue Flats, Liuwa Plain, and Bangweula Swamp was apparently substantial in 2014. As noted in the blue crane's account, the establishment in early 2014 of a 150,000-acre grassland preserve in South Africa, the Chrissiesmeer's Lake District, should be of significance to this crane's survival in South Africa. Crowned crane chicks are often captured and taken into captivity, where they are kept as decorative pets in hotels, restaurants, and private homes. Current overall population estimates and effective conservation measures are badly needed.

SIBERIAN CRANE

(Bugeranus leucogeranus)

The Siberian crane is perhaps the rarest crane in the world and in 2013 was classified by the IUCN as critically world-endangered. In the 1970s, it had a total known population of a few hundred birds, making it almost as rare as the whooping crane. However, in 1980 a major wintering flock was discovered in eastern China, and hopes were raised for the preservation of this beautiful species, which is variously called the "lily of birds" in India, the "snow wreath" in Russia, and the "crane with black sleeves" in China. It has been known to nest in only two areas of Siberia, including a now possibly extirpated population that historically bred between the Ob and Pechora rivers and a second much larger eastern population nesting from the lower Kolyma River basin west to the lower Yana River. The primary surviving flock breeds in the Usi-Yana District of northern Yakutia, which is centered on the Indigirka River, with its western limits near the Yana River (longitude 135° east) and its eastern limits near the Alazeya River (longitude 150° east).

FIGURE 3.3. *Siberian crane,*
adult display posture

If it still survives, the fragmented western population is now limited to one or two tiny relict groups, one breeding along the lower Ob River. The westernmost part of this population, with a breeding area historically west of the Urals and centered on the Pechora River, traditionally wintered along the south shore of the Caspian Sea area in northern Iran. However, only four birds from this westernmost flock were still present in the early 2000s, and only a single bird was seen in Iran as recently as the winter of 2011–12. A more centrally located group, whose breeding grounds were east of the Urals and centered on the Ob River, traditionally wintered in Rajasthan, India, at the Keoladeo Ghana Sanctuary. However, only nine individuals were found there in the early 2000s. Unless other wintering areas are found, it is probable that the western population is now essentially extirpated, although a few have been seen in recent years on the species' historic West Siberian breeding grounds.

It winters in the swampy portions of northern Jiangxi Province at Poyang and Dongting lakes, along the lower Yangtze (Changjiang) River in eastern China, with a major spring and fall stopover area at Momoge National Nature Reserve in Jilin Province. This flock was estimated in 2013 to consist of about 3,400 birds and was judged as stable or increasing (Mirande and Harris, in press).

Siberian cranes are distinctly different from all the other cranes of the world and probably are not close relatives of any of these. Their unison-call behavior and their foraging adaptations suggest affinities with the African wattled crane. Like that species, they have a rather high-pitched and somewhat goose-like voice, and the unison-call ceremony is characterized by its strong wing-lowering and extreme neck-stretching, especially by the male. Both species also have tracheae (windpipes) that only slightly penetrate the front of the sternal breastbone. They are also the most aquatic of all living cranes.

In northern Yakutia these cranes nest in arctic tundra, often in tidal flat areas or in flat and swampy depressions of ancient lakebeds covered by short grasses and sedges, sometimes in company with sandhill cranes. In western Siberia they breed in mossy marshland areas of the northern taiga forest, especially in bogs surrounded by stunted pines. During other seasons Siberian cranes occupy more diverse habitats, but typically occur where the birds can wade in shallow waters and where there is an abundance of aquatic plant roots. They especially like the tubers of sedges, which they can easily reach and grub out with their long and serrated bills. A small amount of animal life may be consumed at times, especially when snow cover makes plant life unavailable early in the breeding season.

Sexual maturity is apparently attained during the third year in this species, judging from the limited information available. The birds arrive at their arctic nesting grounds in late May and begin to lay as soon as their nesting sites become snow-free. Their breeding territories are scattered (an average density of about four pairs per 100 square kilometers, or ca. 40 square miles, has been estimated in northeastern Siberia), with conspecific pairs typically separated by distances of several miles. As a result, direct territorial encounters are unlikely to occur. Nests are often built at the edge of a large wetland, especially where stands of pendant grass are present. Nests have been found in water about 10–25 inches deep, far enough from land to deter prowling predators such as arctic foxes. Incubation lasts 26–32 (average 29) days. However, foxes, jaegers, and arctic gulls may be serious predators on young chicks prior to fledging over the next 70–75 days. The wing molt occurs during the chicks' fledging period in late summer, when the adult birds are also flightless for a time, probably a few weeks.

The discovery and improved protection of the large wintering flock in southeastern China has, however, greatly improved the species' conservation outlook. The establishment by the Chinese Ministry of Forestry of a national nature preserve at Poyang Lake, Jiangxi Province, has been of critical importance to the Siberian crane, as that site supports nearly all of the species' known population during winter.

Russia has also been making strong efforts to protect the Siberian crane and its breeding habitat, although most of its breeding grounds are in northeastern China. Preservation of adequate areas of both breeding and wintering habitat types, which are often influenced by agricultural interests, will be necessary for the continued survival of this beautiful crane. Molecular research using DNA hybridization techniques has shown this to be probably a very isolated species in a genetic sense, second only to the crowned cranes in terms of its evolutionary isolation from other living species of cranes. The Siberian crane is currently considered critically endangered by the IUCN and as an endangered species in the Red Book of Russia.

WATTLED CRANE

(Bugeranus carunculatus)

The distinctive wattled crane of Africa is one of the largest cranes of the world (adults weigh up to eighteen to twenty pounds) and, except for the Australian and the two crowned cranes, is one of the few that is distinctly wattled. Unlike these species, however, in the wattled crane's throat feathers mostly cover the wattle, leaving only the anterior portion bare and reddish. The front of the face, extending from the beak back to the eyes, is bare, with wartlike papillae in both sexes, and the innermost flight feathers (the variably modified secondary feathers that are often called "tertials") are greatly elongated, hiding the tail in resting birds. The wattled crane's voice is a high-pitched scream, with the male's slightly lower in pitch. In both sexes the windpipe is not deeply convoluted within the sternum, and the species' voice lacks the power and resonance of the cranes having greater intra-sternal tracheal penetration.

This crane is associated with large areas of shallow wetlands. Foraging is done by probing in wet or moist soil for the underground portions of sedges and by consuming aquatic plants such as water lilies. It may at times also eat such vertebrate prey as frogs and snakes. The wattled crane thus forages in much the same manner as the Siberian crane, a species that is often considered to be the wattled crane's nearest relative. The breeding season of the wattled crane extends throughout the year in Natal and Zambia, while in Ethiopia and Malawi the breeding records range from May to October. Generally, nest-building does not occur until the peak of annual flooding has occurred, when there would be less risk of water-caused nest losses. Breeding territories include nest sites that are situated in open grassy or sedge-covered marshes up to three feet or more in depth, with high, dense, emergent

FIGURE 3.4. *Wattled crane, adult profile*

vegetation. The nest is a substantial pile of such vegetation, with the area around the nest site well stripped of growing plants.

Wattled cranes have the smallest average clutch size of any cranes, averaging only 1.5 eggs per clutch, and single-egg clutches are frequent. In addition, the eggs have an unusually long incubation period of 32–40 (mean 33) days, and the chicks reportedly have an extremely long fledging period of 103–148 days, or rarely even as long as 180 days. This very long fledging period would seem to put the young at considerable risk from predation. Perhaps for such reasons, the reproductive success of wattled cranes appears to be low, with fledged young usually making up less than 5 percent of the postbreeding populations.

Wattled cranes are probably the most severely threatened of the African cranes. They are now mostly limited in their distribution to the area of the upper Zambezi drainage, although in earlier times they occurred south to Cape Province and west nearly to the mouth of the Congo. Besides the Zambezi basin population, there is a small group of about 200 birds centered in Natal and the Transvaal of South Africa, a disjunctive population of similar size in the highlands of southern Ethiopia, and perhaps a relict population of perhaps only a few pairs in Ovambo, northern Namibia. The current status of the Ethiopian population is precarious, and it is perhaps limited to Bale Mountain National Park in southeastern Ethiopia. Several water development projects in the heart of the wattled crane's primary remaining range in the upper Zambezi drainage make its conservation needs a particularly urgent matter.

The total world population of wattled cranes was probably about 8,000 birds and was declining in early 2014, placing them high on the list of cranes that deserve special conservation attention. The declining Zambian population at the Kafue Flats was estimated at about 1,000 individuals in 2002. A 2013 count revealed 780 birds, but these flats, Liuwa Plain National Park, and Bangeuulu Swamp probably collectively support about two-thirds of the world population. The available data also suggest marked declines in Mozambique and possibly Botswana. Other than in Zambia, the Okavango Delta in Botswana may now hold the largest single population of about 1,300 birds. The establishment in early 2014 of a 150,000-acre grassland preserve in South Africa, the Chrissiesmeer's Lake District, should be of importance to the wattled crane's prospects for survival in South Africa. The world population has been recently estimated at from about 6,000 to 8,000 individuals (IUCN 2013).

BLUE CRANE

(Anthropoides paradisea)

This beautiful species, sometimes called the Stanley's crane or paradise crane, is one of only two cranes to have been designated as a country's "national bird" (by the Republic of South Africa). It also has one of the most restricted distributions of any crane, being essentially limited to South Africa, including Swaziland and Lesotho, as well as having a very small and isolated population near the Etosha Pan of Namibia.

FIGURE 3.5. *Blue crane, adult profile*

The blue crane is a close relative of the demoiselle crane and, like it, is particularly adapted to arid grasslands. It is especially characteristic of grass-covered hills and valleys with only scattered trees, where grassy cover is thick and short. In Natal the birds breed in highland "bergveld" grasslands at 3,300–6,500 feet elevation. There the climate is temperate, and most of the precipitation occurs during the summer months, often in the form of hailstorms. During the cold and dry winter season the birds move to lower elevations.

Blue cranes have short and moderately pointed bills and do most of their foraging from the ground surface or from low vegetation. They have not been observed to dig for foods with their bills or to forage in water, although nighttime roosting in water sometimes occurs among wintering flocks. At that time of year they are quite gregarious and may form flocks of up to 300 birds. Also during that season they may forage among herds of ungulates such as springbok antelopes, with which they form an interactive society, the ever-alert cranes sometimes warning the antelopes of possible danger.

Blue cranes are strongly territorial, and although they are too small to expel wattled cranes from their nesting territories, they do not hesitate to attack cattle or most species of birds that too closely approach their nests. When humans approach, they usually simply retreat, though they may call, dance, or circle the intruder with their wings outstretched. During the unison call the male arches his wings, exposing his darker primary feathers, and calls shrilly with his neck tilted far backward and with the bill held vertically. Females assume a less extreme posture during this pair-bonding ceremony.

The breeding season of blue cranes is limited to the summer period between October and March, with a peak of egg records in December. Nests are placed near water, although on shortgrass foothill habitats they may be placed in quite dry locations. There are consistently two eggs in the clutch, which are laid from one to three days apart. The incubation period lasts 29–33 (mean 30) days. Hatching has been reported to be relatively synchronous, but probably the chicks normally hatch on successive days, as is typical of cranes. The nest is abandoned shortly after the last chick has hatched, and the family gradually moves away from the nest site. The fledging period probably requires about eighty-five days, although estimates have varied greatly. The young birds remain with their parents until the following breeding season, when they are evicted from the breeding territory. Very probably families are reunited after the breeding period.

In spite of its small total range, this species is still fairly common locally, no doubt in part because of its special protected status as the national bird of South Africa. In South Africa the national population has fallen by half or more since the 1970s, although local populations in the south and southwestern Western Cape and Kwazulu-Natal have increased as the species has expanded into agricultural areas. Intentional or unintentional poisoning associated with farming activities is believed to be the major cause of an apparent marked population decline in recent years. The population in the central Karoo region is believed to be stable. Tiny relict populations also exist in Namibia and Swaziland. As of the early 2000s the species' population was estimated at about 21,000 individuals (Hughes 2008).

A major boost to this species' chances for survival, as well as those of the wattled crane and the gray crowned crane, was provided by the establishment in early 2014 of a 150,000-acre grassland preserve in South Africa's Lake District, the Chrissiesmeer's Lake District.

Another 50,000 acres is schedule to be added in the future in hopes of providing an economically viable center for livestock production, tourism, and conservation. Lake Chrissie, the largest freshwater lake in South Africa, has been proposed as a Ramsar wetland site of international importance.

DEMOISELLE CRANE

(Anthropoides virgo)

This smallest, "damsel-like," and most elegant of all the cranes of the world is a relative of the blue crane. Like that species, it has a fully feathered crown, distinctly elongated inner wing feathers, and a somewhat shaggy breast. It is adapted to a dry upland and grass-dominated environment. Indeed, the demoiselle crane is perhaps the most arid-adapted of all the cranes. The species' main breeding region extends from Turkey and the Black Sea region through southern Ukraine and Crimea through Kazakhstan, Mongolia, and northeastern China. Its breeding densities across this broad range are low, but the birds are notably abundant throughout the vast grasslands of Mongolia. In Kazakhstan the demoiselle may still enjoy a fairly stable population, but it has declined over much of its original and now rapidly disappearing steppe range. To a limited degree, it has begun to nest in agriculturally modified areas.

The demoiselle crane has a wide winter distribution that once included much of northwestern Africa (Algeria, Tunisia, and eastern Morocco) but is now restricted to a tiny remnant in Morocco. It also winters in small numbers in north-central and northeastern Africa (from Lake Chad east to the Nile Valley) and is especially widespread in the Indian subcontinent, where the largest numbers of birds that breed in central to eastern Asia overwinter. The breeding population in China has been estimated at about 1,000–10,000 pairs (IUCN 2013). In the early 2000s the species' global population was estimated to number about 230,000–280,000 individuals.

Throughout its breeding range the demoiselle crane occurs in steppe-like to semidesert habitats. It moves into marshes and swamps only for foraging or roosting. The birds nevertheless prefer to nest no more than about a mile from water, and nests often are located within a few hundred yards of it. During the winter period flocks gather in rice paddies, along the margins of shallow monsoon-dependent wetlands ("jheels") and reservoirs ("tanks"), and in other open and variably moist habitats. Roosts are often located along the sandbars of large rivers or the margins of shallow ponds, as in sandhill cranes.

The demoiselle is a gregarious crane, at least on its wintering grounds, and flocks numbering in the thousands of birds have been reported during that season. The birds commonly mix with Eurasian cranes on wintering areas and may forage or roost with them in large flocks. Dancing has been observed among wintering birds as well as among migrating spring and fall flocks. Dancing by these small cranes is highly animated, quick, and graceful, with ballet-like movements.

This is a spring-nesting species, with eggs in Russia being laid primarily during April and May but sometimes as late as June in Siberia. Almost invariably two well-camouflaged eggs

FIGURE 3.6. *Demoiselle crane, adult profile*

are laid. The nest is also often located where small stones are present. No plant materials are added, so the surrounding stones help provide visual camouflage. The incubation period is 27–30 (mean 28) days, with the female reportedly undertaking most of the incubation duties. The fledging period is 55–65 days, which is also a notably short duration for cranes, but is correlated with the species' small body mass.

During the fledging period the adults do not become flightless; instead they replace their flight feathers sequentially and continue to molt during the fall migration. This prolonged molt pattern may reflect an adaptation to dryland breeding, where bodies of water in which flightless birds might escape terrestrial predators are rare or lacking. It is not known with certainty how long family bonds last, but very probably they persist at least through the first year of life, with the young temporarily leaving their parents when slightly less than a year of age as the latter prepare for breeding.

WHITE-NAPED CRANE

(Grus vipio)

The white-naped crane is well named; it is the only white-headed crane that has a red facial patch extending far enough backward to encompass the ear opening, and the only one that has a dark grayish stripe extending up each side of the neck to terminate at a point slightly behind the bare facial region. This species has been classified as vulnerable by the IUCN, and its breeding range is centered in Russia, where it is regarded as being very rare and declining. It breeds in small numbers at several different Russian locations, including the middle Amur River basin and the Ussuri River valley, and at least until recently it nested commonly along the shore of Lake Khanka in the upper Ussuri Basin. The crane is not adequately protected in these areas. Perhaps northeastern Mongolia (the Uldz River basin and Khurkh River valley) actually supports the largest area of breeding habitat and the most birds. The total world population was recently estimated at 5,500–6,500 individuals, based on estimates of 1,000–1,500 individuals wintering in China, a 2009 count of 1,920 in Korea, and a maximum count of 3,142 in 2009 at Izumi, Japan (IUCN 2013). A 2014 spring count of 1,330 at Miyun Reservoir near Beijing suggests that this is a major stopover point, situated roughly halfway between the species' breeding grounds and its Chinese wintering areas.

During the winter, this crane is found in eastern China (Yangtze River valley), Korea (mainly near the Demilitarized Zone, where more than two-thirds of the world population stage during migration), and in southern Japan, where it occupies a restricted area in Izumi and Akune districts of southwestern Kyushu. It is in the last-named area that the best opportunities for censusing exist, and in recent years there have been about 2,000 wintering birds present on Kyushu. The concentration of this many birds, as well as substantial numbers of hooded cranes, has caused many local problems of crop damage by the cranes, and sightseers have had disruptive effects on both the local residents and the cranes. It is vital that Japan manage its rare wintering cranes in such a way as to take into account all of these sometimes conflicting interests.

FIGURE 3.7. *White-naped crane, adult display posture*

The birds nest in grassy or swampy areas of wide river valleys or in lake depressions in steppe or forest-steppe habitats. Breeding typically occurs in April and May, with nests consisting of a broad platform of grasses. The usual clutch is of two eggs, which are incubated 30–33 (mean 30) days, mostly by the female. After hatching, 70–75 days are needed to reach fledging. Like other cranes, the young remain with their parents for their first year of life or at least until the next breeding season.

The species' wintering habitats are primarily brackish marshlands and rice paddies, with nearby roosting sites on salt marshes, mud flats, or the edges and sandbars of shallow lakes. Currently the Demilitarized Zone of Korea provides a fortuitous refuge for a few hundred migrating and overwintering cranes, but this is a situation that might change without advance warning. The Poyang Lake national nature sanctuary in southeastern China has been of great value to the white-naped crane; in 1989–90 nearly 3,000 white-naped cranes were counted there during the winter period. The numbers of these birds wintering at Poyang Lake has dropped from about 3,000 birds in 2000 to about 1,500 in the winter of 2013–14, perhaps reflecting a gradual drying up of wetlands in the heart of the white-nape's range since 2000.

AUSTRALIAN CRANE (BROLGA)

(Grus rubicundus)

This crane, which in Australia is usually called the brolga (a corruption of an aboriginal name) or the native companion, is a close relative to the sarus crane. Both are tall, long-billed, predominantly grayish birds, with a head that is mostly bare in adults. However, the Australian crane is feathered somewhat farther up the neck, and it has a more distinct wattle or dewlap on the throat as well as blackish rather than reddish legs. Both species utter strong, resonating calls; during the unison call, displaying males of both species strongly arch their wings and throw back their head and neck to a fully vertical position or beyond. The unison calls of the Australian crane are somewhat stronger and lower in pitch than those of the sarus. Sarus cranes average slightly larger than Australian cranes, adult males averaging about eighteen pounds and the Australian males about fifteen to sixteen.

Mixed pairings of Australian and sarus cranes sometimes occur, even under wild conditions, and natural hybridization has been reported in the northern portions of Australia. In this region the Australian crane had long been abundant, but the sarus crane was first reported in the 1950s. The sarus has gradually colonized the Cape York region, effectively competing with and perhaps partly displacing the Australian crane.

The Australian crane is widespread over the northern portions of Australia and occurs locally as far south as southern Victoria. The largest numbers and densest concentrations are found in Queensland, especially in the region between the Waverly Plains and Rocky River. There the birds seek out freshwater swamps that are dominated by *Eleocharis* sedges, on the tubers of which the cranes forage. For most of the year these tubers, locally called "bulkuru," provide the species' primary food, but in some areas other sedges are also consumed. Various grain crops and some insects or other invertebrates may also be eaten. When natural foods are lacking, such as during Australia's regularly occurring drought cycles, the birds will resort to feeding in agricultural fields, bringing them increasingly into conflict with farmers.

Nesting in this species is timed to coincide with the wet season, which in northern Australia usually begins in December but may begin as early as about July in southern regions. The length and severity of the dry season varies considerably from year to year, so there are considerable variations in the seasonal movements of the cranes. With the onset of the rainy period, there is lowland flooding and filling of seasonal swamps and lagoons. When this occurs, nesting begins immediately, and normally the chicks have already hatched by the time the lagoons begin to dry up once again. At this time there is a gradual movement of adults and young back to the permanent coastal marshes, where some nesting may also occur.

Nests are large piles of vegetation up to about five feet in diameter, located in seasonal wetlands. Those built too early in the wet season are likely to be drowned out. The length of the breeding season in tropical areas may sometimes permit as many as two renesting efforts in the event of early breeding failures. Incubation in this species lasts from 28 to 36 (mean 30) days, and nearly all of the clutches of wild birds contain two eggs. Juveniles are fledged by about 100 days of age. Immatures have been reported to remain with their parents until they are three years old, although they are annually evicted from their parents' territory during each nesting season. Breeding begins when the birds are from three to five years old. No recent overall population estimates of the Australian crane are available, but earlier ones were in the range of 40,000–50,000, and the population has been reported as decreasing (IUCN

FIGURE 3.8. *Australian crane, adult display posture*

2013). The recent proliferation of wind farms in some key habitats of the breeding range is considered to represent a serious threat in Victoria.

SARUS CRANE

(Grus antigone)

The sarus crane is the tallest of the world's cranes and also one of the heaviest, with adult males standing nearly six feet in height and averaging about eighteen pounds. The birds range widely over the Indian Peninsula and at least originally also ranged over much of historic Indochina (Malaysia, Myanmar, Cambodia, Laos, Thailand, and Vietnam) and even the Philippines. In the last few decades, they have managed to colonize a rather large area in northern Australia in northern Queensland and (as uncertain breeders) coastal northern Australia. However, they have been extirpated from the Philippines, Malaysia, and Thailand and perhaps from Laos and Myanmar. They remain common in northern India, where the Hindus consider them sacred. Uncertain numbers apparently also occur in southeastern Pakistan and southern Nepal.

As with the Australian crane, most of the head and upper neck are bare of feathers in the adult sarus crane, and, except for the grayish crown, the entire head region is a startling flesh red. The vernacular name sarus is of Hindi origin. Linnaeus gave the sarus crane its specific name *antigone* through an apparent association between its garishly bright red head and the ill-fated Antigone of Sophocles, the daughter of Oedipus, who hanged herself.

In northern India these birds are associated with a wide variety of wetland habitats, most of which are seasonal wetlands, flooded during the monsoon period. The arrival of the monsoon rains sets off breeding, but during years when there is no lowland flooding, there may be no nesting. During nonbreeding periods the birds flock to a limited degree, although flock sizes of more than 100 birds are rare. The cranes are omnivorous, consuming not only a wide array of plant materials but also animal foods that range in size from grasshoppers to moderately large water snakes.

Territorial activity begins within as little as a week after the start of the rainy season. At that time, flocks disperse, and pairs begin to defend areas that range in size from as little as about 2–3 acres in populated areas to 100–150 acres in protected locations. The nests are constructed in shallow water, consisting of large heaps of vegetation that are placed among stumps or other supporting structures. Two eggs are laid and are incubated 31–36 (mean 30) days. The female does the majority of the incubation, while the male takes most responsibility for nest protection. The adults are large enough to prevent most potential enemies from approaching the nest site, including the numerous raptors that are common in the region. The young are led away from the nest after a few days and require 85–100 days to attain fledging. Juveniles remain with their parents for about ten months, at which time the adults usually begin breeding again. Although the adults are known to undergo a flightless molt during the time that the young are being reared, little is known of its duration, nor has the period of sexual immaturity been well defined.

The largest known breeding populations of sarus crane are centered in northern India in the boundary area of Etawah and Mainpuri districts of southwestern Uttar Pradesh. During the late 1990s and early 2000s about 250 breeding pairs occurred here, but recent construction, conversion of wetland to farmland, human disturbance, and pesticide applications have reduced the breeding population of this single most important wetland for sarus cranes. That any cranes have managed to survive and continue to breed in this densely populated region is certainly to be welcomed, but human population growth throughout the world has resulted in an ever-increasing threat to the long-term survival of all the world's cranes.

The population of the western race of the sarus crane in the early 2000s might have consisted of 8,000–10,000 individuals in India, Nepal, and Pakistan. There may also have been 800–1,000 in Cambodia, Laos, and Vietnam and 500–800 in Myanmar at that time. The Australian population was estimated at 5,000–10,000 breeding adults in 2000. The world population thus then totaled about 19,000–22,000 individuals (IUCN 2013). Because of some ecological advantages over the smaller Australian crane, the sarus may eventually become the dominant crane species over the northern parts of Australia.

FIGURE 3.9. *Sarus crane, adult display posture*

RED-CROWNED (JAPANESE) CRANE

(Grus japonensis)

This marvelous Asian crane is also known by a variety of English names, including Manchurian crane and Japanese crane, but none of these is particularly suitable for such a magnificent bird. It is arguably the most beautiful of all cranes, with a snow-white plumage that is set off by a red crown and jet-black inner flight feathers, plus similar black feathers on its head and upper neck, but with a contrasting white nape and hindneck. Adults are the heaviest of all crane species, with males reportedly weighing as much as twenty-five pounds during autumn. Like the similar whooping crane, adult red-crowned cranes have an extremely loud voice, which may easily carry a mile or more under favorable conditions, and associated extensive intrasternal penetration by the windpipe.

Apparently the preferred foods of this species are quite similar to those of the whooping crane and include a substantial amount of animal materials. The birds obtain most of their animal food by wading and probing for aquatic animals such as snails, crabs, fish, and the like. However, they also rely heavily on artificial feeding of grain during winter in Hokkaido.

Also like whooping cranes, red-crowned cranes defend large territories, measuring from 0.4 to 4.5 square miles, in deep-water marshes, bogs, and wet meadows. Nests are built on wet ground or in standing water, where the surrounding marsh vegetation may be up to eighty inches high. Incubation lasts 29–36 (mean 32) days, with the female doing most of the incubation and the male defending the nest. After hatching, the family may move to drier habitats for foraging. Fledging occurs at about 95 days of age, and it has been found that in Japan's protected population breeding success may be about 12–15 percent.

The red-crowned crane has long been recognized as endangered, and its population in the 1970s was believed to number fewer than 500 birds. The majority of these were then restricted to Hokkaido, Japan, where a resident population still survives and is essentially nonmigratory, although some wander south as far as the Kushiro District of Hokkaido. They are sometimes also seen in eastern Mongolia. The mainland population breeds in the Amur and Ussuri basins of southeastern Russia and in adjoining northeastern China (Heilongjiang, Julin, and Liaoning provinces). The more western breeders winter along coastal China, while the eastern ones winter in the vicinity of the Demilitarized Zone of Korea.

The total Japanese population was recently estimated at about 2,750 birds, with about 1,650 mature individuals. It is probably declining on mainland Asia; the wintering population in China totaled about 400–500 birds. There are another 1,000–1,050 birds scattered at four locations in Korea (IUCN 2013).

The Hokkaido population of the red-crowned crane was for a time believed to be extinct, but a small group of birds was found to be nesting near Kushiro in 1924. Although given protection, this population increased only slowly until the 1950s, when supplemental feeding during winter was begun. By the mid-1960s the population had reached 200 birds, by 2000 it had exceeded 1,000, and by 2014 it numbered about 1,500 individuals.

FIGURE 3.10. *Red-crowned crane, adult wing-lowering posture*

On the Asian mainland the species' primary breeding area is in the vicinity of Russia's Lake Khanka and along the Amur and Ussuri rivers, where it was first discovered nesting more than a century ago. However, its habitat there has become greatly restricted in recent years, and perhaps now it is more common farther west in the drainage of the Sungari and Nun rivers of China. In 2003 it was discovered that some breeding occurs in Mongolia as well. Some of the mainland breeding birds winter in Korea, mainly around the Demilitarized Zone. The other important wintering area for the mainland population is along the coast of China's Jiangsu Province near the mouth of the Yangtze River. Yancheng Nature Reserve in that region now perhaps provides the most critical winter habitat for the red-crowned crane in China.

Although the Japanese must be greatly admired for their efforts at saving this crane on Hokkaido and in protecting a part of Kushiro Marsh from destruction, it is apparent now that the population there is essentially saturated. If the species' world population is to grow more, there must be other areas of suitable breeding habitats preserved for it, especially on the mainland.

EURASIAN (COMMON) CRANE

(Grus grus)

This is the familiar wild crane of Europe, the species having the broadest breeding distribution of any of the Old World cranes. Currently it breeds from Scandinavia and Great Britain on the west to at least the Kolyma River and almost to the Okhotsk Sea on the east. It nests locally south to Germany, Poland, and across the steppes of Russia, Kazakhstan, and Kirghizia to northeastern China. Wintering areas are similarly vast and include France, Spain, Morocco, Tunisia, Ethiopia, Sudan, Israel, Turkey, Iraq, Iran, northern India, and southern China.

Like the fairly closely related sandhill crane, this species is mostly gray, but unlike the sandhill crane, it has a white stripe extending from the cheeks back toward the hindneck and a mostly black face, foreneck, and nape. It is only moderately large, with adults weighing about ten to thirteen pounds, or about the mass of a greater sandhill crane. Its voice is similarly loud and resonant, but not so penetrating as those of the whooping or red-crowned cranes. During the unison call both sexes raise their curved tertial feathers, lower their primaries, and stretch their necks to the vertical.

Judging from studies in Scandinavia, the breeding territories of Eurasian cranes are very large and may range from about 125 to more than 1,000 acres. Nests of adjacent pairs are often as far as ten miles apart and are rarely as close as a mile apart. As with other cranes, visual isolation is apparently a major factor in influencing minimal territory size, and thus an interspersion of wooded areas between suitable nesting marshes tends to facilitate greater nesting densities. As with sandhill cranes, feather-painting using mud or decaying vegetation is common. The two-egg clutch is incubated in turn by both parents, with the female undertaking the larger share. The eggs hatch in 28–31 (mean 30) days, and the young leave the nest soon afterward. They fledge in 65–70 days and remain with their parents for more or all of their first year of life. Nesting success (percentage of nests successfully hatching) reportedly may range from 50 to 77 percent, and twins have been reported as occurring at a rate of 20–30 percent of successful nests.

Although the Eurasian crane may have lost some breeding areas in the westernmost parts of its range, it is still moderately common in Scandinavia. Its range is also expanding in central Europe. In 2006 it was estimated that Germany supported more than 5,400 pairs. It is also now breeding in small numbers in the Czech Republic and Hungary, and since the 1970s a few have begun to reoccupy Great Britain. By 2012, twenty-two pairs were present, and in 2012 and 2013 two pairs successfully reared single chicks in Scotland. No recent efforts have been made to estimate the entire European population of Eurasian cranes, but in Europe up to 70,000 winter on the Iberian Peninsula, which along with the wintering cranes of northwestern Africa, the Nile Valley, Sudan, and Ethiopia, probably include nearly all of the thriving European and Scandinavian breeding populations. Wintering also occurs in Israel (about 20,000 birds winter in the Hula Valley) and the Arabian Peninsula, which probably attracts birds from both eastern Europe and western Russia.

By the early 2000s, the world population was estimated to number about 360,000–370,000 individuals. National population estimates included about 100–10,000 breeding pairs in China and about 100–10,000 breeding pairs in Russia (IUCN 2013). During some years Eurasian cranes winter south to Tunisia, and others that presumably are of Russian origin winter regularly in the river valleys of Sudan and the Ethiopian highlands south of Addis Ababa. Much of the Siberian population apparently funnels into the Indian subcontinent, while those from the easternmost regions of Siberia migrate south to southeastern China. Almost nothing is known of the relative population sizes of these two components.

FIGURE 3.11. *Eurasian crane, adult display posture*

HOODED CRANE

(Grus monachus)

This rather small species of crane is sometimes known by its Latin-based name of "monk crane," in reference to the white "hood" that contrasts with an otherwise dark gray to blackish body. It is a species that has been classified as threatened by the International Council for Bird Preservation (ICBP) and as vulnerable by the IUCN. The best estimates are that 11,000–12,000 birds were alive during the early 2000s, based mostly on counts of wintering birds in Honshu and Kyushu, Japan, and in China. This little-studied species of crane breeds in subarctic forests of south-central and southeastern Siberia. Breeding also occurs very locally in northeastern China and probably also in Mongolia.

In spite of this moderately comforting population size, the breeding grounds of the hooded crane are almost completely undocumented, and only a very few actual breeding records exist for it. For a long time it was believed that the species bred in the vicinity of Lake Baikal and the regions to the west, but this was partly based on the erroneous identification of a nest found in the early 1900s and on wrongly identified eggs that had been found in the vicinity of Tomsk. Indeed, it was not until 1974 that the first documented nesting of the hooded crane was obtained. This occurred in the Bikin River area of the Ussuri Basin, well to the east of the area previously suspected of hosting breeding birds. Other studies in the Vilyuy Basin of Siberia during the early 1970s indicated that regular nesting occurs in that large but little-studied region. In both regions the birds have been found to prefer mossy hammocks or damp moors in boggy larch forests at altitudes of about 600–2,500 feet. Apparent nonbreeding birds have been seen during summer in other locations, such as the open steppes and forest-steppes of Transbaikalia. So far as is known, nearly all breeding is limited to Russia. However, a small amount of nesting habitat occurs in northeastern China, south of the Amur River, where nesting was first reported in the 1990s.

Even in the known breeding areas, nesting densities are apparently extremely low. Breeding probably begins at four or five years of age, and the permanently paired birds usually return to previous territories, often even using the same nest site as in previous years. Nesting occurs during April or May. Evidently breeding densities are influenced by the availability of mossy bogs of the proper size and with suitable degrees of visual and acoustic isolation from other cranes as well as from human disturbance. Nests are constructed of mosses, peat, sedges, and various other wetland plants. Both parents participate in incubation, which lasts 28–30 (mean 29) days. By the time the chicks are a week old, they are able to follow their parents a mile or more to favorable foraging areas. Fledging occurs at about 75 days of age.

Although little is known of breeding-season foods, studies on wintering birds suggest a high percentage of vegetable materials in their diet, and thus it seems likely that hooded cranes are much like Eurasian cranes in their general dietary needs. A few instances of wild hybridization between hooded and Eurasian cranes have been reported, suggesting that these are fairly closely related species that perhaps maintain their reproductive isolation primarily by habitat preference differences during the breeding season.

The majority of the world population winters in Japan, with smaller numbers in China and South Korea. Over 80 percent winter at Izumi, southern Japan, where nearly 10,500 were recorded in 2009, whereas in 1989–90 about 7,200 birds had been wintering at Izumi. Another wintering population at Yashiro in western Honshu has declined considerably in the past half-century and has recently supported only a few birds. In 1989 about 400 were counted at various wetlands in China, including Shengjin (Anhui Province), Poyang Hu (Jiangxi Province), Longgan (Hubei Province), and Dongting (Hunan Province). By the early 2000s an estimated 1,050–1,150 birds were wintering in China, including 300–400 at Poyang Hu, more than 600 at Shengjin Hu and Caizi Hu (Anhui Province), and over 100 at Chongming Dao (Jiangsu Province). About 100 birds were then wintering in South Korea, mainly at Suncheon Bay. The world population was estimated at about 11,500 birds in the early 2000s (IUCN 2103)

This is one of the species of cranes that can be preserved from extinction only by the cooperation of several nations, particularly Russia, China, Korea, and Japan. Some important wintering areas in Korea and eastern China have apparently been abandoned, and the wintering grounds in Japan are extremely localized.

FIGURE 3.12. *Hooded crane, adult taking flight*

BLACK-NECKED CRANE

(Grus nigricollis)

This is the least-studied of all the cranes in the world and the species that has most rarely been maintained in captivity or even observed in the wild. Until recently it had been represented in European bird collections only once, when Jean Delacour brought some birds to France in the mid-1920s, but breeding was never achieved. From then until the 1980s the species has been observed only by visitors to the Himalayas or by those who have visited some of the Chinese zoos, where it has been on display since the 1960s. It was not until 1985 that the species was first brought alive into the United States and soon thereafter to Germany.

The breeding grounds of the black-necked crane are high in the Himalayas at elevations from about 9,000 to 15,000 feet, where tundra-like marshes occur around lake edges and on lake islands. Its breeding-season diet consists of roots, tubers, insects, snails, shrimp, fish, small birds, and rodents. In such locations there are grass- or sedge-dominated areas that have a relatively abundant aquatic life, and grassy mounds in shallow lakes or ponds may serve as nesting sites. There seem to be few mammalian predators present in these bleak habitats and high elevations, and likewise there are few raptors of significance. Although it prefers breeding along alpine lakes, shallow marshes and boggy meadows are the most important habitat for feeding. Nests are often built at sites with a water depth of around twelve inches, thereby probably reducing exposure to nest predators. Furthermore, island nests are constructed well out of reach of humans and most terrestrial predators (IUCN 2013). There is typically a two-egg clutch, which is incubated 30–33 days (mean 30). Fledging has been reported to require 90 days, a very long time for an alpine-breeding species.

The breeding biology of this crane is still little studied, but the birds build their nests in aquatic vegetation or at lake borders, alpine bog meadows, and riverine marshes, especially in lakeside marshes from 8,300 to 15,500 feet. It winters in river valleys and along reservoir shorelines in the vicinity of barley and spring wheat fields. Shallow marshes and meadows are the most important habitat for feeding; the cranes forage on roots, tubers, insects, snails, shrimp, fish, small birds, and rodents (IUCN 2013).

Eggs are usually laid in May or June. Incubation is by both sexes and lasts 31–33 days, with males usually doing the nocturnal incubation. After hatching, the birds gradually move away from the nest site to better foraging areas. Fledging occurs at about 90 days of age.

The breeding season is very short at these high elevations and probably is confined to the period between late May and August. Evidently there is a fall migration out of the region in October, with many of the cranes wintering to the southeast in the Yunnan-Guizhou regions of China or in southern Tibet, with wintering also occurring in west-central Bhutan, where 300–400 birds occur in the Phobjikha Valley and some at least formerly occurred in Assam and Vietnam. During winter the birds mix to some degree with Eurasian cranes and apparently have rather similar ecological requirements to that species'. However, limited information suggests that they have a greater preference for foraging in marshes and other wetlands and thus may feed to a larger degree on animal materials.

FIGURE 3.13. *Black-necked crane, adult calling*

Besides breeding on the Qinghai-Tibetan Plateau, China, there is a small nesting population in adjacent Ladakh, India. This species winters in river valleys and along reservoir shorelines in the vicinity of barley and spring wheat fields. Several wintering areas have been identified at lower altitudes on the Qinghai-Tibetan and Yunnan-Guizhou plateaus, China, including Yunnan and western Guizhou, as well as in Tibet. Small numbers also winter in Bhutan and in Arunachal Pradesh, India, and wintering birds were historically recorded in Vietnam. The global winter population during the early 2000s was estimated at about 10,000–11,000, including about 6,500–7,000 in Tibet, 3,000 in Yunnan, 450 in Bhutan, and a few in India (IUCN 2013).

Nearly all of the breeding range of this species is confined to Tibet, and at least until the Chinese influence became strong in the 1950s the cranes were effectively protected by the Tibetans' sacred treatment of all animals. The current situation is not clear, but the Chinese government is currently affording the black-necked crane its highest level of official protection and has established one sanctuary specifically for it. It is also the subject of biological studies by the Chinese, and Bhutan has recently established two protected areas on that country's restricted wintering grounds. Agricultural development of winter habitats, poisoning by farmers in China, and hunting in Tibet are believed to be serious factors affecting its survival.

FOUR

Epilogue

THE WORLD'S HUMAN POPULATIONS HAVE increased from about 3 billion to roughly 8 billion in the past half-century. Meanwhile, the number of crane taxa that have been classified as endangered, vulnerable, or threatened has markedly increased since 1966, the year the first edition of the IUCN's *Red Data Book* of rare and endangered bird species was published. A summary (Table 5.1) of the generally rather bleak situation that is now facing most of the world's cranes is thus presented here as a mere moment in time, in full awareness that by the time it is printed it will be outdated. We are now in a critical moment in time, when fate is forcing us to make decisions affecting not only our own survival but also that of all the other creatures that happen to be currently sharing our planet with us.

Aldo Leopold was acutely aware of the role of time in the events of both humans and nature; his parable of the "good oak" in *A Sand*

County Almanac provides a keen sense of Wisconsin ecological history. He knew too the terrible silence of a now-deserted place that once gave shelter and sustenance to wild creatures. As he said so eloquently, "The sadness discernible in some marshes arises, perhaps, from their once having harbored cranes. Now they stand humbled, adrift in history" (1949, 97).

We humans, as a species, are also captives of history. Caught up in our daily worries and repetitive patterns of existence, the sounds of migrating cranes or geese overhead are often not heard at all above the noises of the city or, if heard, are recognized by only a few. Similarly, we all too often cannot fully sense the slowly rising tide of our diverse ecological crises until we begin to realize that we are in real danger of losing control of our own destiny. From the subtle but pervasive influence of carbon dioxide on global climate patterns, worldwide warming

FIGURE 4.1. *Siberian crane, pair performing postcopulatory display*

trends, or the invisible but increasingly dangerous effects of atmospheric changes, we are perhaps like that unfortunate apocryphal frog that, unaware of the slowly heating water surrounding it, failed to make its escape before it was fatally boiled alive. By the time that most politicians, as well as the general public, are convinced that a real ecological crisis exists, it may well also be too late to do anything to avert it.

Since World War II we as a North American society have generally successively worried about the possibility of dying in a nuclear holocaust, imagining life under a Communist takeover, and avoiding surprise terrorist attacks. While slowly starting to recover from a series of disastrous and incredibly expensive wars in Vietnam, Iraq, and Afghanistan, perhaps we can turn our attention to issues that are far greater threats to our national survival and the future of our overall planetary ecosystem, those of climate change and population control. That way, we can perhaps avert the wholesale ravaging of natural habitats and salvage at least a credible sample of our ravaged world's habitats and biodiversity. I would also hope that a small part of that salvaged biodiversity might be represented by cranes, a nearly universal symbol of happiness and longevity. If I had to choose between never hearing a chorus of heavenly angels or never again hearing wild cranes, I would most certainly choose the cranes. I have indeed often wondered if the "angels" that were heard high above Bethlehem were not really migrating Eurasian cranes . . . at least that's a tantalizing thought to contemplate.

FIGURE 5.1. *Black-necked crane, adult wing-flapping*

Appendix A
A Summary of the World's Crane Populations

Table 5.1. Summary of the World's Cranes and Their Recent Status

Species and Subpopulations	Approx. Total Population[a]	Breeding Distribution	Conservation Status and Trend[a]
Black Crowned Crane	ca. 50,000	Africa	Vulnerable, decreasing
W. African race	ca. 10,000–15,000	Gambia to Chad	Endangered, decreasing
E. African race	ca. 40,000–50,000	Sudan to Kenya	Vulnerable, uncertain
Gray Crowned Crane	ca 30,000	Africa	Endangered, decreasing
S. African race	ca. 4,000–5,000	Zimbabwe, S. Africa	Endangered, in rapid decline
E. African race	ca. 25,000	Kenya to Malawi	Vulnerable, in rapid decline
Siberian Crane	3,525–3,835	Siberia	Critically endangered
West/Central group	Few or none	Western Siberia	Nearly extirpated
Eastern population	ca. 3,500	Eastern Siberia	Stable or increasing
Wattled Crane	8,060–8,110	Zambia, Botswana	Vulnerable, decreasing?
Blue Crane	25,535	South Africa	Vulnerable, stable or increasing
Demoiselle Crane	225,630–260,760	Central Asia	Least concern, increasing
Sandhill Crane[b]	500,000–600,000	North America, Siberia	Least concern, increasing
Lesser race	ca. 500,000	North America, Siberia	Lower risk, stable
Greater race	80,000	Northern United States	Lower risk, increasing
Florida race	ca. 4,000	Florida	Lower risk, stable
Mississippi race	110	Mississippi	Critically endangered
Cuba race	650	Cuba	Critically endangered
White-naped Crane	5,500–6,500	Northeast China	Vulnerable, decreasing
Australian Crane	25,000–110,000	Australia	Least concern, decreasing
Sarus Crane	24,300–26,800	Asia, Australia	Vulnerable
Indian race	ca. 19,000–21,000	India, Nepal	Endangered, decreasing
Eastern race	ca. 1,000	Southeast Asia	Endangered
Australian race	ca. 5,000	Northern Australia	Uncertain
Red-crowned Crane	2,910–3,100	China, Russia, Japan	Endangered
Whooping Crane[c]	634	North America	Endangered, increasing
Great Plains	304	Canada, Texas	Increasing
Eastern US	125	Wisconsin-Florida	Increasing
Florida	20	Central Florida	Decreasing
Louisiana	32	Southwestern Louisiana	Uncertain
Captive flock	153	five facilities	Increasing
Eurasian Crane	491,200–503,200	Eurasia	Least concern, increasing
Hooded Crane	11,550–11,650	Eastern Asia	Vulnerable, increasing
Black-necked Crane	10,000– 11,000	Tibetan Plateau	Vulnerable, stable or increasing

a   Species estimates and population trends based on Harris and Mirande (2013), except for whooping and sandhill cranes. Subspecies populations and trends from racial and subpopulations in part after Meine and Archibald (1996a). Conservation status category after IUCN (2013).

b   Population estimates as of 2014; the lesser sandhill population estimate includes the Canadian race *rowani.*

c   Population estimates as of 2014.

Appendix B
Useful Internet Sources of Information

Aransas National Wildlife Refuge (Austwell, Texas): http://www.fws.gov/southwest/REFUGES/texas/aransas/

Bernard W. Baker Sanctuary (Bellevue, Michigan): http://www.bakersanctuary.org/

Bosque Del Apache National Wildlife Refuge (Socorro, New Mexico): http://www.fws.gov/southwest/refuges/newmex/bosque/

The Crane Trust (Wood River, Nebraska): http://www.cranetrust.org/

Friends of the Wild Whoopers, Inc.: http://friendsofthewildwhoopers.org/

International Crane Foundation (Baraboo, Wisconsin): http://www.savingcranes.org/

Lillian Annette Rowe Sanctuary (Gibbon, Nebraska): http://rowe.audubon.org/

Majestic and Endangered Whooping Cranes: http://raysweb.net/specialplaces/pages/crane.html

Mississippi Sandhill Crane National Wildlife Refuge (Gautier, Mississippi): http://www.fws.gov/mississippisandhillcrane/

Necedah National Wildlife Refuge (Necedah, Wisconsin): http://www.fws.gov/refuges/profiles
/index.cfm?id=32530

North American Crane Working Group: http://www.nacwg.org/

Operation Migration: http://www.operationmigration.org/

Patuxent Wildlife Research Center (Laurel, Maryland): http://www.pwrc.usgs.gov/birds/

Platte River Recovery Implementation Program (Kearney, Nebraska, and Denver, Colorado):
http://www.platteriverprogram.org/

West Coast Crane Working Group: http://www.wccwg.nacwg.org/

Whooping Crane Conservation Association: http://www.whoopingcrane.com/

Whooping Crane Eastern Partnership (WCEP): http://www.bringbackthecranes.org/

Wood Buffalo National Park (Alberta and Northwest Territories, Canada): http://www.pc.gc.ca
/pn-np/nt/woodbuffalo/index

References

The following list of nearly 400 references may serve as an introduction to the vast technical and semitechnical literature on cranes, which probably now numbers well over 4,000 citations, judging from Reeves (1975), Walkinshaw (1981a), and the International Crane Foundation's *Comprehensive Crane Bibliography* (2005). The Ron Sauey Memorial Library for Bird Conservation of the International Crane Foundation (ICF), in Baraboo, Wisconsin, is very extensive, with many unique holdings and translations and lending privileges for members. The ICF also has helped sponsor and publish the proceedings of several workshops on crane research around the world, and it developed the first *Status Survey and Conservation Action Plan* for the cranes of the world (Meine and Archibald 1996a, 1996b).

The ICF has also played a major role in developing avicultural techniques for breeding rare cranes in captivity and has promoted research on and the conservation of all fifteen species of cranes worldwide. The ICF has a very useful website (www.savingcranes.org) and publishes a popularly written and informative quarterly newsletter for its members, titled *The Bugle*. Information on membership in the ICF and its activities can be obtained from the International Crane Foundation, E–11376 Shady Lane Road, Baraboo, WI 53913. *The Unison Call*, the twice-yearly newsletter of the North American Crane Working Group, provides valuable information on current North American crane research and related news. It totals fourteen volumes as of 2014, and it can be downloaded from the group's website (www.nacwg.org). This and many other websites with useful crane information are listed in Appendix B. I earlier (2001) listed more than 125 locations in North America where wild sandhill or whooping cranes might be observed, and von Treuenfels (2006) described over 50 notable crane-watching locations for the Old World cranes in Europe and Asia.

World Surveys and Crane Bibliographies

Ackerman, J. 2004. "'No mere Bird': Cranes." *National Geographic* 205 (4): 39–55.
    (A photographic essay and a distribution map of all the world's cranes.)

Archibald, G. W., and C. D. Meine. 1996. "Family Gruidae." In *Handbook of the Birds of the World*. Vol. 3,
    Hoatzins to Auks, ed. J. del Hoyo, A. Elliott, and J. Sargatal, 60–89. Barcelona: Lynx Editions.
    (Brief technical accounts and paintings of all the extant species and subspecies of cranes of the
    world. See also Meine and Archibald 1996a, 1996b.)

Ellis, D. H., G. F. Gee, and C. M. Mirande, eds. 1996. *Cranes: Their Biology, Husbandry and
    Conservation*. Washington, DC: National Biological Service; Baraboo, WI: International Crane
    Foundation.
    (A review of all the crane species, with an emphasis on captive husbandry and conservation.)

Harris, J., and C. Mirande. 2013. "A Global Overview of Cranes: Status, Threats and Conservation
    Priorities." *Chinese Birds* 4 (3): 189–209. http://dx.doi.org/10.5122/cbirds.2013.0025.

Hughes, J. 2008. *Cranes: A Natural History of a Bird in Crisis*. Tonawanda, NY: Firefly Books.
    (A photographically-rich account of cranes, with a primary emphasis on the whooping crane.
    Includes brief summaries of all the cranes of the world, with range maps and population
    estimates.)

International Crane Foundation (ICF). 2005. *Comprehensive Crane Bibliography*. https://www
    .savingcranes.org/comprehensive-crane-bibliography.html.
    (An online bibliography, organized by topic and species, with over 4,000 references to 2005,
    including about 300 whooping crane and over 500 sandhill crane references. Many library
    holdings of the ICF can also be accessed at the ICF website.)

Johnsgard, P. A. 1983. *The Cranes of the World*. Bloomington: Indiana University Press.

Johnsgard, P. A. 2014. *Musica de las Grullas: Una historia natural de las Grullas de America*. Translated by E. Weir and Karine Gil-Weir. University of Nebraska Digital Commons. http://digitalcommons. unl.edu/zeabook/.

King, W. B., ed. 1981. *Endangered Birds of the World. The ICBP Bird Red Data Book*. Washington, DC: Smithsonian Institution Press and International Council for Bird Preservation.
    (Includes Mississippi and Cuban sandhill, whooping, red-crowned, Siberian, hooded, white-naped, and black-necked cranes.)

Meine, C. D., and G. W. Archibald, eds. 1996a. *The Cranes: Status Survey and Action Plan*. Gland, Switzerland: International Union for Conservation of Nature and Natural Resources.
    (A comprehensive survey of the distribution and status of all fifteen crane species, with about 900 references. See also Mirande and Harris, in press.)

Meine, C. D., and G. W. Archibald. 1996b. "Ecology, Status and Conservation." In *Cranes: Their Biology, Husbandry and Conservation*, ed. D. H. Ellis, G. F. Gee, and C. M. Mirande, 263–92. Washington, DC: National Biological Service; Baraboo, WI: International Crane Foundation.
    (Range, status, and population trends of all crane species and subspecies.)

Mirande, C. M., and J. Harris, eds. In press. *WI/IUCN Crane Conservation Plan*. Baraboo, WI: International Crane Foundation.

Walkinshaw, L. H. 1973. *Cranes of the World*. New York: Winchester Press.

Walkinshaw, L. H. 1981a. "Cranes of the World: A Partial Bibliography." In *Crane Research around the World*, ed. J. Lewis and H. Masatomi, 24–45. Baraboo, WI: International Crane Foundation.

General Topics and Taxonomic Works

Archibald, G. W. 1975. "The Unison Call of Cranes as a Useful Taxonomic Tool." PhD diss., Cornell University, Ithaca.

Bent, A. C. 1926. *Life Histories of North American Marsh Birds*. US National Museum Bulletin 135. Washington, DC: Smithsonian Institution.

Carver, E., and J. Caudill. 2013. *Economic Benefits to Local Communities of National Wildlife Refuge Visitation*. Washington, DC: Dept. of Economics, US Fish and Wildlife Service.

Dahl, T. E. 1990. *Wetlands—Losses in the United States 1780s to 1980s*. Washington, DC: US Dept. of Interior, Fish and Wildlife Service.

Dessauer, H. C., G. F. Gee, and J. S. Rogers. 1992. "Allozyme Evidence for Crane Systematics and Polymorphism within Populations of Sandhill, Sarus, Siberian and Whooping Cranes." *Molecular Phylogenetics and Evolution* 1 (4): 279–88. http://dx.doi.org/10.1016/1055-7903(92)90003-Y.

Drewien, R. C., and L. C. Lewis. 1987. "Status and Distribution of Cranes of North America." In *Proceedings of the 1983 International Crane Workshop*, 469–77. Baraboo, WI: International Crane Foundation.

Ellis, D. H., G. W. Archibald, S. R. Swegel, and C. B. Kepler. 1991. "Compendium of Crane Behavior, Part 1: Individual (Nonsocial) Behavior." In *Proceedings of the 1987 International Crane Workshop*, ed. J. Harris, 225–34. Baraboo, WI: International Crane Foundation.

Gee, G. F., H. C. Dessauer, J. Longmire, W. E. Briles, and R. C. Simon. 1992. "The Study of Relatedness and Genetic Diversity in Cranes." In *Proceedings of the 1988 North American Crane Workshop*, ed. D. A. Wood, 225–30. Tallahassee: Florida Game and Freshwater Fish Commission.

Harris, J. T. 2008. "Cranes Respond to Climate Change." *ICF Bugle* 34 (3):1–3, 14–15.

Harrison, G. H. 1978. "Crane Saviors of Baraboo." *Audubon* 80 (3): 25–30.
    (Work of the International Crane Foundation.)

IUCN. 1994. *IUCN Red List Categories*. Gland, Switzerland: International Union for Conservation of Nature and Natural Resources.

IUCN. 2007. *IUCN Red List of Threatened Species*. Gland, Switzerland: International Union for Conservation of Nature and Natural Resources.

IUCN. 2013. *IUCN Red List of Threatened Species*. Version 2013.1. Gland, Switzerland: International Union for Conservation of Nature and Natural Resources. www.iucnredlistorg.

Johnsgard, P. A. 1991. *Crane Music: A Natural History of American Cranes*. Washington, DC: Smithsonian Institution Press.

Johnsgard, P. A. 2002. "A Chorus of Cranes." *Zoonooz* 65 (5): 6–11.
    (A general account of the world's cranes.)

Johnsgard, P. A. 2003. *Great Wildlife of the Great Plains*. Lawrence: University Press of Kansas.

Johnsgard, P. A. 2011. *The Sandhill and Whooping Cranes: Ancient Voices over America's Wetlands*. Lincoln: University of Nebraska Press.

Johnsgard, P. A. 2012. *Nebraska's Wetlands: Their Wildlife and Ecology*. Water Survey Paper 78. Lincoln: Conservation and Survey Division, Institute of Agriculture and Natural Resources, University of Nebraska–Lincoln.

Johnsgard, P. A. 2012. *Wetland Birds of the Central Plains: South Dakota, Nebraska and Kansas*. Lincoln: Zea E-Books and University of Nebraska Digital Commons. http://digitalcommons.unl.edu/zeabook/8/.

Johnsgard, P. A. 2012. *Wings over the Great Plains: The Central Flyway*. Lincoln: Zea E-Books and University of Nebraska Digital Commons. http://digitalcommons.unl.edu/zeabook/13/.

Johnsgard, P. A. 2014. *Musica de las Grullas. Una historia natural de las Grullas de America*. Spanish translation of Johnsgard 1991. Lincoln: University of Nebraska Digital Commons. http://digital commons.unl.edu/zeabook/25/.

Jones, K. L. 2003. "Genetic Variation and Structure in Cranes: A Comparison among Species." PhD diss., University of Illinois, Chicago.
    (Taxonomic recognition of *G. c. rowani* is not supported by mitochondrial data.)

Jones, K. L., G. L. Krapu, D. A. Brandt, and M. V. Ashely. 2005. "Population Genetic Structure in Migratory Sandhill Cranes and the Role of Pleistocene Glaciations." *Molecular Ecology* 14 (9): 2645–57. http://dx.doi.org/10.1111/j.1365-294X.2005.02622.x.

Krajewski, C. 1988. "Phylogenetic Relationships among Cranes (Aves: Gruiformes) Based on DNA Hybridization (Abstract)." *American Zoologist* 28:172A.

Krajewski, C., and J. W. Fetzner Jr. 1994. "Phylogeny of Cranes (Gruiformes: Gruidae) Based on Cytochrome-B DNA Sequences." *Auk* 111 (2): 351–65. http://dx.doi.org/10.2307/4088599.
    (The Gruidae are divided into the crowned cranes, Balearicinae, and the remaining species in the subfamily Gruinae. The genus *Leucogeranus* is genetically isolated and the sister to all the other Gruinae. The sandhill crane and Siberian crane represent isolated genetic branches within *Grus*. The whooping crane is part of a group of central *Grus* species that also includes *G. grus, G. monachus, G. japonensis*, and *G. nigricollis*.)

Leopold, A. 1949. *A Sand County Almanac and Sketches from Here and There*. New York: Oxford University Press.

Love, J., and P. Deininger. 1992. "Characterization and Phylogenetic Significance of a Repetitive DNA Sequence from Whooping Crane." *Auk* 109 (1): 73–79. http://dx.doi.org/10.2307/4088267.
    (The whooping crane's nearest relative is probably *Grus japonensis*.)

Mathiessen, P. 2001. *The Birds of Heaven: Travels with Cranes*. New York: North Point Press.
    (Observations of cranes around the world.)

McMillen, J. L. 1988. "Conservation of North American Cranes." *American Birds* 42:1212–21.

Peterson, J. L., R. Bischoff, G. L. Krapu, and A. L. Szalanski. 2003. "Genetic Variation in the Mid-Continent Population of Sandhill Cranes, *Grus canadensis*." *Biochemical Genetics* 41 (1/2): 1–12. http://dx.doi.org/10.1023/A:1020985427461.

Reeves, H. R. 1975. *A Contribution to an Annotated Bibliography of North American Cranes, Rails, Woodcock, Snipe, Doves and Pigeons*. Washington, DC: US Fish and Wildlife Service.
(Distributed by National Technical Information Service, US Dept. of Commerce; ref. code PB–240 999. Literature survey through 1971, with approximately 600 crane references.)

Russell, N., and K. J. McGowan. 2003. "Dance of the Cranes: Crane Symbolism at Çatalhöyük and Beyond." *Antiquity* 77 (297): 445–55. http://dx.doi.org/10.1017/S0003598X00092516.

von Treuenfels, C.-A. 2006. *The Magic of Cranes*. New York: Harry Abrams.
(A personal account of observing and photographing the cranes of the world, translated from the German.)

Wessling, B. n.d. "Individual Recognition, Territorial and Partnership Fidelity of Cranes Evaluated by Sonography: Acoustic Individual Monitoring over Six Years." Unpublished manuscript.

Wood, D. C. 1979. "Phenetic Relationships within the Family Gruidae." *Wilson Bulletin* 91:284–300.

Proceedings of Crane Workshops and Symposia

Several of the crane workshop proceedings are available as for-sale hardcopies (6th–12th) or free-access pdf files (6th–8th) through the North American Crane Working Group's website: http://www.nacwg .org/index.html.

Aborn, D. A., and R. A. Urbenek, eds. 2014. *Proceedings of the Twelfth North American Crane Workshop*. Madison, WI: North American Crane Working Group.

Archibald, G. W., and R. F. Pasquier, eds. 1987. *Proceedings of the 1983 International Crane Workshop*. Baraboo, WI: International Crane Foundation.

Chavez-Ramirez, F., ed. 2005. *Proceedings of the Ninth North American Crane Workshop*. Sacramento, CA: North American Crane Working Group.

Ellis, D. H., ed. 2001. *Proceedings of the Eighth North American Crane Workshop*. Seattle, WA: North American Crane Working Group.
(For the online version see https://www.savingcranes.org/proceedings-of-the-eighth-north -american-crane-workshop.html.)

Feldt, R. D., comp. 1977. *Papers of the Symposium on the Eastern Population of Greater Sandhill Cranes*. Indianapolis: Indiana Division of Fish and Wildlife.

Folk, M. J., and S. A. Nesbitt, eds. 2008. *Proceedings of the Tenth North American Crane Workshop*. Gambier, OH: North American Crane Working Group.

Hartup, B. K., ed. 2010. *Proceedings of the 11th North American Crane Workshop*. Baraboo, WI: International Crane Foundation.

Lewis, J. C., ed. 1976. *Proceedings of the 1975 International Crane Workshop*. Stillwater: Oklahoma State University Publishing and Printing Dept.

Lewis, J. C., ed. 1979. *Proceedings of the 1978 Crane Workshop*. Fort Collins: Colorado State University Printing Service.

Lewis, J. C., ed. 1982. *Proceedings of the 1981 Crane Workshop*. Tavernier, FL: National Audubon Society.

Lewis, J. C., ed. 1987. *Proceedings of the 1985 Crane Workshop*. Grand Island, NE: Platte River Whooping Crane Habitat Maintenance Trust and US Fish and Wildlife Service.

Lewis, J. C., and H. Masatomi, eds. 1981. *Crane Research around the World: Proceedings of the International Crane Symposium*. Baraboo, WI: International Crane Foundation.

Schimmel, C., ed. 1995. *Proceedings of the Third Annual International Crane Symposium: People, Water and Wildlife: Human Population Impacts on Cranes*. Boulder, CO: National Audubon Society.

Stahlecker, D. W., and R. P. Urbanek, eds. 1992. *Proceedings of the Sixth North American Crane Workshop*. Grand Island, NE: North American Crane Working Group.
   (For the online version see https://www.savingcranes.org/proceedings-of-the-sixth-north -american-crane-workshop-1992.html.)

Urbanek, R. P., and D. W. Stahlecker, eds. 1997. *Proceedings of the Seventh North American Crane Workshop*. Grand Island, NE: North American Crane Working Group.

Whitaker, H., ed. 1992. *Proceedings of the International Crane Symposium. People, Water and Wildlife: Human Population Impacts on Cranes*. Washington, DC: National Audubon Society.

Whitaker, H., and C. Schimmel, eds. 1994. *Proceedings of the Second Annual International Crane Symposium. People, Water and Wildlife: Human Population Impacts on Cranes*. Boulder, CO: National Audubon Society.

Wood, D. A., ed. 1992. *Proceedings of the 1988 North American Crane Workshop*. Nongame Wildlife Program Technical Report 12. Tallahassee: Florida Game and Fresh Water Fish Commission.

Platte River Valley References

Breckenridge, W. J. 1945. "Nebraska Crane Flight." *Flicker* 17:79–81.
   (Early sandhill crane observations on the Platte.)

Brown, M. B., S. J. Dinsmore, and C. R. Brown. 2012. *Birds of Southwestern Nebraska*. Lincoln: Conservation and Survey Division, Institute of Agriculture and Natural Resources, University of Nebraska–Lincoln.
   (Ornithological history and an annotated bird list of 363 species reported in the North Platte Valley.)

Brown, M. B., and P. A. Johnsgard. 2013. *Birds of the Central Platte Valley, Nebraska*. Lincoln: Zea E-Books and University of Nebraska Digital Commons. http://digitalcommons.unl.edu/zeabook/17/.
   (Ornithological background and an annotated regional list of 373 species.)

Colt, C. J. 1996. "Breeding Bird Use of Riparian Forests along the Central Platte River: A Spatial Analysis." MS thesis, University of Nebraska, Lincoln.

Cunningham, D. 1983. "River Portraits: The Platte." *Nebraskaland* 63 (1): 29–30.

Currier, P. J., G. R. Lingle, and J. G. VanDerwalker. 1985. *Migratory Bird Habitat on the Platte and North Platte Rivers in Nebraska*. Grand Island, NE: Whooping Crane Habitat Maintenance Trust.

Davis, C. A. 2005a. "Breeding Bird Communities in Riparian Forests along the Central Platte River, Nebraska." *Great Plains Research* 15:199–211.

Davis, C. A. 2005b. "Breeding and Migration Bird Use of a Riparian Woodland along the Platte River in Central Nebraska." *North American Bird Bander*, July–Sept:109–14.

Faanes, C. E., and G. R. Lingle. 1995. *Breeding Birds of the Platte Valley of Nebraska*. Jamestown, ND: Northern Prairie Wildlife Research Center. http://www.npwrc.usgs.gov/resources/distr/birds /platte/platte.

Farrar, J. 1985. "Partners on the Platte." *Nature Conservancy News* 35:13–38.

Farrar, J. 1989. "Lillian Annette Rowe Sanctuary: Way-Station on the Platte." *Nebraskaland* 67 (2): 18–34.

Grier, R. 2009. "Cranes on the North Platte." *Nebraskaland* 87 (2): 42–45.

Gruchow, P. 1989. "The Ancient Faith of Cranes." *Audubon Magazine* 91 (3): 40–54.
    (Part of a special issue primarily devoted to the Platte River.)

Jenkins, A., ed. 1993. *The Platte River: An Atlas of the Big Bend Region*. Kearney: University of Nebraska–Kearney.
    (A broad survey of the region and its history.)

Johnsgard, P. A. 1983. "The Platte: A River of Birds." *Nature Conservancy News* 33:6–10.

Johnsgard, P. A. 1984. *The Platte: Channels in Time*. Lincoln: University of Nebraska Press.
    (Historical review of the Platte Valley and its ecology.)

Johnsgard, P. A. 1991. *Crane Music: A Natural History of American Cranes*. Washington, DC: Smithsonian Institution Press.

Johnsgard, P. A. 2001. *The Nature of Nebraska: Ecology and Biodiversity*. Lincoln: University of Nebraska Press.
    (The ecology of Nebraska's major ecoregions, including the Platte Valley and its crane usage.)

Johnsgard, P. A. 2003. "Great Gathering on the Great Plains." *National Wildlife* 41 (3): 20–29. http://digitalcommons.unl.edu/johnsgard/38.
    (Sandhill and whooping cranes in the Platte Valley.)

Johnsgard, P. A. 2007. "The Platte: River of Dust or River of Dreams?" *Prairie Fire* 1 (5): 12–13, 17–19. http://www.prairiefirenewspaper.com/2007/11/the-platte.
    (Recent water usage and water priorities in the Platte Valley.)

Johnsgard, P. A. 2011. *The Sandhill and Whooping Cranes: Ancient Voices over America's Wetlands*. Lincoln: University of Nebraska Press.
    (Biology of the American species.)

Johnsgard, P. A. 2012. "Nebraska's Magical Sandhill Crane Migration." *Prairie Fire* 6 (2): 1, 3–5. http://prairiefirenewspaper.com/2012/02/nebraskas-magical-sandhill-crane-migration.

Johnsgard, P. A. 2012. *Wings over the Great Plains: The Central Flyway*. Lincoln: Zea E-Books and University of Nebraska Digital Commons. http://digitalcommons.unl.edu/zeabook/13/.

Johnsgard, P. A. 2013. *The Birds of Nebraska*. Rev. ed. Lincoln: Zea E-Books and University of Nebraska Digital Commons. http://digitalcommons.unl.edu/zeabook/17/.

Johnsgard, P. A., and K. Gil-Weir. 2011. "Sandhill Cranes: Nebraska's Avian Ambassadors at Large." *Prairie Fire* 5 (3): 14, 15, 20. http://www.prairiefirenewspaper.com/2011/02/sandhill-cranes-our-avian-ambassadors-at-large.

Johnson, K. A. 1982. "Whooping Crane Use of the Platte River, Nebraska—History, Status and Management Recommendations." In *Proceedings of the 1981 Crane Workshop*, ed. J. C. Lewis, 33–44. Tavernier, FL: National Audubon Society.

Johnson, W. C. 1994. "Woodland Expansion in the Platte River, Nebraska: Patterns and Causes." *Ecological Monographs* 64 (1): 45–84. http://dx.doi.org/10.2307/2937055.

Jorgensen, J. G. 2004. *An Overview of the Shorebird Migration in the Eastern Rainwater Basin, Nebraska*. Occasional Paper 8. Lincoln: Nebraska Ornithologists' Union.

Klataske, R. 1972. "Wings across the Platte." *National Wildlife* 10 (5): 44–47.

Krapu, G. L. 1981. *The Platte River Ecology Study: Special Research Report*. Jamestown, ND: Northern Prairie Wildlife Research Center.

Krapu, G. L., D. E. Facey, E. K. Fritzell, and D. H. Johnson. 1984. "Habitat Use by Migrant Sandhill Cranes in Nebraska." *Journal of Wildlife Management* 48 (2): 407–17. http://dx.doi.org/10.2307/3801172.

Krapu, G. L., D. Facey, B. Gehring, and M. I. Meyer. 1987. "Resource Inventory of Sandhill Crane Staging Areas in Nebraska." In *Proceedings of the 1985 North American Crane Workshop*, ed. J. C. Lewis, 364–70. Grand Island, NE: Platte River Whooping Crane Habitat Maintenance Trust and US Fish and Wildlife Service.

Krapu, G. L., G. C. Iverson, K. J. Reinecke, and C. M. Boise. 1985. "Fat Deposition and Usage by Arctic-Nesting Sandhill Cranes during Spring." *Auk* 102 (2): 362–68. http://dx.doi.org/10.2307/4086780.

Krapu, G. L., K. J. Reinecke, and C. R. Frith. 1982. "Sandhill Cranes and the Platte River." *Transactions of the North American Wildlife and Natural Resources Conference* 47:542–52.

Krapu, G., K. J. Reinecke, D. G. Jorde, and S. G. Simpson. 1995. "Spring Staging Ecology of Midcontinent Greater White-Fronted Geese." *Journal of Wildlife Management* 59 (4): 736–46. http://dx.doi.org/10.2307/3801950.

Lewis, J. C. 1979. "Taxonomy, Food, and Feeding Habitat of Sandhill Cranes, Platte Valley, Nebraska." In *Proceedings of the 1978 International Crane Workshop*, ed. J. C. Lewis, 21–28. Fort Collins: Colorado State University Printing Service.

LaGrange, T. 2005. *Guide to Nebraska's Wetlands and Their Conservation Needs*. 2nd ed. Lincoln: Nebraska Game and Parks Commission.

Line, L. 2007. "New Dawn for a Prairie River." *National Wildlife* 34:22–29.
(Platte River restoration.)

Madson, J. 1974. "Day of the Crane." *Audubon* 74 (2): 46–63.
(Sandhill cranes and the Platte River.)

Nagel, H. G., K. Geisler, J. Cochran, J. Fallesen, B. Hadenfelt, J. Mathews, J. Nickel, S. Stec, and A. Walters. 1980. "Platte River Island Succession." *Transactions of the Nebraska Academy of Sciences* 8:77–90.

Pearse, A. T., G. L. Krapu, D. A. Brandt, and P. J. Kinzel. 2010. "Changes in Agriculture and Abundance of Snow Geese Affect Carrying Capacity of Sandhill Cranes in Nebraska." *Journal of Wildlife Management* 74 (3): 479–88. http://dx.doi.org/10.2193/2008-539.

Platte River Recovery Implementation Program (PRRIP). 2013. *Bi-Annual Report, 2011–2012*. Kearney, NE: Platte River Recovery Implementation Program.

Reinecke, K. J., and G. L. Krapu. 1986. "Feeding Ecology of Sandhill Cranes during Spring Migration in Nebraska." *Journal of Wildlife Management* 50 (1): 71–79. http://dx.doi.org/10.2307/3801490.

Safina, C., L. Rosenbluth, C. Pustmueller, K. Strom, R. Klataske, M. Lee, and J. Beyea. 1989. *Threats to Wildlife and the Platte River*. Environmental Policy Analysis Department Report 33. New York: National Audubon Society.

Sharpe, R. W., R. Silcock, and J. G. Jorgensen. 2001. *The Birds of Nebraska, Their Distribution and Temporal Occurrence*. Lincoln: University of Nebraska Press.

Shoemaker, T. G. 1988. "Wildlife and Water Projects on the Platte River." In *Audubon Wildlife Report 1988/1989*, ed. W. J. Chandler, 285–34. San Diego, CA: Harcourt, Brace, Jovanovich. http://dx.doi.org/10.1016/B978-0-12-041001-9.50018-2.

Sidle, J. G. 1989. "A Prairie River Roost." *Living Bird Quarterly* 8 (2): 8–13.
(Sandhill cranes and the Platte River.)

Shoumatoff, G. 2014. "Flight Club." *Smithsonian* 44 (11): 56–67.
(Sandhill cranes and the Platte River.)

Smith, C. 2007. "The Platte River Recovery Implementation Program: Adaptive Management and Collaboration on the Platte." *Prairie Fire* 1 (6): 12–14.
(Habitat restoration program resulting from the Platte River Cooperative Agreement among Nebraska, Wyoming, and Colorado.)

Soine, J. 1982. "Roost Habitat Selection by Sandhill Cranes in Central North Dakota." In *Proceedings of the 1981 Crane Workshop*, ed. J. C. Lewis, 88–94. Tavernier, FL: National Audubon Society.

Van der Valk, A., ed. 1989. *Northern Prairie Wetlands*. Ames: Iowa State University Press.

Vogt, W. 1978. "Now, the River Is Dying." *National Wildlife* 16 (4): 4–11.
(Platte River flows.)

Sandhill Crane References

Aikens, R. 2009. "The Southwest's Triple Crown of Wintering Cranes." *Arizona Wildlife Views* 52 (1): 12–6.

Aldrich, J. W. 1972. "A New Subspecies of Sandhill Crane from Mississippi." *Proceedings of the Biological Society of Washington* 5:63–70.

Aldrich, J. W. 1979. "Status of the Canadian Sandhill Crane." In *Proceedings of the 1978 Crane Workshop*, ed. C. Lewis, 139–48. Fort Collins: Colorado State University Printing Service.

Bailey, R. J. 1979. *Lesser and Canadian Sandhill Crane Populations, Age Structure, and Harvest.* Special Scientific Report—Wildlife 221. Washington, DC: US Department of the Interior, Fish and Wildlife Service

Baldwin, J. H. 1977. "A Comparative Study of Sandhill Crane Subspecies." PhD diss., University of Wisconsin, Madison.

Ball, J., T. E. Austin, and A. Henry. 2003. *Populations and Nesting Ecology of Sandhill Cranes at Grays Lake, Idaho, 1997–2000.* Missoula, MT: US Geological Survey, Cooperative Wildlife Research Unit.

Ballard, B. M., and J. E. Thompson. 2000. "Winter Diets of Sandhill Cranes from Central and Coastal Texas." *Wilson Bulletin* 112 (2): 263–68. http://dx.doi.org/10.1676/0043-5643(2000)112[0263:WDOSCF]2.0.CO;2.

Ballard, B. M., J. E. Thompson, M. T. Meredino, J. D. Ray, J. A. Robertson, and T. C. Tacha. 1999. "Demographics of the Gulf Coast Subpopulation of Mid-Continent Sandhill Cranes." In *Proceedings of the Annual Conference of the Southeast Association of Fish and Wildlife Agencies*, 449–63.

Bennett, A. 1989. "Movements and Home Range of Florida Sandhill Cranes." *Journal of Wildlife Management* 53 (3): 830–36. http://dx.doi.org/10.2307/3809221.

Bennett, A. J., and L. A. Bennett. 1990. "Productivity of Florida Sandhill Cranes in the Okefenokee Swamp, Georgia." *Journal of Field Ornithology* 61:224–31.

Benning, D. S., R. C. Drewien, D. H. Johnson, W. M. Brown, and E. L. Boeker. 1997. "Spring Population Estimates of Rocky Mountain Greater Sandhill Cranes in Colorado." In *Proceedings of the Seventh North American Crane Workshop*, ed. R. P. Urbanek and D. W. Stahlecker, 165–72. Grand Island, NE: North American Crane Working Group.

Boise, C. M. 1977. "Breeding Biology of the Lesser Sandhill Crane *(Grus canadensis canadensis* L.) on the Yukon-Kuskokwim Delta, Alaska." MS thesis, University of Alaska, College.

Carlisle, M. J. 1982. "Nesting Habitat of Sandhill Cranes in Central Alberta." In *Proceedings of the 1981 Crane Workshop*, ed. J. Lewis, 44–55. Tavernier, FL: National Audubon Society.

Carlisle, M., and T. C. Tacha. 1983. "Fall Migration of Sandhill Cranes in West Central North Dakota." *Journal of Wildlife Management* 47 (3): 818–21. http://dx.doi.org/10.2307/3808617.

Central Flyway Migratory Shore and Upland Game Bird Technical Committee. 1993. *Management Guidelines for Mid-Continent Sandhill Cranes.* Golden, CO: Central Flyway Waterfowl Council, Pacific Flyway Waterfowl Council, and US Fish and Wildlife Service.

Central Flyway Webless Migratory Game Bird Technical Committee. 2006. *Management Guidelines for the Mid-Continent Population of Sandhill Cranes.* Golden, CO: US Fish and Wildlife Service, Migratory Bird Management Office.

Chavez-Ramirez, F. 2005. "New Locations and Range Extension of Wintering Sandhill Cranes in Central Northern Mexico." In *Proceedings of the Ninth North American Crane Workshop*, ed. F. Chavez-Ramirez, 173–78. Sacramento, CA: North American Crane Working Group.

Conant, B., J. King, and H. Hansen. 1985. "Sandhill Cranes in Alaska: A Population Survey 1957–1985." *American Birds* 39:855–58.

Drewien, R. C. 1973. "Ecology of Rocky Mountain Greater Sandhill Cranes." PhD diss., University of Idaho, Moscow.

Drewien, R. C., and E. G. Bizeau. 1974. "Status and Distribution of Greater Sandhill Cranes in the Rocky Mountains." *Journal of Wildlife Management* 38 (4): 720–42. http://dx.doi.org/10.2307/3800039.

Drewien, R. C., W. M. Brown, and D. S. Benning. 1996. "Distribution and Abundance of Sandhill Cranes in Mexico." *Journal of Wildlife Management* 60 (2): 270–85. http://dx.doi.org/10.2307/3802225.
    (Chihuahua and Durango wetlands.)

Drewein, R. C., W. M. Brown, and K. R. Clegg. 2010. "Longevity Records of Rocky Mountain Greater Sandhill Cranes Banded during 1969–1987 in Idaho, Montana, Utah and Wyoming." In *Proceedings of the 11th North American Crane Workshop*, ed. B. Hartup, 199. Baraboo, WI: International Crane Foundation.

Drewien, R. C., W. M. Brown, and W. L. Kendall. 1995. "Recruitment in Rocky Mountain Greater Sandhill Cranes and Comparison with Other Crane Populations." *Journal of Wildlife Management* 59 (2): 339–56. http://dx.doi.org/10.2307/3808948.
    (This race had an estimated fall recruitment rate of 8.1%, as compared with 5–24% for various other sandhill crane races and 13.9% for the whooping crane. Summarized recruitment estimates for mid-continent lesser sandhills averaged 9.8%. Estimated annual adult survival rates for some nonhunted North American crane populations have ranged from about 85% to 90%.)

Drewien, R. C., W. M. Brown, J. D. Varley, and D. C. Lockman. 1999. "Seasonal Movements of Sandhill Cranes Radiomarked in Yellowstone National Park, Jackson Hole, Wyoming." *Journal of Wildlife Management* 63 (1): 126–36. http://dx.doi.org/10.2307/3802493.

Fields, R. C., A. K. Trout, and D. T. Walls. 1974. "Recent Breeding of the Sandhill Crane in North Dakota." *Wilson Bulletin* 86:285–86.

Forsberg, M. 2004. *On Ancient Wings: The Sandhill Cranes of North America*. Lincoln, NE: Michael Forsberg Photography.
    (A popular, color-illustrated account.)

Glenn, T. C., J. E. Thompson, B. M. Ballard, J. A. Roberson, and J. O. French. 2002. "Mitochondrial DNA Variation among Wintering Midcontinent Gulf Coast Sandhill Cranes." *Journal of Wildlife Management* 66 (2): 339–48. http://dx.doi.org/10.2307/3803166.

Grooms, G. 1991. *Cry of the Sandhill Crane*. Minaqua, WI: North Word Press.
    (A popular, color-illustrated account.)

Happ, C. Y., and G. Happ. 2011. *Sandhill Crane Display Dictionary*. Waterford, CT: Waterford Press. www.AlaskaSandhillCrane.com.
    (Fold-out photo brochure of display postures.)

Hereford, S. G., and L. E. Bilodeaux. 2010. "Mississippi Sandhill Crane Conservation Update, 2006–2009." In *Proceedings of the 11th North American Crane Workshop*, ed. B. Hartup, 189–91. Baraboo, WI: International Crane Foundation.

Herter, D. R. 1982. "Staging of Sandhill Cranes on the Eastern Copper River Delta, Alaska." In *Proceedings of the 1981 Crane Workshop*, ed. J. C. Lewis, 273–80. Tavernier, FL: National Audubon Society.

Hoffman, R. H. 2014. "Annual Recruitment and Brood Size of Greater Sandhill Cranes in Michigan (Abstract)." In *Proceedings of the Twelfth North American Crane Workshop*, ed. D. A. Aborn and R. A. Urbenek, 93. Madison, WI: North American Crane Working Group.

Iverson, G. C., P. A. Vohs Jr., and T. C. Tacha. 1985. "Distribution and Abundance of Sandhill Cranes Wintering in Western Texas." *Journal of Wildlife Management* 49 (1): 250–55. http://dx.doi.org/10.2307/3801880.

Iverson, G. C., P. A. Vohs, and T. C. Tacha. 1987. "Habitat Use by Mid-Continent Sandhill Cranes during Spring Migration." *Journal of Wildlife Management* 51 (2): 448–58. http://dx.doi.org/10.2307/3801033.

Ivey, G. L., and B. D. Dugger. 2008. "Factors Influencing Greater Sandhill Crane Nest Success in Malheur National Wildlife Refuge, Oregon (Abstract)." In *Proceedings of the Tenth North American Crane Workshop*, ed. M. J. Folk and S. A. Nesbitt, 157. Gambier, OH: North American Crane Working Group.
(Among 508 nests studied, mean apparent nest success was 72% [range 51–87%], with success higher during warmer springs, in deeper water, and in years of moderate precipitation. Haying, grazing, and predator control did not influence nest success.)

Ivey, G. L., B. D. Dugger, L. Casazza, J. P. Fleskes, and C. P. Herziger. 2014. "Movements and Home Range Size of Greater and Lesser Sandhill Cranes Wintering in Central California (Abstract)." In *Proceedings of the Twelfth North American Crane Workshop*, ed. D. A. Aborn and R. A. Urbenek, 94. Madison, WI: North American Crane Working Group.

Ivey, G. L., B. D. Dugger, C. P. Herziger, M. L. Casazza, and J. P. Fleskes. 2014. "Distribution, Abundance, and Migration Timing of Greater and Lesser Sandhill Cranes Wintering in the Sacramento–San Joaquin River Delta Region of California." In *Proceedings of the Twelfth North American Crane Workshop*, ed. D. A. Aborn and R. A. Urbenek, 1–11. Madison, WI: North American Crane Working Group.

Ivey, G. L., J. D. Engler, M. J. St. Louis, M. A. Stern, and S. Cross. 2010. "Winter Distribution of Greater Sandhill Cranes Marked at Breeding Areas in California, Washington and Oregon (Abstract)." In *Proceedings of the 11th North American Crane Workshop*, ed. B. Hartup, 206. Baraboo, WI: International Crane Foundation.

Ivey, G. L., C. P. Herzinger, and T. J. Hoffmann. 2005. "Annual Movements of Pacific Coast Sandhill Cranes." In *Proceedings of the Ninth National Crane Workshop*, ed. F. Chavez-Ramirez, 25–35. Sacramento, CA: North American Crane Working Group.

Johnsgard, P. A. 1979. *Birds of the Great Plains: Breeding Species and Their Distribution*. Lincoln: University of Nebraska Press.

Johnsgard, P. A. 1981. *Those of the Gray Wind: The Sandhill Cranes*. New York: St. Martin's Press.
(A fictionalized account of sandhill crane life history, told over a 150-year [1850–2000] time span and from four seasonal and cultural perspectives.)

Johnsgard, P. A. 1982. *Teton Wildlife: Observations by a Naturalist*. Boulder: University Press of Colorado.
(Greater sandhill crane nesting biology.)

Johnsgard, P. A. 2002. "Nebraska's Sandhill Crane Populations; Past, Present and Future." *Nebraska Bird Review* 70:175–77.
(Historic and recent mid-continent crane populations and predictions of probable future trends.)

Johnsgard, P. A. 2013. *Yellowstone Wildlife: Ecology and Natural History of the Greater Yellowstone Ecosystem*. Boulder: University Press of Colorado.
(Greater sandhill crane breeding.)

Johnsgard, P. A. 2014. "The Allure of Cranes." *Prairie Fire* 8 (3): 1, 3, 4. http://prairiefirenewspaper.com/2014/03/the-allure-of-cranes.

Johnsgard, P. A. 2014. *Seasons of the Tallgrass Prairie: A Nebraska Year*. Lincoln: University of Nebraska Press.
(Sandhill crane migrations.)

Johnson, D. H. 1976. "The Status of the Sandhill Crane in North Dakota." In *Proceedings of the International Crane Workshop*, ed. J. C. Lewis, 69–77. Baraboo, WI: International Crane Foundation

Johnson, D. H., J. E. Austin, and J. A. Shaffer. 2005. "A Fresh Look at the Taxonomy of Midcontinental Sandhill Cranes." In *Proceedings of the Ninth National Crane Workshop*, ed. F. Chavez-Ramirez, 37–45. Sacramento, CA: North American Crane Working Group.
(The three regional subspecies are morphologically definable, but exhibit intergrading features.)

Johnson, D. H., and R. E. Stewart. 1973. "Racial Composition of Migrant Populations of Sandhill Cranes in the Northern Plains States." *Wilson Bulletin* 85:148–62.

Johnson, J. W. 1963. "The Dispossessed Sandhill Cranes." *Audubon Magazine* 65 (4): 213–17.

Kendall, W. L., D. H. Johnson, and S. C. Kohn. 1997. "Subspecies Composition of Sandhill Crane Harvest in North Dakota, 1968–94." In *Proceedings of the Seventh North American Crane Workshop*, ed. R. P. Urbanek and D. W. Stahlecker, 201–8. Grand Island, NE: North American Crane Working Group.

Kessel, B. 1984. "Migration of Sandhill Cranes, *Grus canadensis*, in East-Central Alaska, with Routes through Alaska and Western Canada." *Canadian Field Naturalist* 98:279–92.

King, S. L., A. R. Pierce, K. R. Hershey, and N. A. Winstead. 2010. "Migration Patterns and Movements of Sandhill Cranes Wintering in Central and Southwestern Louisiana." In *Proceedings of the 11th North American Crane Workshop*, ed. B. Hartup, 57–61. Baraboo, WI: International Crane Foundation.

Kinzel, P. J., J. M. Nelson, R. S. Parker, and L. R. Davis. 2006. "Spring Census of Mid-Continent Sandhill Cranes Using Aerial Infrared Videography." *Journal of Wildlife Management* 70 (1): 70–77. http://dx.doi.org/10.2193/0022-541X(2006)70[70:SCOMSC]2.0.CO;2.

Krapu, G. L. 1987a. "Sandhill Recovery." *Birder's World* 1 (1): 4–8.
   (Population trends in sandhill cranes.)

Krapu, G. L. 1987b. "Use of Staging Areas by Sandhill Cranes in the Midcontinent Region of North America." In *Proceedings of the 1983 International Crane Workshop*, ed. G. Archibald and R. F. Pasquier, 451–62. Baraboo, WI: International Crane Foundation.

Krapu, G. L. 2001. "Satellite Telemetry: A Powerful New Tool for Studying Sandhill Cranes." *Braided River* 14:1–5. (newsletter of the Crane Trust)
   (Results of radio-tracking the northward migrations of sandhill cranes trapped in the Platte Valley.)

Krapu, G. L. 2005. "Satellite Telemetry Provides a Revealing Look at the Phantom of the Plains." *Braided River* 21:6–9.
   (A summary of sandhill crane migration information based on telemetry data.)

Krapu, G. L., and D. A. Brandt. 2008. "Spring Migratory Habits and Breeding Distribution of Lesser Sandhill Cranes That Winter in West-Central New Mexico and Arizona." In *Proceedings of the Tenth North American Crane Workshop*, ed. M. J. Folk and S. A. Nesbitt, 43–49. Gambier, OH: North American Crane Working Group.

Krapu, G. L., and D. A. Brandt. 2010. "Population Status and Geographic Distribution of Greater Sandhill Cranes in the Midcontinent Population." In *Proceedings of the 11th North American Crane Workshop*, ed. B. Hartup, 72–81. Baraboo, WI: International Crane Foundation.

Krapu, G. L., D. A. Brandt, and R. R. Cox, Jr. 2004. "Less Waste Corn, More Land in Soybeans, and the Switch to Genetically Modified Crops, Trends with Important Implications for Wildlife Management." *Wildlife Society Bulletin* 32 (1): 127–36. http://dx.doi.org/10.2193/0091-7648(2004)32[127:LWCMLI]2.0.CO;2.

Krapu, G. L., D. A. Brandt, and R. R. Cox Jr. 2005. "Do Arctic-Nesting Geese Compete with Sandhill Cranes for Waste Corn in the Central Platte Valley, Nebraska?" In *Proceedings of the Ninth National Crane Workshop*, ed. F. Chavez-Ramirez, 185–91. Sacramento, CA: North American Crane Working Group.

Krapu, G. L., D. A. Brandt, D. A. Buhl, and G. W. Lingle. 2005. "Evidence of a Decline in Fat Storage in Mid-Continent Sandhill Cranes in Nebraska during Spring: A Preliminary Assessment." In *Proceedings of the Ninth National Crane Workshop*, ed. F. Chavez-Ramirez, 179–84. Sacramento, CA: North American Crane Working Group.

Krapu, G. L., D. A. Brandt, K. L. Jones, and D. H. Johnson. 2011. "Geographic Distribution of the Mid-Continent Population of Sandhill Cranes and Related Management Applications." *Wildlife Monographs* 175 (1): 1–38. http://dx.doi.org/10.1002/wmon.1.

Krapu, G. L., D. E. Facey, E. K. Fritzell, and D. H. Johnson. 1984. "Habitat Use by Migrant Sandhill Cranes in Nebraska." *Journal of Wildlife Management* 48 (2): 407–27. http://dx.doi.org /10.2307/3801172.

Krapu, G. L., G. C. Iverson, K. J. Reineke, and C. M. Boise. 1985. "Fat Deposition and Usage by Arctic-Nesting Sandhill Cranes in Spring." *Auk* 102 (2): 362–68. http://dx.doi.org/10.2307/4086780.

Krapu, G. L., and D. H. Johnson. 1990. "Conditioning of Sandhill Cranes during Fall Migration." *Journal of Wildlife Management* 54 (2): 234–38. http://dx.doi.org/10.2307/3809035.

Kruse, K. L., J. A. Dubovsky, and T. R. Cooper. 2012. *Status and Harvests of Sandhill Cranes: Mid-Continent, Rocky Mountain, Lower Colorado River Valley and Eastern Populations*. Denver, CO: US Fish and Wildlife Service.

Kruse, K. L., D. E. Sharp, and J. A. Dubovsky. 2008. "Population Status, Hunting Regulations and Harvests of the Rocky Mountain Population of Sandhill Cranes, 1981–2005." In *Proceedings of the Tenth North American Crane Workshop*, ed. M. J. Folk and S. A. Nesbitt, 71–75. Gambier, OH: North American Crane Working Group.

Kruse, K. L., D. E. Sharp, and J. A. Dubovsky. 2010. *Status and Harvests of Sandhill Cranes: Mid-Continent, Rocky Mountain, Lower Colorado River Valley Populations.* Denver, CO: US Fish and Wildlife Service.

Layne, J. N. 1982. "Status of Sibling Aggression in Florida Sandhill Cranes." *Journal of Field Ornithology* 53:272–74.

Lewis, J. C. 1974. "Ecology of Sandhill Cranes in the Southeastern Central Flyway." PhD diss., Oklahoma State University, Stillwater.

Lewis, J. C. 1977. "Sandhill Crane." In *Management of Migratory Shore and Upland Game Birds in North America*, ed. G. C. Sanderson, 5–44. Washington, DC: International Association of Fish and Wildlife Agencies.
(See also Tacha, Nesbitt, and Vohs 1994.)

Lewis, J. C. 1979. "Field Identification of Juvenile Sandhill Cranes." *Journal of Wildlife Management* 43 (1): 211–14. http://dx.doi.org/10.2307/3800655.

Littlefield, C. D., and R. A. Ryder. 1968. "Breeding Biology of the Greater Sandhill Crane on Malheur National Wildlife Refuge, Oregon." *Transactions of the North American Wildlife and Natural Resources Conference* 33:444–54.

Littlefield, C. D., and S. P. Thompson. 1979. "Distribution and Status of the Central Valley Population of Greater Sandhill Cranes." In *Proceedings of the 1978 International Crane Workshop*, ed. J. C. Lewis, 113–20. Fort Collins: Colorado State University Printing Service.

Littlefield, C. D., and S. P. Thompson. 1982. "The Pacific Coast Population of Lesser Sandhill Cranes in the Contiguous United States." In *Proceedings of the 1981 Crane Workshop*, ed. J. C. Lewis, 288–94. Tavernier, FL: National Audubon Society.

Lovvorn, J. R., and J. M. Kirkpatrick. 1981. "Roosting Behavior and Habitat of Migrant Greater Sandhill Cranes." *Journal of Wildlife Management* 45 (4): 842–57. http://dx.doi.org/10.2307/3808093.

Lumsden, H. G. 1971. "The Status of the Sandhill Crane in Northern Ontario." *Canadian Field Naturalist* 85:285–93.

Madsen, C. R. 1967. "Food and Habitat Selection by Fall Migrant Sandhill Cranes in Kidder County, North Dakota." MS thesis, Michigan State University, East Lansing.

Manning, T. H., and A. H. MacPherson. 1961. "A Biological Investigation of Prince of Wales Island, N.W.T." *Transactions of the Royal Canadian Institute* 33 (part 2): 116–239.

Martin, E. M. 2006. "Sandhill Crane Harvest and Hunter Activity in the Central Flyway during the 2005–2006 Hunting Season." http://digitalcommons.unl.edu/usfwspubs/387/.

Maxson, S. J., J. R. Fieberg, and M. R. Riggs. 2008. "Sandhill Crane Nest Habitat Selection and Factors Affecting Nest Success in Northwestern Minnesota." In *Proceedings of the Tenth North American*

Crane Workshop, ed. M. J. Folk and S. A. Nesbitt, 90–97. Gambier, OH: North American Crane Working Group.

Melvin, S. M. 2010. "First Breeding Records and Historical Status of Sandhill Cranes in New England (abstract)." In *Proceedings of the 11th North American Crane Workshop*, ed. B. Hartup, 209. Baraboo, WI: International Crane Foundation.

Melvin, S. M. 2014. "Sandhill Cranes Nesting in New England: An Update (Abstract)." In *Proceedings of the Twelfth North American Crane Workshop*, ed. D. A. Aborn and R. A. Urbenek, 97. Madison, WI: North American Crane Working Group.

Melvin, S. M., W.J.D. Stephen, and S. A. Temple. 1990. "Population Estimates, Nesting Biology, and Habitat Preferences of Interlake, Manitoba, Sandhill Cranes, *Grus canadensis*." *Canadian Field Naturalist* 104:354–61.

Mickelson, P. G. 1987. "Management of Lesser Sandhill Cranes Staging in Alaska." In *Proceedings of the 1985 Crane Workshop*, ed. J. C. Lewis, 264–75. Grand Island, NE: Platte River Whooping Crane Habitat Maintenance Trust and US Fish and Wildlife Service.

Montgomery, J. B., Jr. 1997. "Sandhill Crane Use of the Mid-Pecos Valley of Eastern New Mexico." In *Proceedings of the Seventh North American Crane Workshop*, ed. R. A. Urbanek and D. W. Stahlecker, 157–64. Grand Island, NE: North American Crane Working Group.

Morekill, A. E., and S. H. Anderson. 1993. "Effectiveness of Yellow Aviation Balls in Reducing Sandhill Crane Collisions with Powerlines." In Proceedings of Avian Interactions with Utility Structures International Workshop, 21.1–21.17. Pleasant Hill, CA: Electric Power Research Institute.

Mullens, W. H., and E. G. Bizeau. 1978. "Summer Foods of Sandhill Cranes in Idaho." *Auk* 95 (1): 175–78. http://dx.doi.org/10.2307/4085509.

Nesbitt, S. 1988. "Nesting, Renesting and Manipulated Nesting of Florida Sandhill Cranes." *Journal of Wildlife Management* 52 (4): 758–63. http://dx.doi.org/10.2307/3800943.

Nesbitt, S. 1989. "The Significance of Mate Loss in Florida Sandhill Cranes." *Wilson Bulletin* 101:648–51.

Nesbitt, S. 1992. "First Reproductive Success and Individual Productivity in Sandhill Cranes." *Journal of Wildlife Management* 56 (3): 573–77. http://dx.doi.org/10.2307/3808874.
(The modal age for initial reproduction in Florida sandhill cranes was five years for the Florida race and four years for the greater. Both subspecies averaged 0.35 young fledged per pair per year, and the expected lifetime reproductive success for birds reaching sexual maturity was 1.86 young.)

Nesbitt, S. A. 1997. "Florida Sandhill Crane *(Grus canadensis pratensis)*, Family Gruidae, Order Gruiformes." In *Rare and Endangered Biota of Florida.* Vol. 5, *Birds*, ed. J. A. Rogers, H. Kale, and H. Smith, 219–29. Gainesville: University Press of Florida.
(A review of this endemic subspecies' biology.)

Nesbitt, S. A., and G. Archibald. 1981. "The Agonistic Repertoire of Sandhill Cranes." *Wilson Bulletin* 93:99–103.

Nesbitt, S. A., M. J. Folk, S. T. Schwikert, and J. A. Schmidt. 2001. "Aspects of Reproduction and Pair Bonds in Florida Sandhill Cranes." In *Proceedings of the Eighth National Crane Workshop*, ed. D. Ellis, 31–35. Seattle, WA: North American Crane Working Group.

Nesbitt, S. A., P. S. Kubilis, and S. T. Schwikert. 2008. "Interaction of Young Sandhill Cranes with Their Parents." In *Proceedings of the Tenth North American Crane Workshop*, ed. M. J. Folk and S. A. Nesbitt, 107–10. Gambier, OH: North American Crane Working Group.

Nesbitt, S. A., and S. T. Schwikert. 2008. "Timing of Molt in Florida Sandhill Cranes." In *Proceedings of the Tenth North American Crane Workshop*, 125–27. Gambier, OH: North American Crane Working Group.

Nesbitt, S. A., and S. T. Schwikert. 2014. "Territory Histories of Florida Sandhill Cranes, 1980–2006." In *Proceedings of the Twelfth North American Crane Workshop*, ed. D. A. Aborn and R. A. Urbenek, 98. Madison, WI: North American Crane Working Group.

Nesbitt, S. A., S. T. Schwikert, and M. G. Spalding. 2008. "Survival and Sources of Mortality in Florida Sandhill Crane Chicks—Hatching to Fledging." In *Proceedings of the Tenth North American Crane Workshop*, ed. M. J. Folk and S. A. Nesbitt, 86–89. Gambier, OH: North American Crane Working Group.

    (Of 38 chicks produced from 25 successful nests of 45 pairs, 21 survived to fledging. Predation caused 81% of the identified sources of mortality.)

Nesbitt, S. A., and A. S. Wenner. 1987. "Pair Formation and Mate Fidelity in Sandhill Cranes." In *Proceedings of the 1985 Crane Workshop*, ed. J. Lewis, 117–22. Grand Island, NE: Platte River Whooping Crane Habitat Maintenance Trust and US Fish and Wildlife Service.

Nesbitt, S. A., and K. S. Williams. 1990. "Home Range and Habitat Use of Florida Sandhill Cranes." *Journal of Wildlife Management* 54 (1): 92–96. http://dx.doi.org/10.2307/3808907.

    (Territorial adult cranes had average home ranges of about 1,100 acres [447 hectares], which were smallest during the nesting season.)

Ness, K. H., and A. E. Lacey. 2010. "Assessing Sandhill Crane Flight Alterations to Power Lines in South-Central Wisconsin (Abstract)." In *Proceedings of the 11th North American Crane Workshop*, ed. B. Hartup, 217. Baraboo, WI: International Crane Foundation.

Parmalee, D. F., and S. D. MacDonald. 1960. *The Birds of West-Central Ellesmere Island and Adjacent Areas*. National Museum of Canada Bulletin 169. Ottawa, Ontario: Queen's Printer.

Petrula, M. J., and T. C. Rothe. 2005. "Migration Chronology, Routes, and Distribution of Pacific Flyway Population Lesser Sandhill Cranes." In *Proceedings of the Ninth National Crane Workshop*, ed. F. Chavez-Ramirez, 53–67. Sacramento, CA: North American Crane Working Group.

Pogson, T. H., and S. M. Lindstedt. 1991. "Distribution and Abundance of Large Sandhill Cranes, *Grus canadensis*, Wintering in California's Central Valley." *Condor* 93 (2): 266–78. http://dx.doi.org/10.2307/1368942.

Reed, J. R. 1988. "Arctic Adaptations in the Breeding Biology of Sandhill Cranes, *Grus canadensis*, on Banks Island, Northwest Territories." *Canadian Field Naturalist* 102:643–48.

Phymer, Judith M., Mathew G. Fain, Jane E. Austin, Douglas H. Johnson, and Carey Krajewski. 2001. "Mitochondrial Phylogeography, Subspecific Taxonomy, and Conservation Genetics of Sandhill Cranes (*Grus canadensis*; Aves, Gruidae)." *Conservation Genetics* 2 (3): 203–18. http://dx.doi.org/10.1023/A:1012203532300.

Safina, C. 1993. "Population Trends, Habitat Utilization, and Outlook for the Future of Sandhill Cranes in North America: A Review and Synthesis." *Bird Populations* 1:1–27.

Schlorff, R. W. 2005. "Greater Sandhill Crane: Research and Management in California since 1978." In *Proceedings of the Ninth National Crane Workshop*, ed. F. Chavez-Ramirez, 155–65. Sacramento, CA: North American Crane Working Group.

Schmitt, C. G., and B. Hale. 1997. "Sandhill Crane Hunts in the Rio Grande Valley and Southwest New Mexico." In *Proceedings of the Seventh North American Crane Workshop*, ed. R. P. Urbanek and D. W. Stahlecker, 219–31. Grand Island, NE: North American Crane Working Group.

Sharp, D. E. 1995. *Status and Harvests of Sandhill Cranes: Mid-Continent and Rocky Mountain Populations*. Golden, CO: Office of Migratory Bird Management, US Fish and Wildlife Service.

Sharp, D. E., and J. E. Comely. 1997. "Summary of Sandhill Crane Hunting Seasons in North Dakota, 1968–94." In *Proceedings of the Seventh North American Crane Workshop*, ed. R. P. Urbanek and D. W. Stahlecker, 209–18. Grand Island, NE: North American Crane Working Group.

Sharp, D. E., J. D. Dubovsky, and K. L. Kruse. 2003. *Status and Harvests of the Midcontinent and Rocky Mountain Populations of Sandhill Cranes*. Denver, CO: US Fish and Wildlife Service; http://fws.gov/migratorybirds/.

    (Data for the 2002–3 hunting season, with a calculated Central Flyway kill of 16,650 birds exclusive of Mexico, Canada, and Alaska, and an estimated 2003 Platte Valley crane population of about 376,000 birds.)

Sharp, D. E., K. L. Kruse, and J. A. Dubovsky. 2007. *Status and Harvests of Sandhill Cranes: Mid-Continent and Rocky Mountain Populations*. Denver, CO: US Fish and Wildlife Service.

Sharp, D. E., and W. O. Vogel. 1992. "Population Status, Hunting Regulations, Hunting Activities, and Harvest of Mid-Continental Sandhill Cranes." In *Proceedings of the Sixth North American Crane Workshop*, ed. D. W. Stahlecker, 24–32. Grand Island, NE: North American Crane Working Group. (Hunter-kill data for 1975–90. For online version see http://www.savingcranes.org/proceedings -of-the-sixth-north-american-crane-workshop-1992.html.)

Stephen, W.J.D. 1967. *Bionomics of the Sandhill Crane*. Report Series 2. Ottawa, ON: Canadian Wildlife Service.

Tacha, T. C. 1988. *Social Organization of Sandhill Cranes from Midcontinental North America*. Wildlife Monographs 99. Bethesda, MD: Wildlife Society.

Tacha, T. C., D. E. Haley, and P. A. Vohs. 1989. "Age of Sexual Maturity in Sandhill Cranes from Midcontinental North America." *Journal of Wildlife Management* 53 (1): 43–46. http://dx.doi.org /10.2307/3801303.

Tacha, T. C., C. Jorgenson, and P. S. Taylor. 1985. "Harvest, Migration, and Condition of Sandhill Cranes in Saskatchewan." *Journal of Wildlife Management* 49 (2): 476–80. http://dx.doi.org/10 .2307/3801556.

Tacha, T. C., S. A. Nesbitt, and P. A. Vohs. 1992. *Sandhill Crane*. Birds of North America 31. Philadelphia: Academy of Natural Sciences. (A literature summary of the species, with 155 citations.)

Tacha, T. C., S. A. Nesbitt, and P. A. Vohs. 1994. "Sandhill Crane." In *Migratory Shore and Upland Game Bird Management in North America*, ed. T. C. Tacha and C. E. Braun, 76–94. Washington, DC: International Association of Fish and Wildlife Agencies. (A summary of biology and management.)

Tacha, T. C., and P. A. Vohs. 1984. "Some Population Parameters of Sandhill Cranes from Midcontinental North America." *Journal of Wildlife Management* 48 (1): 89–98. http://dx.doi.org /10.2307/3808456.

Tacha, T. C., P. A. Vohs, and G. C. Anderson. 1984. "Migration Routes of Sandhill Cranes from Midcontinental North America." *Journal of Wildlife Management* 48:1023–33.

Tacha, T. C., P. A. Vohs, and W. D. Warde. 1985. "Morphometric Variation of Sandhill Cranes from Mid-Continent North America." *Journal of Wildlife Management* 49 (1): 246–50. http://dx.doi.org /10.2307/3801879.

Toepfer, J. E., and R. A. Crete. 1979. "Migration of Radio-Tagged Greater Sandhill Cranes from Minnesota and Wisconsin." In *Proceedings of the 1978 Crane Workshop*, ed. J. C. Lewis, 159–74. Fort Collins: Colorado State University Printing Service.

Valentine, J. M. 1982. "Breeding Ecology of the Mississippi Sandhill Crane in Jackson County, Mississippi." In *Proceedings of the 1981 Crane Workshop*, ed. J. C. Lewis, 63–72. Tavernier, FL: National Audubon Society.

Voss, K. S. 1976. "Behavior of the Greater Sandhill Cranes." MS thesis, University of Wisconsin, Madison.

Walkinshaw, L. H. 1949. *The Sandhill Cranes*. Bloomfield Hills, MI: Cranbrook Institute of Science.

Walkinshaw, L. H. 1965a. "A New Sandhill Crane from Central Canada." *Canadian Field Naturalist* 79:181–84.

Walkinshaw, L. H. 1965b. "Sandhill Crane Studies on Banks Island, N.W.T." *Blue Jay* 23:66–72.

Walkinshaw, L. H. 1981b. "The Sandhill Cranes." In *Crane Research around the World: Proceedings of the International Crane Symposium*, ed. J. C. Lewis, and H. Masatomi. Baraboo, WI: International Crane Foundation.

Walkinshaw, L. H. 1986. *The Sandhill Crane and I*. No. LD01109. Ann Arbor, MI: University Microfilms. (History of the sandhill crane in Michigan.)

Walkinshaw, L. H. 1987. "Nesting of the Florida and Cuban Sandhill Cranes." No. LD01165. Ann Arbor, MI: University Microfilms.

Weekley, F. 1985. "Individual and Regional Variations in the Calls of the Greater Sandhill Crane." Master's thesis, University of Wisconsin, Madison.

Windingstad, R. M. 1988. "Nonhunting Mortality in the Sandhill Crane." *Journal of Wildlife Management* 52 (2): 260–63. http://dx.doi.org/10.2307/3801231.
(Cholera, botulism, and mycotoxins were major causes of death in a sample of 170 wild birds.)

Zickafoose, J. 2008. "Love and Death among the Cranes." *Bird Watcher's Digest* 21 (2): 92–99. (Hunting the eastern population of greater sandhill cranes.)

Whooping Crane References

Ackerman, J. 2004. "'No mere Bird': Cranes." *National Geographic* 205 (4): 39–55.

Allen, R. P. 1952. *The Whooping Crane*. Research Report 3. New York: National Audubon Society.

Allen, R. P. 1956. *A Report on the Whooping Crane's Northern Breeding Grounds: A Supplement to the Research Report No. 3*. New York: National Audubon Society.

Armbruster, M. J. 1990. "Characterization of Habitat Used by Whooping Cranes during Migration. U.S. Dept. Of Interior, Fish and Wildlife Service." *Biology of Reproduction* 90 (4): 1–16.

Austin, J. E., and A. L. Richert. 2001. *A Comprehensive Review of Observational and Site Evaluation Data of Migrant Whooping Cranes in the United States, 1943–99*. Jamestown, ND: Northern Prairie Research Center.

Austin, J. E., and A. L. Richert. 2005. "Patterns of Habitat Use by Whooping Cranes during Migration: Summary from 1977–1999 Site Data Evaluation." In *Proceedings of the Ninth North American Crane Workshop*, ed. F. Chavez-Ramirez, 79–104. Sacramento, CA: North American Crane Working Group.

Binkley, C. S., and R. S. Miller. 1983. "Population Characteristics of the Whooping Crane, *Grus americana*." *Canadian Journal of Zoology* 61 (12): 2768–76. http://dx.doi.org/10.1139/z83-363.

Bishop, M. A. 1984. "The Dynamics of Subadult Flocks of Whooping Cranes Wintering in Texas, 1978–79 through 1982–83." Master's thesis, Texas A&M University, College Station.

Blankinship, D. R. 1976. "Studies of Whooping Cranes on the Wintering Grounds." In *Proceedings of the International Crane Workshop*, ed. J. C. Lewis, 197–205. Tavernier, FL: National Audubon Society.

Brown, W. M., and R. C. Drewien. 1995. "Evaluation of Two Powerline Markers to Reduce Crane and Waterfowl Collision Mortality." *Wildlife Society Bulletin* 23:217–37.

Bysykatova, I., S. Slepsov, and N. Vasilev. 2011. "Current Status of Lesser Sandhill Cranes in Yakutia (Abstract)." In *Proceedings of the 11th North American Crane Workshop*, ed. B. Hartup, 198. Baraboo, WI: International Crane Foundation.

Carlson, G. 1991. "The Feasibility of Individual Identification and Sex Determination of Whooping Cranes (*Grus americana)* by Vocalizations." Master's thesis, Idaho State University, Pocatello.

Chavez-Ramirez, F. 2004. "Whooping Cranes in Nebraska: Historical and Recent Trends." *Braided River* 20:1–9. (newsletter of the Crane Trust)

Chavez-Ramirez, F., M. Dumesnil, and E. Smith. 2013. "A Thousand Whoopers: The Nature Conservancy." http://www.gcbo.org/html/1000Whoopers.pdf.

Chavez-Ramirez, F., and R. D. Slack. 1999. "Movements and Flock Characteristics of Whooping Cranes Wintering on the Texas Coast." *Texas Journal of Science* 51 (1): 3–14.

Chavez-Ramirez, F., and W. Wehtje. 2012. "Potential Impact of Climate Change Scenarios on Whooping Crane Life History." *Wetlands* 32 (1): 11–20. http://dx.doi.org/10.1007/s13157-011-0250-z.

Conover, A. 1998. "Fly Away Home." *Smithsonian* 29 (1): 62–70.
(Early efforts to establish the Wisconsin-Florida migratory whooping crane flock.)

Converse, S. J., and R. P. Urbenek. 2010. "Demography of Whooping Cranes in the Eastern Migratory Population (Abstract)." In *Proceedings of the 11th North American Crane Workshop*, ed. B. Hartup, 198. Baraboo, WI: International Crane Foundation.

Dellinger, T., M. Folk, S. Bayncs, and K. Chappell. 2014. "Video Surveillance of Nesting Whooping Cranes (Abstract)." In *Proceedings of the Twelfth North American Crane Workshop*, ed. D. A. Aborn and R. A. Urbenek, 84. Madison, WI: North American Crane Working Group.

Dellinger, T., M. Folk, S. Baynes, K. Chappell, and M. Spalding. 2014. "Copulation of Non-Migratory Whooping Cranes in Florida (Abstract)." In *Proceedings of the Twelfth North American Crane Workshop*, ed. D. A. Aborn and R. A. Urbenek, 85. Madison, WI: North American Crane Working Group.

Doughty, R. W. 1989. *Return of the Whooping Crane*. Austin: University of Texas Press.
(An account of early whooping crane restoration efforts.)

Drewien, R. C., and E. G. Bizeau. 1981. "Use of Radiotelemetry to Study the Movements of Juvenile Whooping Cranes." In *Crane Research around the World*, ed. J. C. Lewis and H. Masatomi, 130–35. Baraboo, WI: International Crane Foundation.

Drewien, R. C., and E. Kuyt. 1979. "Teamwork Helps the Whooping Crane." *National Geographic* 155 (5): 680–92.

Duff, J. 2014. "Reintroducing an Endangered Species Is Complicated." *Prairie Fire* 8 (2): 9–12.

Ellis, D. H., G. F. Gee, K. R. Clegg, J. W. Duff, W. A. Lishman, and W.J.L. Sladen. 2001. "Lessons from the Motorized Migrations." In *Proceedings of the Eighth National Crane Workshop*, ed. D. H. Ellis, 139–44. Seattle, WA: North American Crane Working Group.

Ellis, D. H., J. C. Lewis, G. F. Gee, and D. G. Smith. 1992. "Population Recovery Efforts of the Whooping Crane with Emphasis on Reintroduction Efforts: Past and Future." In *Proceedings of the Sixth North American Crane Workshop*, ed. D. W. Stahlecker, 142–50. Grand Island, NE: North American Crane Working Group. https://www.savingcranes.org/proceedings-of-the-sixth-north-american-crane-workshop-1992.html.

Folk, M. J., S. A. Nesbitt, J. M. Parker, M. G. Spalding, S. B. Baynes, and K. L. Candelora. 2008a. "Current Status of Nonmigratory Whooping Cranes in Florida." In *Proceedings of the Tenth North American Crane Workshop*, ed. M. J. Folk and S. A. Nesbitt, 7–12. Gambier, OH: North American Crane Working Group.

Folk, M. J., S. A. Nesbitt, J. M. Parker, M. G. Spalding, S. B. Baynes, and K. L. Candelora. 2008b. "Feather Molt of Nonmigratory Whooping Cranes in Florida." In *Proceedings of the Tenth North American Crane Workshop*, ed. M. J. Folk and S. A. Nesbitt, 128–32. Gambier, OH: North American Crane Working Group.

Folk, M. J., S. A. Nesbitt, S. T. Schwikert, J. A. Schmidt, K. A. Sullivan, T. J. Miller, S. B. Baynes, and J. M. Parker. 2005. "Breeding Biology of Re-Introduced Non-Migratory Whooping Cranes in Florida." In *Proceedings of the Ninth National Crane Workshop*, ed. F. Chavez-Ramirez, 105–9. Sacramento, CA: North American Crane Working Group.

Gil-Weir, K. 2006. "Whooping Crane (*Grus americana*) Demography and Environmental Factors in a Population Growth Simulation Model." PhD diss., Texas A&M University, College Station.

Gil-Weir, K., F. Chavez-Ramirez, B. W. Johns, L. Craig-Moore, T. V. Stehn, and R. Silva. 2014. "Historical Breeding, Stopover, and Wintering Distributions of a Whooping Crane Family (Abstract)." In *Proceedings of the Twelfth North American Crane Workshop*, ed. D. A. Aborn and R. A. Urbenek, 87. Madison, WI: North American Crane Working Group.

Gil-Weir, K., F. Chavez-Ramirez, B. W. Johns, T. V. Stehn, and R. Silva. 2010. "An Individual Whooping Crane Life History (Abstract)." In *Proceedings of the 11th North American Crane Workshop*, ed. B. Hartup, 201. Baraboo, WI: North American Crane Working Group.

Gil-Weir, K., W. E. Grant, R. D. Slack, H. H. Wang, and M. Fujiwara. 2012. "Demography and Population Trends of Whooping Cranes." *Journal of Field Ornithology* 83 (1): 1–10. http://dx.doi.org /10.1111/j.1557-9263.2011.00349.x.

Gil-Weir, K., and P. A. Johnsgard. 2010. "The Whooping Cranes: Survivors against All Odds." *Prairie Fire* 4 (9): 12, 13, 16, 22. http://www.prairiefirenewspaper.com/2010/09/ the-whooping-cranes-survivors-against-all-odds.

Gomez, G. M. 2014. "The History and Reintroduction of Whooping Cranes at White Lake Wetlands Conservation Area, Louisiana." In *Proceedings of the Twelfth North American Crane Workshop*, ed. D. A. Aborn and R. A. Urbenek, 76–78. Madison, WI: North American Crane Working Group.

Hartup, B. K., M. G. Spalding, N. J. Thomas, G. A. Cole, and Y. J. Kim. 2010. "Thirty Years of Mortality Assessment in Whooping Crane Reintroductions: Patterns and Assessments (Abstract)." In *Proceedings of the 11th North American Crane Workshop*, ed. B. Hartup, 204. Baraboo, WI: International Crane Foundation.

Holland, J. 2014. "Counting Cranes." *National Geographic* (June): 69–79.

Horwich, R. H. 2001. "Developing a Migratory Whooping Crane Flock." In *Proceedings of the Eighth National Crane Workshop*, ed. D. H. Ellis, 85–95. Albuquerque NM: North American Crane Working Group.
    (See also updates at the following URLs: www.operationmigration.org; www.savingcranes.org; and www.bringbackthecranes.org.)

Howe, M. A. 1989. *Migration of Radio-Tagged Whooping Cranes from the Aransas–Wood Buffalo Population: Patterns of Habitat Use, Behavior and Survival.* Report 20. Washington, DC: US Fish and Wildlife Service.

Johns, B. 2005. "Whooping Cranes: The Canadian Connection." *Braided River* 21:1–5. (newsletter of the Crane Trust)
    (Breeding ground and migration information for the Wood Buffalo–Aransas flock.)

Johns, B. W., J. P. Gossen, E. Kuyt, and L. Craig-Moore. 2005. "Philopatry and Dispersal in Whooping Cranes." In *Proceedings of the Ninth National Crane Workshop*, ed. F. Chavez-Ramirez, 117–25. Sacramento, CA: North American Crane Working Group.

Johnsgard, P. A. 1982. "Whooper Recount." *Natural History* 91 (2): 70–75. http://digitalcommons.unl. edu/biosciornithology/19.
    (Population trends in whooping cranes.)

Johnsgard, P. A. 2014. "Aransas National Wildlife Refuge: The Whooping Crane's Vulnerable Winter Retreat." *Prairie Fire* 8 (5): 12–13.

Johnsgard, P. A., and R. Redfield. 1977. "Sixty-Five Years of Whooping Crane Records in Nebraska." *Nebraska Bird Review* 45:54–56. *http://digitalcommons.unl.edu/johnsgard/9.*

Johnson, A. S. 1987. "Will Bosque's Whoopers Make It?" *Defenders* 62 (1): 20–27.
    (Threats to cross-fostered whoopers from hunting, collisions with power lines, and avian cholera.)

Kepler, C. B. 1976. "Dominance and Dominance-Related Behavior in the Whooping Cranes." In *Proceedings of the International Crane Workshop*, ed. J. C. Lewis, 177–96. Stillwater: Oklahoma State University Press.

Kuyt, E. 1981a. "Clutch Size, Hatching Success and Survival of Whooping Crane Chicks, Wood Buffalo Park, Canada." In *Crane Research around the World*, ed. J. C. Lewis and H. Masatomi, 126–29. Baraboo, WI: International Crane Foundation.

Kuyt, E. 1981b. "Population Status, Nest-Site Fidelity, and Breeding Habitat of Whooping Cranes." In *Crane Research around the World*, ed. J. C. Lewis and H. Masatomi, 119–25. Baraboo, WI: International Crane Foundation.

Kuyt, E. 1987. "Whooping Crane Migration Studies, 1981–82." In *Proceedings of the 1983 International Crane Workshop*, ed. G. Archibald and R. Pasquier, 371–79. Baraboo, WI: International Crane Foundation.

Kuyt, E. 1992. *Aerial Radio-Tracking of Whooping Cranes Migrating between Wood Buffalo National Park and Aransas National Wildlife Refuge*. Occasional Papers. Ottawa: Canadian Wildlife Service.

Kuyt, E. 1993. "Whooping Crane, *Grus americana,* Home Range and Breeding Range Expansion in Wood Buffalo National Park, 1976–1991." *Canadian Field Naturalist* 107:1–12.

Kuyt, E., and P. Gossen. 1987. "Survival, Sex Ratio, and Age at First Breeding of Whooping Cranes in Wood Buffalo National Park, Canada." In *Proceedings of the 1985 Crane Workshop*, ed. J. C. Lewis, 230–44. Grand Island, NE: Platte River Whooping Crane Habitat Maintenance Trust and US Fish and Wildlife Service.

Labuda, S. E., and K. O. Butts. 1979. "Habitat Use by Wintering Whooping Cranes on the Aransas National Wildlife Refuge." In *Proceedings of the 1978 International Crane Workshop*, ed. J. C. Lewis, 152–57. Fort Collins: Colorado State University.

Lewis, J. C. 1993. *Whooping Crane*. Birds of North America. 153. Philadelphia: Academy of Natural Sciences. (A literature summary of the species, with 95 citations.)

Lewis, J. C., E. Kuyt, K. E. Schmidt, and T. V. Stehn. 1992. "Mortality in Fledging Cranes of the Aransas-Wood Buffalo Population." In *Proceedings of the 1988 North American Crane Workshop*, ed. D. A. Wood, 145–48. Tallahassee: Florida Game and Freshwater Fish Commission.

Lingle, G. R., K. J. Strom, and J. W. Ziewitz. 1986. "Whooping Crane Roost Site Characteristics on the Platte River, Buffalo County, Nebraska." *Nebraska Bird Review* 54:36–39.

Lingle, G. R., G. A. Wingfield, and J. W. Ziewitz. 1991. "The Migration Ecology of Whooping Cranes in Nebraska." In *Proceedings of the International Crane Foundation Workshop*, ed. J. Harris, 395–401. Qiqhar, People's Republic of China.

Longmire, J. L., G. F. Gee, C. L. Hardeknopf, and G. A. Marks. 1992. "Establishing Paternity in Whooping Cranes (*Grus americana*) by DNA analysis." *Auk* 109:522–29.

McCoy, J. J. 1966. *The Hunt for the Whooping Cranes: A Natural History Detective Story*. New York: Lothrop, Lee and Shepard.

McNulty, F. 1966. *The Whooping Crane: The Bird That Defies Extinction*. New York: E. P. Dutton. (History of early whooping crane conservation efforts.)

Nedelman, J., A. Thompson, and R. J. Taylor. 1987. "The Statistical Demography of Whooping Cranes." *Ecology* 68 (5): 1401–11. http://dx.doi.org/10.2307/1939224.

Nesbitt, S., M. J. Folk, K. A. Sullivan, S. T. Schwikert, and M. G. Spalding. 2001. "An Update of the Florida Whooping Crane Release Project through June, 2000." In *Proceedings of the Eighth National Crane Workshop*, ed. D. H. Ellis, 62–72. Seattle, WA: North American Crane Working Group. (First-year mortality averaged 50%, with bobcats and alligators the major predators.)

Novakowski, N. S. 1966. *Whooping Crane Population Dynamics on the Nesting Grounds, Wood Buffalo National Park, Canada.* Report Series 1. Ottawa, ON: Canadian Wildlife Service Research.

Olsen, D. L., D. R. Blankinship, R. C. Erickson, R. Drewien, H. D. Irby, R. Lock, and L. S. Smith. 1980. *Whooping Crane Recovery Plan*. Washington, DC: US Fish and Wildlife Service.

Pittman, C. 2003. "Making Whoopee." *Smithsonian* 33 (10): 92–95. (Breeding of Florida whooping cranes.)

Richert, A. L. 1999. "Multiple Scale Analyses of Whooping Crane Habitat in Nebraska." PhD diss., University of Nebraska, Lincoln. (See also Austin and Richert, 2001.)

Sherwood, G. 1971. "If It's Big and Flies—Shoot It." *Audubon Magazine* 73 (November): 72–99.

Smith, E. H. 2014. "What Do Whooping Cranes Do in the Winter?" *Prairie Fire* 7 (4): 1, 3, 4. (Aransas National Wildlife Refuge.)

Stap, D. 1998. "A Population Reinstated: Establishing a New Population of Whooping Cranes in Central Florida Improves the Prospects for the Birds' Long-Term Survival." *Audubon* 100 (4): 92–97.

Stehn, T. V. 1992a. "Behavior of Whooping Cranes during Initiation of Migration." In *Proceedings of the Sixth North American Crane Workshop*, ed. D. W. Stalnecker and R. P. Urbanek, 102–5. Grand Island, NE: North American Crane Working Group.

Stehn, T. V. 1992b. "Re-Pairing of Whooping Cranes at Aransas National Wildlife Refuge." In *Proceedings of the Sixth North American Crane Workshop*, ed. D. W. Stalnecker and R. P. Urbanek, 185–87. Grand Island, NE: North American Crane Working Group.

Stehn, T. V., and C. L. Haralson-Strobel. 2014. "An Update on Mortality of Fledged Whooping Cranes in the Aransas-Wood Buffalo Population." In *Proceedings of the Twelfth North American Crane Workshop*, ed. D. A. Aborn and R. A. Urbenek, 43–50. Madison, WI: North American Crane Working Group.

Stehn, T. V., and F. Prieto. 2010. "Changes in Winter Whooping Crane Territories and Range 1950– 2006." In *Proceedings of the 11th North American Crane Workshop*, ed. B. Hartup, 30–56. Baraboo, WI: International Crane Foundation.

Stehn, T. V., and T. E. Taylor. 2008. "Aerial Census Techniques for Whooping Cranes on the Texas Coast." In *Proceedings of the Tenth North American Crane Workshop*, ed. M. J. Folk and S. A. Nesbitt, 146–51. Gambier, OH: North American Crane Working Group.

Stehn, T. V., and T. Wassenich. 2008. "Whooping Crane Collisions with Power Lines: An Issue Paper." In *Proceedings of the Tenth North American Crane Workshop*, ed. M. J. Folk and S. A. Nesbitt, 25–36. Gambier, OH: North American Crane Working Group.

Stephenson, J. D. 1971. "Plumage Development and Growth of Young Whooping Cranes." Master's thesis, Oregon State University, Corvallis.

Stevenson, J. O., and R. E. Griffith. 1946. "Winter Life of the Whooping Crane." *Condor* 48 (4): 160– 78. http://dx.doi.org/10.2307/1363971.

Tacha, M., A. Bishop, and J. Brei. 2010. "Development of the Whooping Crane Tracking Project Geographic Information System." In *Proceedings of the 11th North American Crane Workshop*, ed. B. Hartup, 96–104. Baraboo, WI: International Crane Foundation.

Temple, S. A. 1978. *Endangered Birds: Management Techniques for Preserving Threatened Species*. Madison: University of Wisconsin Press.
   (Cross-fostering of whooping cranes.)

Thoemke, K. W., and P. M. Prior. 2004. "A Crane Called Lucky: A Major Milestone in the Reintroduction of Whooping Cranes to Florida." *Living Bird* 23 (1): 28–35.

Turner, M. 1989. "Trouble at Aransas." *Defenders* 64 (3): 30–34.
   (Threats to the Aransas National Wildlife Refuge from the Intracoastal Waterway.)

Urbanek, R. P., L. A. Fondow, and S. E. Zimorski. 2010. "Survival, Reproduction and Movements of Migratory Whooping Cranes during the First Seven Years of Reintroduction." In *Proceedings of the 11th North American Crane Workshop*, ed. B. Hartup, 133–41. Baraboo, WI: International Crane Foundation.

Urbanek, R. P., S. E. Zimorski, A. Fasoll, and E. Syskoski. 2010. "Nest Desertion in a Reintroduced Flock of Migratory Whooping Cranes." In *Proceedings of the 11th North American Crane Workshop*, ed. B. Hartup, 133–41. Baraboo, WI: International Crane Foundation.

US Fish and Wildlife Service. 1986. *Endangered and Threatened Wildlife and Plants, January 1, 1986*. Washington, DC: Government Printing Office.

Zimmerman, D. R. 1975. *To Save a Bird in Peril*. New York: Coward, McCann and Geoghegan.
   (Early whooping crane conservation history.)

Zimmerman, D. R. 1978. "A Technique Called Cross-Fostering May Help Save the Whooping Crane." *Smithsonian* 9 (6): 62–63.

References on the Old World Species of Cranes

Many of the following references may be found in the ICF's Ron Sauey Memorial Library for Bird Conservation. For a more comprehensive bibliography of the Old World cranes, see Meine and Archibald, 1996 (under "World Surveys and Bibliographies").

Allan, D. G. 1993. "Aspects of the Biology and Conservation Status of the Blue Crane *Anthropoides paradiseus*, and the Ludwig's *Neotis ludwigii* and Stanley's *N. denhami stanleyi* Bustards in Southern Africa." Master's thesis, University of Cape Town, Cape Town, South Africa.

Archibald, G. W., and R. F. Pasquier, eds. 1987. *Proceedings of the 1983 International Crane Workshop, 1983, Bharatpur, India*. Baraboo, WI: International Crane Foundation.

Bankovics, A., ed. 1987. *Proceedings of the International Crane Foundation Working Group on European Cranes, 1985, Orosháza-Kardoskiit, Hungary*. Aquila: Budapest, Hungary.

Beilfuss, R. D., T. Dodman, and E. K. Urban. 2007. "The Status of Cranes in Africa in 2005." *Ostrich* 78 (2): 175–84. http://dx.doi.org/10.2989/OSTRICH.2007.78.2.11.91.

Beilfuss, R., W. Tarboton, and N. Gichuki, eds. 1994. *Proceedings of the 1993 African Crane and Wetland Training Workshop, 1993, Maun, Botswana*. (Includes papers from the 1992 International Conference on the Black Crowned Crane and Its Habitats in West and Central Africa.) Baraboo, WI: International Crane Foundation.

Bento, C. M. 2002. "The Status and Prospects of Wattled Cranes *Grus carunculatus* in the Marromeu Complex of the Zambezi Delta." Master's diss., University of Cape Town, Cape Town, South Africa.

Blahy, B. 2004. *Das Lächeln des Kranichs. Ein Tagebuch*. Berlin: Neunplusı.
    (A daily journal account of Eurasian crane observations.)

Britton, D., and T. Hayashida. 1981. *The Japanese Crane: Bird of Happiness*. Tokyo: Kodansha International.
    (A photo-essay on the red-crowned cranes of Hokkaido.)

Bysykatova, I. P., G. L. Krapu, N. I. Germogenov, and D. A. Buhl. 2014. "Distribution, Densities and Ecologies of Siberian Cranes in the Khroma River Region of Northern Yakutia in Northeastern Russia." In *Proceedings of the Twelfth North American Crane Workshop*, ed. D. A. Aborn and R. A. Urbenek, 51–64. Madison, WI: North American Crane Working Group.

Glutz von Blotzheim, U. N., ed. 1973. *Handbuch der Vogel Mitteleuropas*. Vol. 5. Weisbaden, Germany: Akademische Verlagegellschaft.

Halvorson, C. H., J. T. Harris, and S. M. Sniirenski, eds. 1995. *Cranes and Storks of the Amur River: The Proceedings of the International Workshop, 1992, Khaborovsk and Poyarkovo, Russia*. Amur Program of the Socio-Ecological Union, International Crane Foundation, and Moscow State University. Moscow, Russia: Arts Literature Publishers.

Harris, J., ed. 1991. *The Cranes of China: Proceedings of the 1987 International Crane Workshop, 1987, Qiqihar, Heilongjiang Province, People's Republic of China*. Baraboo, WI: International Crane Foundation.
    (In English; see also Heilongjiang Forest Bureau 1987, 1990).

Harris, J., ed. 2012. "Cranes, Agriculture, and Climate Change (Abstract)." In *Proceedings of a Workshop Organized by the International Crane Foundation and Muraviovka Park for Sustainable Land Use*. Baraboo, WI: International Crane Foundation.

Hayashida, T. 2002. *Cranes of Japan*. Tokyo: Heibonsha.
    (Photographic essay.)

Heilongjiang Forest Bureau. 1987. *Proceedings of the 1987 International Crane Workshop (Summaries), 1987, Qiqihar, Heilongjiang Province, China*. Beijing, People's Republic of China: China Forestry Press.
    (In Chinese; see also Heilongjiang Forest Bureau, 1990, and Harris, 1991.)

Heilongjiang Forest Bureau. 1990. *International Crane Protection and Research: Proceedings of the 1987 International Crane Workshop, 1987, Qiqihar, Heilongjiang Province, China*. Beijing, People's Republic of China: China Forestry Press.
(In Chinese; see also Harris 1991.)

Higuchi, H., and J. Minton, eds. 1994. *The Future of Cranes and Wetlands: Proceedings of the International Symposium, June 1993, Tokyo and Sapporo*. Tokyo: Wild Bird Society of Japan.

Ilyashenko, E. I., A. F. Kovshar, and S. V. Winter, eds. 2008. *Cranes of Eurasia (Biology, Distribution, Migrations)*. Vol. 3. Moscow, Russia: Moscow Zoo.

Johnson, D. N., and P. R. Barnes. 1991. "The Breeding Biology of the Wattled Crane in Natal." In *Proceedings of 1987 International Crane Workshop, Qiqihar, People's Republic of China*, ed. J. Harris, 377–86. Baraboo, WI: International Crane Foundation.

Johnson, R. L., Zou Hongfei, and R. C. Stendell, eds. 2001. *Cranes in East Asia: Proceedings of the Symposium held in Harbin, People's Republic of China, June 9–18, 1998*. Fort Collins, CO: Geological Survey, Midcontinent Ecological Science Center.

Krajewski, C., J. T. Sipiorski, and F. E. Anderson. 2010. "Complete Mitochondrial Genome Sequences and the Phylogeny of Cranes." *Auk* 127:440–52.

Li, F., J. Wu, J. Harris, and J. Burnham. 2012. "Number and Distribution of Cranes Wintering at Poyang Lake, China during 2011–2012." *Chinese Birds* 3 (3): 180–90. http://dx.doi.org/10.5122/cbirds .2012.0027.

Litvinenko, N. M., and I. A. Neufeldt, eds. 1982. *Cranes of East Asia*. Vladivostok, USSR: Far East Branch, Academy of Sciences of the USSR.
(In Russian, with English abstracts.)

Litvinenko, N. M., and I. A. Neufeldt, eds. 1988. *The Palearctic Cranes: Biology, Morphology, and Distribution: Papers from the Fifth Meeting of the Soviet Working Group on Cranes, 1986, Arkhara, USSR*. Vladivostok, USSR: Far East Branch, Academy of Sciences of the USSR; Amur-Ussuri Branch of the USSR Ornithological Society.
(In Russian, with English abstracts.)

Liu, Q., F. Li, P. Buzzard, F. Qian, F. Zhang, J. Zhao, J. Yang, and X. Yang. 2012. "Migration Routes and New Breeding Areas of Black-Necked Cranes." *Wilson Journal of Ornithology* 124 (4): 704–12. http://dx.doi.org/10.1676/1559-4491-124.4.704.

Masatomi, H. 1989. *International Censuses on Wintering Cranes in East Asia, 1987–88*. Bibai, Japan: International Crane Research Unit in Eastern Asia.

Masatomi, H. 2004. "Individual (Non-Social) Behavioral Acts of Hooded Cranes *Grus monachus* Wintering in Izumi, Japan." *Journal of Ethology* 22 (1): 69–83. http://dx.doi.org/10.1007/s10164 -003-0103-1.

Masatomi, H., and T. Kitagawa. 1974. "Bionomics and Sociology of Tancho or the Japanese Crane, *Grus japonensis*. I. Distribution, Habitat and Outline of Annual Cycle." *Journal of the Faculty of Science, Hokkaido University, Series 6, Zoology* 19 (3): 777–802

Masatomi, H., and T. Kitagawa. 1975. "Bionomics and Sociology of Tancho or the Japanese Crane, *Grus japonensis*. II. Ethogram." *Journal of the Faculty of Science, Hokkaido University, Series 6, Zoology* 19 (4): 834–78.

Matthiessen, P. 1994. "At the End of Tibet." *Audubon*, March–April.
(Red-crowned crane.)

Matthiessen, P. 1995. "The Cranes of Hokkaido." *Audubon*, July–August.
(Black-necked crane.)

Matthiessen, P. 1996. "Accidental Sanctuary." *Audubon*, July–August.
(Wintering Asian cranes.)

Matthiessen, P. 2001. *The Birds of Heaven: Travels with Cranes*. New York: North Point Press.

Ma Yiqing, ed. 1986. *Crane Research and Conservation in China: Proceedings of the First Symposium on Crane Research in China, 1984*. Harbin, China: Heilongjiang Education Press.
    (In Chinese, with English abstracts.)

Neufeldt, I. A., ed. 1982. *Cranes of the USSR. Papers presented at the Second Meeting of the Soviet Working Group on Cranes, 1981, Leningrad, USSR*. Leningrad, USSR: Zoological Institute of the Academy of Sciences of the USSR.
    (In Russian, with English titles.)

Neufeldt, I. A., and J. Kespaik, eds. 1987. *Crane Studies in the USSR. Papers presented at the Fourth Meeting of the Soviet Working Group on Cranes, 1984. Matsulu Nature Reserve, USSR (Estonia)*. Communications of the Baltic Commission for the Study of Bird Migration 19. Tartu, USSR (Estonia):
    (In Russian, with English titles.)

Neufeldt, I. A., and J. Kespaik, eds. 1989. *Common Crane Research in the USSR: Papers Prepared by the USSR Working Group on Cranes*. Communications of the Baltic Commission for the Study of Bird Migration 21. Tartu, USSR (Estonia).
    (In Russian, with English summaries.)

Porter, D. J., H. S. Craven, D. N. Johnson, and M. J. Porter, eds. 1992. *Proceedings of the First Southern African Crane Conference, 1989, Natal, Republic of South Africa*. Durban, South Africa: Southern African Crane Foundation.

Prange, H., ed. 1995. *Crane Research and Protection in Europe*. Halle-Wittenberg, Germany: European Crane Working Group and Martin Luther-Universität.

Prange, H. 2008. "The Status of the Common Crane (*Grus grus*) in Europe—Breeding, Resting, Migration, Wintering and Protection." In *Proceedings of the Tenth North American Crane Workshop*, ed. M. J. Folk and S. A. Nesbitt, 69–77. Gambier, OH: North American Crane Working Group.
    (160,000 Eurasian cranes stop over in northeastern Germany between August and December, with 80% of their roosts under protection.)

Shaw, J. M., A. R. Jenkins, J. J. Smallie, and P. J. Ryan. 2010. "Modeling Power-Line Collision Risk for Blue Cranes *Anthropoides paradiseus* in South Africa." *Ibis* 152 (3): 590–59. http://dx.doi.org/10.1111/j.1474-919X.2010.01039.x.

Yang, R., H. Q. Wu, X. J. Yang, W. G. Jiang, L. Zuo, and Z. R. Xiang. 2005. "A Preliminary Observation on Breeding Behavior of Black-Necked Cranes at Ruoergai, Sichuan Province." In *Status and Conservation of Black-Necked Cranes on the Yunnan and Guizhou Plateau*, ed. F. S. Li, X. J. Yang, and F. Yang, 163–69. Kunming, People's Republic of China: Yunnan Nationalities Publishing House.
    (In Chinese.)

Zimmerman, D. R. 1981. "A Fragile Victory for Beauty on an Old Asian Battleground." *Smithsonian* 12 (7): 57–60.
    (Crane conservation in Korea.)

Index

Note: Entries shown in bold indicate illustrations or maps. Latin names of non-crane species are shown here after their English names. Both the Latin and English names of cranes are indexed.

FIGURE 6.1. *Gray crowned crane, three adults in flight*